"This is an outstanding practical introduction to
kinds – news, features, print, online. Starting with most p
ability through exercises at each stage and a structured progression to more
complex issues like interviews, data, science and business. With contributions
from leading journalism teachers and professional journalists it is a timely update of previous introductions taking full account of the digital transition in
newsrooms and the expectations from employers of multimedia competence.
At a time when journalists are under scrutiny for their professionalism and high
standards are at a premium it offers an excellent introduction to key skills for
those entering the business."

Richard Sambrook, *Professor of Journalism and*
Director of the Centre for Journalism at
Cardiff University, formerly Director of Global News at the BBC

"In the summer of 2018, when we, a group of mainly print and TV journalists
at *The Telegraph India* and other brands of India's top media group ABP were
struggling to adjust to a native digital newsroom, Matt came to our rescue. His
clear vision of how to approach a multimedia story was immensely beneficial.
This book is an extension of those practical tips. A much needed book for both
journalists and journalism educators. I have used many of Matt's tips like how
to approach a feature, decide on multimedia content among others in my class
and my students found them interesting. The real-life examples and exercises
through out the book adds much value to it. It also covers a wide spectrum of
journalistic writing which sets the principles of journalism straight."

Sambit Pal, *Assistant Professor at the Indian*
Institute of Mass Communications,
formerly journalist at The Telegraph India

"Early in my career I would have loved to be able to draw on the diverse, rigor-
ous advice you'll find in these pages, and even now I found so much in here to
challenge and encourage."

Peter Grunert, *Group Editor, Magazines for Lonely Planet*

Writing for Journalists

Thoroughly revised and updated, the fourth edition of *Writing for Journalists* focuses on the craft of journalistic writing, offering invaluable insight on how to hook readers and keep them to the end of your article.

The book offers a systematic approach to news and feature writing that starts with the basics and builds to more complex and longer pieces. The authors give the reader the tools they need to deliver engaging and authoritative writing that works across print and digital. Drawing on professional insight from writers across the industry, the book guides readers through the essential elements needed to write powerful and effective news stories, from hard news pieces to features on business, science and travel, and entertainment reviews. New to this edition are hands-on writing exercises accompanying each chapter to help reinforce key points; chapters on how to build a professional profile, pitch stories and get commissioned; and a section on online writing, SEO, analytics and writing for social media.

This is an essential guide for all journalism students and early-career journalists. It also has much to offer established journalists looking to develop their writing and lead editorial teams.

Matt Swaine is the Course Director for the MA in International Journalism at Cardiff University, where he teaches multimedia news and long-form feature writing. As a journalist he edited *BBC Wildlife* and *Trail* magazines and launched websites and magazines such as *Trail Running* and *Outdoor Fitness*. He spent two years as Lonely Planet's Editorial and Product Development Director, and has written for titles as diverse as *Mother and Baby*, *Sunday Times Travel*, *Guitarist*, *The Telegraph* and *Cycling Plus*.

@MattSwaine

Harriett Gilbert is a broadcaster, journalist and novelist. She was literary editor of the *New Statesman* and has reviewed the arts for, among others, *Time Out*, the *Listener*, the *Independent* and the BBC. She presents *A Good Read* on BBC Radio 4 and *World Book Club* on BBC World Service Radio. She was for many years a senior lecturer in the Department of Journalism at City University London.

@HarriettSG

Gavin Allen is a Digital Journalism Lecturer at Cardiff University School of Journalism, Media and Culture. He has been a journalist for 20 years, latterly as Associate Editor of *Mirror.co.uk*, having previously worked at *MailOnline*, MSN and *WalesOnline*.

@Gavinallen

Media Skills

Edited by Richard Keeble, Lincoln University

The *Media Skills* series provides a concise and thorough introduction to a rapidly changing media landscape. Each book is written by media and journalism lecturers or experienced professionals and is a key resource for a particular industry. Offering helpful advice and information and using practical examples from print, broadcast and digital media, as well as discussing ethical and regulatory issues, *Media Skills* books are essential guides for students and media professionals.

For more information about this series, please visit: https://www.routledge.com/Media-Skills/book-series/SE0372

Writing for Journalists

FOURTH EDITION

Matt Swaine
with Harriett Gilbert
and Gavin Allen

Routledge
Taylor & Francis Group

LONDON AND NEW YORK

Fourth edition published 2022
by Routledge
2 Park Square, Milton Park, Abingdon, Oxon, OX14 4RN

and by Routledge
605 Third Avenue, New York, NY 10158

Routledge is an imprint of the Taylor & Francis Group, an informa business

First edition published by Routledge 1999
Third edition published by Routledge 2016

British Library Cataloguing-in-Publication Data
A catalogue record for this book is available from the British Library

Library of Congress Cataloging-in-Publication Data
Names: Swaine, Matt, author. | Gilbert, Harriett, 1948- author. |
Allen, Gavin L., author.
Title: Writing for journalists / Matt Swaine with
Harriett Gilbert and Gavin Allen.
Description: 4th edition. | London; New York : Routledge, 2021. |
Series: Media skills |
Includes bibliographical references and index. |
Identifiers: LCCN 2020053272 | ISBN 9780367368562 (hardback) |
ISBN 9780367368579 (paperback) | ISBN 9780429351761 (ebook)
Subjects: LCSH: Journalism—Authorship.
Classification: LCC PN4783.H53 2021 | DDC 808.06/607—dc23
LC record available at https://lccn.loc.gov/2020053272

ISBN: 9780367368562 (hbk)
ISBN: 9780367368579 (pbk)
ISBN: 9780429351761 (ebk)

Typeset in Goudy
by codeMantra

This book would not have happened without the input of colleagues and editorial experts; Wynford Hicks, Tim Holmes, Dr Aidan O'Donnell; Nigel Stephenson; Guy Procter; Richard Sambrook; Anna Walker; Simon Ingram; Simon Hemelryk; Paul Rees; Jonathan Swift; Jheni Osman; Ben Hoare; Oliver Berry; Phoebe Smith; Bethan Rose Jenkins; Richard Eccleston; Louise Parker; Kat Smith; Dr Janet Harris; Mike Hill; Dr Savyasaachi Jain; Tony O'Shaughnessy; Dr David Dunkley Gyimah; James Stewart; Dr Linda Mitchell; Dr Gavin Evans; Simon Williams Clare Savage and BAFTA award-winning image scanner Mick Connaire.

Thank you to Clare, Artie, Charlie and Hazel

Contents

Contributors

Aidan O'Donnell lectures in data journalism at Cardiff University and is the director for the MSc in Computational and Data Journalism. He has worked in broadcast and online journalism and has reported from Africa and France.

@aodhanlutetiae

Nigel Stephenson is a highly experienced international journalist with an expertise in reporting business and finance. He has reported from 21 countries and has trained journalists around the world. He teaches business journalism at Cardiff University and City University of London.

1
How to read like a journalist

Introduction

The job of a journalist can be broken into two key functions: finding things out and then telling people what it is that they have discovered. That does not do justice to one of the most rewarding and diverse careers you can have, but it is a useful starting point to explain the scope of this book. Within the following chapters we are going to focus on the second of these roles: communicating stories, through the written word.

We won't spend a great deal of time on how to find news, interview sources or dig for information. We will focus on the craft of writing: understanding how to structure a story that other people are going to read.

We live in an era of free content, so why wouldn't people want stories they can often access for free through their mobile devices? Rather than handing money to your local newsagent, payment comes in the form of your attention: time that could be spent on a multitude of distractions from social media and mobiles games, to podcasts, video, other stories and even the odd conversation with real people.

This great proliferation of content means that every story has to be clearer on its purpose and work harder to get and retain people's attention.

If you want to understand the challenge you are up against, spend a morning watching commuters on their train journey to work, scrolling and swiping through stories on their phones. Get a sense of how little time they spend on one article before they swipe to the next. What was it that put them off? A poorly constructed intro? A line that didn't make sense? A joke that didn't hit the mark? An impenetrable wall of data? Or an article that didn't deliver on its promise?

Perhaps this morning's commuters aren't even reading stories, but scrolling idly through news feeds or Facebook and Twitter posts. What does a headline have to do to grab their attention and get them to click and read a piece of journalism?

The web and mobile devices we increasingly use to access journalism have radically changed the way we find, read and engage with stories. In Chapter 5 we explain how to get your articles as high as possible on a Google search, how to write for social media and make your articles work across print, desktops and mobile devices.

But the essentials of good writing haven't changed that much and the fundamentals are arguably more important than ever. So we start with a traditional approach to constructing news. It aims to be "platform agnostic," because good writing shines through whether it's being read on a small screen, on a laptop or in print.

The chapters that follow will focus on the craft of writing news and features that make the issues you want to cover interesting and accessible to the widest possible audience. It will tell you how to write reviews, develop your own editorial voice, build your personal brand, write travel, interview, science and business articles.

This book aims to equip you with the skills and confidence to succeed in the world of journalism, whether you are starting a course, trying to get your first job, leading a team of writers or looking for your next professional challenge.

You know how to tell stories

If you're new to writing, here's the good news: you are already hardwired to tell stories and it's something you probably do on a daily basis. What's more, your potential readers are instinctively interested in hearing about other people and the challenges they face. We have evolved a desire and ability to share information that has given our species a unique evolutionary advantage.

Just imagine the scene on a frosty moorland as the last Ice Age was drawing to a close. Two cave-persons stumble upon each other as their day of hunting and/ or gathering draws to a close.

"Hey Ugg, you hear about Dave? He attacked by bear, in cave! He don't come out."

"Thank you, Thagg. I'll certainly avoid that cave in future."

Thankfully, Ugg is now less at risk of bear attack and is more likely to pass on her genes to future generations. And although Thagg, her friend and proto-journalist, is clearly struggling with the rudiments of grammar, he has delivered information that is both timely and of value to his audience, which in this case is Ugg, and any other Troglodytes who get to hear the tale of Dave, who died in a cave.

Some 12,000 years later and we are still telling stories: "You'll never guess what happened to me last night"; "Did you hear about the new shop opening on the high street?"; "I bumped into Mandy Jenkins from school this morning. You won't believe who she married…"

Jonathan Gottschall, the author of *The Storytelling Animal*, says that we are a species addicted to storytelling. No one knows whether story is an evolutionary adaptation or a side effect, he says, but his book explores the benefits that we as a species derive from telling stories. An appreciation of why we tell stories and what makes them so compelling is vital for any journalist.

Most of the stories we share are told directly to small groups, often just one other person. That means that, whether you are conscious of it or not, you are able to continually monitor their reaction and adapt your story accordingly. If someone scrunches their forehead, it's likely they haven't understood what you are saying. That would be your cue to offer more information or explain something more clearly. If they start yawning, then you need to throw in more excitement or get to the point. Most of us respond to a host of prompts like this every day, without ever registering how we are being influenced by our audience.

When you write as a journalist you are attempting to communicate with a far larger group of people, the vast majority of whom you will never meet. You have little idea about their knowledge of the subject. You don't see any of the visual cues you might get when you're telling a story in person. You won't be there as they read to gauge their interest or offer extra explanation.

So the art of good writing starts by really thinking about who your reader is and what they need to know. You cannot make assumptions about their knowledge, so you will need to explain key details clearly. You certainly won't be able to make your story more interesting if it looks like they are about to click to another article. So you need a plan to engage your reader from the top of your piece.

Learning to write well involves a significant shift in thinking and that requires hard work and a great deal of practice. For that reason, each chapter in this book features exercises to develop the basics, but that is not going to be enough to turn you into a professional writer.

Writing for a student paper, setting up your own blog, getting work experience at your local paper, or taking a practical course in journalism are all ways to develop your skills. Writing regularly means you are thinking about how you construct sentences, build stories, explain complex ideas and engage your readers.

These days analytics offer incredible insights into how readers engage with content online. Google Analytics is an easily available tool that can tell you which stories on a website are the most popular and how long people spend on them. Organisations like Chartbeat or sites like Dataminr can give even more detailed data that help publications sharpen their editorial strategy (see Chapter 5).

You probably won't have access to that level of information at the moment, and there aren't that many opportunities to sit with readers and question them on the way they read a piece of journalism. But there is one person who you can observe at length, and that is yourself. To do that effectively, you need to identify what sparks your interest, what keeps you reading or makes you turn to another article.

Reading to develop good writing

There are many reasons to read widely and one of the most important is to develop a sense of what constitutes good writing. Every time you read a piece of journalism, you should consider how the writer is trying to engage you as a reader. Here are three questions you should start asking from today…

1. **Why am I reading this story?** Get in the habit of identifying the reader value in every story. What was it that made you want to read this piece? What was it in the headline or sell line that encouraged you to open the paper or click from an online link? Thinking about your own motivation will help you to understand why other people might engage with your work.
2. **What tone is the writer trying to strike with their readers?** The readership of each publication is different. People who buy *The Economist* clearly do so for different reasons than subscribers to *Your Horse* magazine. So ask how the writer aims to engage the audience of this publication. Where did they start the story and why? What kind of language do they use? What relationship are they trying to forge with the reader?
3. **When did you stop reading?** As we will learn in Chapter 2, news is constructed to deliver the most important information at the top, so it is possible to stop reading at any point in the article. So where did you stop in a particular news story and why? Did you read to the end of a feature and if not, why not? What might have kept you reading longer? You want to keep your readers till the final paragraph, so start to develop an understanding of exactly what that involves.

Good writing starts by thinking about your readers. Examining your own motivation and your own response to stories is a good place to start.

Read to develop a love of words

As a writer, words are your raw material. You need to use them with precision. Confidence with words means you should know the difference between affect and effect. You should know that a cache is a hidden horde, for example of treasure or weapons, while cachet is something worthy of respect or admiration. You should know that a city that is genuinely "decimated" has lost 10% of its buildings but also that its meaning has evolved and that some publications may use it to suggest more significant destruction.

You will need to be able to use words to communicate complex ideas; to describe how events unfolded; to bring characters in your stories to life and to give readers a ring-side view of the action. Words matter and the way you use them will determine how effective you are as a writer. Reading is the quickest way to sharpen your understanding of language and your ability to select exactly the right word for the job.

Reading is also a good way to identify the kind of writer you want to be. You might do that by following particular journalists who impress you with their tone, content and style. By analysing what it is they do well, you will find it easier to develop your own voice. Who do you admire as a writer? It's a question that I'd always ask an applicant for a staff writing position. You may well be asked the same thing in the future, so I suggest you have an answer ready to go.

Read to understand the world

Being a journalist gives you licence to call anyone up and ask them questions, to go where the action is taking place and to find things out first-hand. Editors want to employ writers who are inquisitive, well informed and will dig for answers, and journalism is an incredible job for anyone who wants to find out about the world. Reading is the quickest way to satisfy (or develop) that curiosity.

As an aspiring journalist, you should have a good handle on world events, a sense of how international institutions work, how local government operates and the ways that people find to fill the gaps in democracy. You should have some sense of how Artificial Intelligence (AI) could impact on jobs in the next decade; what austerity is doing to social care; the debate around gender pricing and the campaign to reintroduce lynx into the UK. Consuming journalism, whether in written or broadcast format, is an efficient way to build that knowledge.

Don't think everything needs to be in *The Economist*, the *Financial Times* or *Newsweek*. You should be equally aware of modern culture, sport, music and comedy. It doesn't hurt to have an opinion on what made the Marvel superhero series so popular, what the Kardashians have been up to and the tribulations of boxing champions and football teams.

Good journalists understand the importance of impartiality. We can never fully escape our own biases, and our view of what constitutes "unbiased reporting" is unlikely to correspond to anyone else's. But there is a great deal to be said for reading widely to challenge your own preconceived ideas.

So if you tend towards left-wing papers, you should aim to read articles each week from publications on the right of the political spectrum. If you only read publications from Western media outlets, then look for stories from English-language papers from China, Africa or South America. Global perspectives on current events will broaden your world view and give you a sense of different voices, political ideas and other approaches to writing.

If you genuinely want to succeed as a writer and a journalist, then you should be a voracious consumer of news and features from a variety of sources. But don't do this passively. Always ask what the writer is trying to do. Develop a sense of what works for you as a reader, and try to build that into your writing.

Exercise 1: Direct your reading

Here is your weekly challenge for the next month:

1) Find a writer whose style and approach you like. Identify what appeals about their writing.

2) Read at least five articles from a publication at the opposite end of the political spectrum from your usual reading. What surprised you about these pieces?

3) Make a note of five new words you discover each week and their precise definitions.

4) Find a news article about the World Bank. What does this organisation do and how does this story connect to that role? In subsequent weeks do the same with these acronyms: the UN, WHO, IMF, WTO and OECD.

5) What are the top five issues that are being covered in your local newspaper each week? Why are they important to readers?

6) Read three stories from a source from overseas. My students recommend the following as good starting points. Sierra Leone: www.ayvnewspaper.com, Kenya: www.standardmedia.co.ke, Cyprus: www.cyprus-mail.com, India: www.scroll.in, Japan: www3.nhk.or.jp

7) What celebrities are featured in news stories in the *Daily Mail* and why? In subsequent weeks do the same with *VICE*, *Empire*, *Hello*, *Buzzfeed*, *Grazia* and *OK!* magazine.

The role of the journalist

Above all, a journalist's role is one of witness and watchdog. The BBC's definition of public interest journalism includes stories that expose corruption, crime and injustice; prevent people being misled by individuals or organisations; and highlight incompetence and negligence. Journalism can have real impact on society, our laws and people in positions of power.

Good journalism informs the way we engage with society: how we vote, where we spend our money, how we discuss and take action to solve problems. It is increasingly important in a polarised world awash with fake news. "The purpose of journalism is to help people make informed choices about their lives," says Richard Sambrook, former director of BBC News. "As such it should be led by evidence, not overwhelmed by opinion."

As a journalist, the way you communicate is vital. If people are going to be informed, then your writing needs to be sufficiently clear and engaging for people to read. This book aims to be a guide on that journey. Continue to read widely and you will make far quicker progress (see our recommended reading list on page 232 for ideas).

Bibliography

Gottschall, J. (2013) *The Storytelling Animal: How Stories Make Us Human*, Mariner Books.

2
The news intro

What is news?

Over the next two chapters we are going to learn how to construct the opening pars of a basic news story. You don't need to have studied journalism to distinguish between news and features, as they often appear in specific sections of a publication. Even without the help of a headline or picture, you can probably spot which of these is the opening for a news story.

> GPs will be encouraged to prescribe cycling as a way for patients to lose weight, as part of a new government strategy to tackle the nation's obesity crisis to be announced on Monday.

Or…

> While ABBA filled the airwaves and the hottest summer in living memory broiled the tarmac on the road outside our house, my brother and I spent a fortnight in 1976 terrorising the occupants of rock pools along the Dorset coast. Clumsy juvenile fingers churned the glistening water, greedily corralling crustaceans into a sun-bleached bucket.

The second example is clearly not news. It is the opening paragraph of a feature about walking in Dorset. While the first intro is an information-rich summary of the whole story, very little of this feature's first paragraph is central to the story that follows, which has nothing to do with ABBA, 1976 or the writer's brother.

For something to be news it has to be factual, new and interesting, and only the first example, from *The Guardian*, fulfils those criteria. In the news intro above this announcement has just happened. If a historian makes a discovery about the eating habits of the ancient Britons, this could be a news story for *BBC History* magazine, even though the people concerned lived hundreds of years ago. This research provides new information of interest to this readership.

Good writing is about understanding your readers. What is news for one pub-lication may not be news for another. Being able to identify stories that will interest a specific group of readers is what we describe as having "news sense." However, when you ask a journalist why a particular story is news, you may find that even they struggle to offer a satisfying answer.

There is a degree of gut instinct, but there are some useful guides that will help.

News is something that doesn't happen every day: News is the unusual rather than the usual. The classic example is that "Dog bites man" isn't news, because we assume this happens quite often, but that the headline "Man bites dog" has a surprise factor that gives it news value.

A sense that something is unusual is important, but rarity value alone is not sufficient.

News is something someone doesn't want you to know…: When award-winning journalist Carole Cadwalladr investigated the funding of the Vote Leave campaign in the run-up to the EU referendum, this was a story that a number of pro-Brexit campaigners did not want people to know about. It was news because it potentially influenced the democratic process in the UK.

For readers in Britain, wherever they stood on Brexit, this was a story that re-vealed new information of political importance. You will find plenty of examples of hard news stories that fit this category: from claims of sexual harassment against a CEO, MPs' expenses, a big oil company's records on pollution and even celeb-rities whose lucrative public image does not match their extra-marital behaviour.

Getting to the truth is what helps people to be engaged citizens and allows the democratic process to function. Reporting "without fear or favour" is at the heart of public service journalism that aims to inform and contribute to debate about issues that matter.

Not every news story is something that someone is trying to hide. When a sci-entist publishes new research, they want people to know about it. When a new airline offers cheaper flights to ski destinations in Europe, they may have a PR team to spread the message. These still qualify as "news" to certain publications and may have value to readers of a science website or travel publication.

News is people: As we noted in Chapter 1, readers are interested in other people. Quite often that is the rich and famous. At one end of the spectrum that might be celebrity gossip but at the other it might be a disagreement be-tween two former political allies.

Conflict between people and organisations is often at the heart of news sto-ries: strike action that puts workers at odds with management; governments involved in international trade wars; parents who want to see greater funding for education; or patients who want a new drug provided through the health service.

Understanding how to tell stories in terms of people is vital. This doesn't mean only writing about people who are in the public eye, or those who work for government and business. New laws and legislation are crafted by politicians, but they have an impact on the lives of ordinary people. Telling the story from their perspective will often deliver a much stronger story. In the words of Arthur Christiansen, late editor of the *Daily Express (1933–1957)*: "There is no subject… that cannot be translated in terms of people."

Scale, impact and proximity: There are three factors worth considering in terms of news value.

Scale: what is the size of this event?
Impact: what does it mean for readers?
Proximity: how close is this to the readership either geographically or in terms of a community or interest group?

If a volcano kills hundreds of people on the other side of the world, the magnitude and rarity of the event would make it news. But if a bomb explodes in the capital city of a neighbouring country, with no loss of life, the proximity and potential impact on readers could push the previous story off the front page.

Equally if the largest employer in your town is about to go into receivership, with the potential loss of thousands of jobs, this is what will feature as the lead story of your local paper. But if your neighbour breaks their arm falling off the roof of their extension, then you can be pretty sure that this (rather than job losses, bombs and volcanoes) will be the subject of conversation at the dinner table tonight.

Proximity, scale and impact are useful ways to assess news value and then identify the best way to tell the story.

Exercise 1: Identifying news value

What makes each of the following intros newsworthy? Does the story rely on celebrity, conflict or something surprising? Does it potentially impact on the readers? Is there a human story at the heart of the piece or a combination of factors?

> Seven people have been killed and at least 48 injured in a terror incident in London in which three male attackers were shot dead by police.
> *BBC online*

The Duke and Duchess of Cambridge are expecting their third child, Kensington Palace has announced.

BBC online

A prisoner who was given nearly £4,000 damages because his cell light went out for almost 40 minutes has won the latest round of a legal fight.

Wales Online

Rail workers at three train operators are staging fresh strikes on Monday in disputes over the role of guards and driver-only trains.

The Guardian

Astronomers searching for signals from alien civilisations have detected 15 powerful, repeated radio pulses coming from a dwarf galaxy 3 billion light years away from Earth.

The Guardian

So how do we write news?

In each of the examples above you have the "news in a nutshell" approach. The key facts required to understand the story are delivered in a single sentence under 30 words, and often far less.

Journalists use an inverted triangle to explain the structure of news, with the key details at the top, and the remaining facts delivered in order of importance. So it is essential to get your opening paragraph right.

News intro

Opening par contains all the information essential to understanding the story in a single sentence
Who; What; Where; Why; How; When

The rest of the story delivers information in descending order of importance

This approach aims to grab the reader's attention, with the most interesting elements in the intro, not buried in the middle. It allows readers to scan stories and to stop reading at any point, knowing they have the key information.

It also helps the efficient running of a newsroom, by allowing sub-editors to cut a story from the bottom up. This means they don't have to invest time in restructuring to make sure important details are not lost. So if a story is moved to a smaller slot in the print version of a newspaper, the production team can quickly cut it from 800 to 500 words, by taking out the final six to seven paragraphs.

Space is less of an issue for an online platform. For digital-first publishers, there may still be a need to edit some stories in this manner as they move from web to their print version. In a digital-only world, getting your reader's attention becomes the priority. It is your job to get to the point and ensure that stories have impact rather than to blame readers for their decreasing attention spans.

While we are on the subject, concerns about short attention spans are nothing new. Consider this quote from influential American journalist and editor Edwin Lawrence Godkin in 1890: "Nothing can be more damaging to the habit of continuous attention than newspaper-reading… It never requires the mind to be fixed on any topic more than three or four minutes.…"

Identifying key facts

Rudyard Kipling, journalist, poet and author of *Just So Stories*, identified six questions as a useful checklist for any journalist – Who, What, Where, Why How and When. He called them his "six serving men" and the textbook example is as follows:

> Lady Godiva (WHO) rode (WHAT) naked (HOW) through the streets of Coventry (WHERE) yesterday (WHEN) in a bid to cut taxes (WHY).

This news intro comes in at 16 words long but manages to include each of Kipling's key questions. It is simple, clear and tells the whole story in a single sentence.

In general, the six questions should be answered somewhere in the story – but there is no requirement to cram them all into your intro paragraph. Go back to Exercise 1 and identify the Who, What, Where, Why, How and When in each intro.

Two of these questions – Who and What – are essential. In all news intros, somebody or something must do or experience something. All the examples above have a Who and a What in the intro. In the second example, about the royal baby, that's really all we get.

Only one intro answers the question When. For the story about rail strikes, readers need to know that strikes start on Monday, so they can plan for disruptions. In the other three stories, the implication is that the event happened recently, exactly when will be answered later in the story.

In stories two and three, there is no Where, because it's either not important or not relevant to the story (Kensington Palace is the source of the announcement, not the location).

You will also notice that all four of these examples start with the Who: "Seven people"; "The Duke and Duchess"; "A prisoner"; "Rail workers." I have chosen these intros for a reason. "News is people," and where possible you should aim to bring people to the front of your news story.

The six questions are a checklist, not a straitjacket. Use it as a guide to help you select the facts that are important. When you've written a news story, check whether you've missed something out and weakened your story. If there is no point including it, then don't.

The news intro should be able to stand on its own. Usually one sentence, it conveys the essence of the story in a clear, concise, punchy way: general enough to be understood; precise enough to be distinguished from other stories.

Exercise 2: Local news

Buy a copy of your local paper, and for each news story, identify what makes it newsworthy. Then ring the Who, What, Where, Why, How and When in the opening paragraph. Note any that do not fit our news-in-a-nutshell approach; we will return to these in Chapter 4.

Get in the habit of identifying the news value and key facts in any story you read. Doing this will help you to understand good news structure.

Planning your news intro

Writing your own news story can be significantly more challenging, especially when you are faced with a large amount of information. You may find there are multiple Whos and Whats that all offer different starting points or potential angles.

So before you start to write, take a notepad and plan your story. The first question you need to answer is, why is this news? What impact will it have on your readers? Why would they be interested in this story? Is this a story about conflict or tragedy, corruption or success against the odds? When you have answered this question, it will be easier to identify the facts needed to tell your story.

Let's imagine that a coach has crashed somewhere near Manchester this morning. It was foggy and the crash happened during rush hour, near junction 19 on the M62. Five people on the Damesbury Travel coach were killed in the accident and another seven people were seriously injured. Three other cars were involved in the incident (a Fiat, a red Audi and a Skoda). No one else was seriously hurt.

Here's our plan…

Why is this news: local tragedy
Who: five people
What: died
Why: involved in a motorway crash
Where: Manchester
How: during poor weather and rush hour
When: this morning

We want to tell the story clearly and bring people to the front of our intro, which might look like this…

> Five people were killed when the coach they were travelling in was involved in a motorway pile-up outside Manchester during this morning's rush hour.

Planning this story has allowed us to identify the key facts. Other details will appear later in the story: a more precise location, the number of people injured, the name of the coach company, etc. Keeping them out of the first par keeps our intro clutter-free and easy to understand.

The more complex your story the harder it can be to identify your focus. Let's imagine that a jewellery shop in Birmingham was raided by three armed attackers last night and that the manager was shot but only slightly injured. They made away with almost £250,000 worth of goods and police are now asking for help from the public. You need to write this story for the *Birmingham Mail*.

This is clearly news: as an unusual and violent crime has taken place locally. There are three groups of people here, so which is your "Who?" Is it the shop manager, the police or the armed attackers?

> A woman was shot by armed attackers who stole over £250,000 worth of jewellery from a city centre store last night.

There is clearly human interest but this intro pushes the armed robbery down in the story.

An alternative could be…

> Police are searching for three armed men who stole £250,000 worth of jewellery from a city centre store, after shooting the manager.

This has the advantage of leading with the latest development, but it is the job of the police to search for criminals. It also relegates the unique element of this story.

This would be my preferred way in…

> Three armed attackers shot a woman and made away with £250,000 worth of jewellery from a Birmingham city centre store last night.

The four opening words of this intro are the strongest of these three examples. This version places emphasis on the "armed attackers" and the crime.

Write in the active voice

This intro is written in the active voice. This means that the subject of the sentence (three armed attackers) are the people who performed the action ("shot a woman and made away with…").

The first example uses the passive voice. Here the woman did not do the shooting. Passive voice is when someone has something done to them.

"The window was washed by the boy" is passive voice, because the subject of the sentence (the window) did not do the washing.

"The boy washed the window" is active voice because the subject of the sentence (the boy) is the one who performed the action.

As journalists, we want our writing to be dynamic. We want to bring people to the front and emphasise what they have done. So where possible you should use the active voice. It encourages tighter writing, is more conversational and is less likely to deliver grammatical errors.

There are reasons for breaking this rule. This story from NBC News in America starts with the victim whose identity may be relevant to the story.

> A 22-year-old Black transgender woman was fatally shot in Dallas on Tuesday, according to police.
>
> NBC News

The following intro has three potential subjects but decides to emphasise the "heroics" of the police officer involved.

> A hero policeman who was stabbed trying to protect victims from a knifeman who attacked six people at a hotel in Glasgow yesterday is fighting for his life. (28 words)
>
> *Daily Mail*

As an intro it works, but it is overly complex. You could tighten and deliver it in the active voice, and with simpler sentence construction. You might feel that "knifeman" sounds rather odd, and do we need "A hero policeman" as his actions speak for themselves?

> A policeman is fighting for his life after he was stabbed by a man who attacked six people at a Glasgow hotel yesterday. (23 words)

Your first five words matter

With our jewellery story (above) we have three ways of delivering the same intro. Each one fits our formula: one sentence and under 30 words. By changing the opening of the sentence we also change the emphasis on the story.

News writing is not a formula that tells you how to cram facts into a single sentence. It is about making editorial decisions on the story you want to tell.

Your news intro may be 16 words long, but you should aim to catch your reader's attention with your opening five to seven words.

This story about job losses at a major employer does that by emphasising its proximity to the reader…

> Birmingham's John Lewis store will never reopen after lockdown in a huge blow to the city's economy.
>
> *Birmingham Live*

In this story, it is the age of the victim of an attack that is likely to hook readers…

> A 10-year-old boy was rushed to hospital after being stabbed in a "distressing" and "isolated" incident, leaving neighbours in shock.
>
> *Mirror*

News about the death of a celebrity may emphasise the reason for their fame. This story brings national sporting achievements to the front of this intro.

> England 1966 World Cup hero Jack Charlton has died at the age of 85.
>
> *Daily Mail*

As the story develops later in the day, this update emphasises the latest developments.

> Tributes have poured in for former England and Leeds defender Jack Charlton who has died aged 85.
>
> *Yahoo News*

While the Yorkshire Post emphasises his connection to Leeds United...

> World Cup winner and Leeds United legend Jack Charlton has died, aged 85, following a long-term illness.
>
> *Yorkshire Post*

Clarity and simplicity

Clarity is vital: news intros should contain only the key facts required to summarise the story and nothing else. The words used in all these examples are easily understood. You will not have had to reach for a dictionary for any of them. This is not an accident. Good journalistic writing should favour conversational language and commonly used words.

Sentence construction is also very simple. Our shortest intro above is just 14 words and our longest is 27. Only a few of the examples in this chapter contain a comma. If you need to use more than one comma and a full-stop in your news intro, then consider rewriting. Your job is to make it as easy as possible for your reader to understand the story in the intro.

Things to avoid

- Don't start with questions, direct quotes or abbreviations (except the most common).
- Don't start with things that create typographical problems, such as numbers, italics and speech marks.
- Don't start with things that slow the sentence, such as subordinate clauses; participles; parentheses; long, difficult or foreign words.
- Don't start with When, Where, How or Why.

Dealing with the Who

Picking up a random copy of the *Independent*, almost every story conforms to our news-in-a-nutshell approach. If I look at the sports section, then most articles start with a Who: (often a well-known sports star or football manager). In the business section, most intros begin with an organisation ("The UK construction industry...," "Pret a Manger...," "Barratt Developments..."), but even here there are some that start with a person ("The boss of Lloyds Bank..."). With more general news stories, there is a slight bias towards stories that lead with people.

A well-written news intro should not assume knowledge on the part of the reader. Don't expect them to know the name of a politician or the post they hold, the type of goods a particular business produces or the location of a particular town. Your intro needs to be precise enough to tell the story you want but accessible enough for it to work for all of your readers.

If everybody were equal in news terms, all intros might be general and start: "A man," "A company," "A football team." But people are not equally interesting. Some are so well known that their name is enough to sell a story. Others will only get into the paper by winning the national lottery or dying in a car crash.

Here is a typical Who intro about a celebrity – without his name there would be no national paper story:

> Comic Eddie Izzard fought back when he was attacked in the street by an abusive drunk, a court heard yesterday.
>
> *Daily Mail*

Note the contrast with

> A crown court judge who crashed his Range Rover while five times over the drink-drive limit was jailed for five months yesterday
>
> *Telegraph*

He may be a crown court judge but not many *Telegraph* readers would recognise his name. It is his occupation that makes this story newsworthy.

And finally the anonymous figure "A man" – his moment of infamy is entirely due to what he has done:

> A man acquitted of murder was convicted yesterday of harassing the family of a police officer who helped investigate him.
>
> *The Guardian*

There are few people well known enough to carry a story. Even Eddie Izzard requires the descriptive prefix of "comic" to make it clear who he is. The crown court judge's name adds nothing to the intro, and this will appear in the second or third paragraph.

Never start with When?

The Who and What elements of a story tend to be the most important, but your job is to tell the strongest possible story in a way that will engage the widest possible audience. For most stories you shouldn't begin with a When question, but there are exceptions. For example,

> Two years after merchant bank Barings collapsed with £830m losses, it is back in hot water.
>
> *Daily Mail*

If starting this way gives the story a strong angle, by all means do it.

Intros that make a claim

A vital distinction in news is whether you are reporting something as fact, or reporting that somebody has said something in a speech or a written report. A great deal of news comes through reports and surveys; courts, councils and tribunals; public meetings and conferences.

Finding a story from these sources requires you to spot something sufficiently significant and important to your readership. Some of these statements will be facts, some predictions and some opinions. All of them need to be clearly attributed in the intro: this means making it clear to the reader where the statement comes from. Tabloids sometimes delay the attribution to the second or third par – but this risks confusion in the reader's mind.

These kinds of stories can come from newly released reports. In this example, the source of these figures is from the Ministry of Justice, which is named in the second paragraph.

> Thousands of rape and murder cases were waiting to be dealt with as courts closed because of the coronavirus lockdown, according to new figures.
>
> *Independent*

Stories of this nature can also be sourced from statements from politicians, such as...

> The UK's aid budget is to be slashed by more than £2bn as a result of the coronavirus downturn, the International Development Secretary Anne-Marie Trevelyan has confirmed.
>
> *Independent*

Others can come from organisations that want to highlight issues or bring about change.

> A huge increase in litter and fly-tipping in woodlands during lockdown is harming the countryside and putting nature at risk, a charity has warned.
>
> *Independent*

Others can come from newly published research.

> The number of flying insects has plummeted by 75 per cent in the last 25 years, according to a study that suggests we are approaching an "ecological Armageddon."
>
> *Independent*

The last two examples only give a general attribution; specific mention of the charity and source of the study comes later in each story. Only give a name in the intro when it is likely to be recognised by the reader.

The general rule is to start with what is said – as with all three examples above – unless the person saying it is well known.

> Sir Jackie Stewart, the former motor-racing world champion, has accused his fellow Scots of being lazy and overdependent on public sector "jobs for life."
>
> *Sunday Times*

If your story is based on a speech or written report you give the detail (e.g. Where) lower in the story. But if it is based on a press conference or routine interview, there is no need to mention this. Writing "said at a press conference" or "in a telephone interview" is like nudging the reader and saying "I'm a journalist, really."

Linking ideas in an intro using "after"

"After" is a useful way of linking two stages of a story without having to say "because." Always use "after" rather than "following" to do this: it is shorter, clearer – and not journalistic jargon.

> A Cambridge student who killed two friends in a drunken car crash left court a free man yesterday after a plea for clemency from one of the victims' parents.
>
> *The Guardian*

In this case, the judge may have been influenced by the plea for clemency – but even if he was, that would still not enable the reporter to say "because."

In some stories the "after" links the problem with its solution...

> A six-year-old boy was rescued by firemen after he became wedged under a portable building being used as a polling station.
>
> *Telegraph*

In others the "after" helps to explain the first part of the intro:

> An Aboriginal man was yesterday speared 14 times in the legs and beaten on the head with a nulla nulla war club in a traditional punishment after Australia's courts agreed to recognise tribal justice.
>
> *The Guardian*

Sometimes "after" seems too weak to connect the two parts of an intro...

> Examiners were accused of imposing a "tax on Classics" yesterday after announcing they would charge sixth formers extra to take A-levels in Latin and Greek.
>
> *Daily Mail*

It is certainly true that A happened after B – but it also happened because of B. There should be a stronger link between the two parts of the intro.

Linking ideas with "as and when"

"As" is often used in intros to link two events that occur at the same time:

> A National Lottery millionaire was planning a lavish rerun of her wedding last night as a former colleague claimed she was being denied her rightful share of the jackpot.
>
> *Telegraph*

This approach rarely works. Here the main point of the story is not story A (the planned second wedding) but B (the dispute) – as is shown by the fact that the next ten pars develop this story; the 11th par covers the wedding plans; and the final four pars return to the dispute.

In contrast to "as," "when" is often used for intros that have two bites at the cherry: the first grabs the reader's attention; the second justifies the excitement:

> A crazed woman sparked panic in the High Court yesterday when she burst in and held a gun to a judge's head.
>
> *The Sun*

> A naive Oxford undergraduate earned a double first from the university of life when he was robbed by two women in one day, a court heard today.
>
> *London Evening Standard*

Exercise 3: News intros

Rewrite each of these news stories following the rules we have outlined above: one sentence and under 26 words. Where possible bring the Who to the front of the story, use the active voice, commonly used words and simple sentence construction. You'll find our suggested answers on page 242.

1) Mavis Watkins, 45, who teaches maths to year five children at the Westfield Primary in Leeds was awarded the first prize for her debut novel in a leading literary competition for aspiring nature writers and won a cheque for £10,000 pounds.

2) In a press conference today the government minister Keith Hounslow said that Russian interference in our elections posed the biggest threat to UK democracy.

3) The latest research from Sheffield University says that people who have strong northern or rural accents are less likely to be offered jobs.

4) The M4 was closed today when a coach crashed through the barriers and hurtled off the road. Police and medical crews arrived on the scene and although no one died, 11 people had to be taken to nearby Swindon hospital and one of them, a woman, is seriously injured.

5) Due to a very dry summer, the farmer's union (the NFU) has said their members will struggle to get a good harvest of hops, which means that beer prices are going to go up in the UK.

6) A coastal village in Indonesia was flooded and a number of houses collapsed when the area experienced over a month's worth of rain in just three days: at least 450 people had to be evacuated and are now homeless.

7) "It's a hidden crisis that not enough people are talking about," said researcher Paul Winslow from Bristol University. His latest research has found that air pollution has a disproportionate impact on vulnerable groups such as the elderly and the very young. His research found that it is the cause of over 40,000 early deaths each year.

Developing your news sense

News is not an abstract idea. A story is not news because it has been written but because people want to read it. Both of these stories relate to a proposed inquiry into the government's handling of the Covid-19 crisis. They take a different line on the story that is aimed at their readership...

> Boris Johnson has confirmed that he will organise an independent inquiry into his handling of Covid-19 – but not yet.
>
> *Mirror*

An independent inquiry into Covid-19 must be done urgently and with the input of nurses across all settings and sectors, according to the Royal College of Nursing.

Nursing Times

The better you understand your readers, the sharper your news writing will be. The quickest way to get to know them is to listen to what they have to say. Read their letters, emails and comments on stories. Even better, get out and meet them for yourself. No matter what publication you write for, there are ways to meet your readers.

If you aspire to write for your local newspaper or website, go out and talk to local people. What are their biggest challenges? What are they most worried about? What do they want local politicians to deal with? These are the stories that you should be covering. Get out and talk to potential readers and you may spot an opportunity for a story that your local paper has missed.

3
The first three paragraphs

What happens next?

When you write a news intro, precision, simplicity and clarity are key. We have seen how to achieve that in the intro paragraph: an opening sentence of under 30 words with the key facts required to understand the story. So what comes next?

In this chapter we are going to look at a simple formula for your first three to four paragraphs that will develop the angle of your story, deliver key information and keep the reader engaged. Not every news story conforms to this approach, but you will see a number of examples that do. It is a useful foundation that will help you build your story one paragraph at a time.

At 41 words long, this example is longer than the formula we are working to. All of the information here is important, but not all of it needs to be in the opening paragraph.

> Six-year-old Jack Moore was rescued by firemen after he became wedged under a portable building where he was playing with friends, near his home in Nevilles Cross Road, Hebburn South Tyneside, that was being used as a polling station.

Information we can cut from intro...

1. Jack Moore: few people will know who this is. We can leave his name till later but keep "A six-year-old boy" at the front of the intro to emphasise his age.
2. Nevilles Cross Road: few people will know where this is, so it will only clutter the intro. A local paper might use Hebburn, but does a national paper even need a location in the intro?
3. The boy was playing with friends and the portable building was being used as a polling station. As this story happened around the time of an election, we might focus on that aspect.

You have already seen this intro in the previous chapter...

> A six-year-old boy was rescued by firemen after he became wedged under a portable building being used as a polling station.
>
> *Telegraph*

Your second paragraph

The first paragraph of your news story has delivered the news-in-a-nutshell approach, but what happens next? The best guide to developing a news story is to ask, what does the reader need to know now?

A common approach in the classic news pyramid is to take the story in the intro par and to extend it, adding useful information to build the story, like this:

> Jack Moore was playing with friends near his home in Nevilles Cross Road, Hebburn, South Tyneside, when curiosity got the better of him and he crawled into the eight-inch space under the building, where he became firmly wedged.

This second paragraph tells us how he got stuck, and it also adds key information that we took out of the original 41-word intro: his name, where he is from and that he was playing with friends.

While the intro gives us headline information that will work for all our readers, the second paragraph is where we can explain, reinforce and add information. Note that this paragraph is also a single sentence.

Also note that the subject in the first and second par are the same: "A six-year-old boy" and "Jack Moore." This makes it easier for the reader to digest the story. Good news writers use simple sentence construction and accessible, conversational language, and deliver facts in a logical manner. You will often find this approach being used as a story develops.

Firemen are also mentioned in the intro par and we could have started the second paragraph... "Fireman took over four hours to release Jack Moore..." That could work, but it would have shifted the emphasis and would not have been quite as easy to take in.

You can see that much of the information that we took out of the original 41-word intro now appears in the second paragraph. These two paragraphs work together to layer information, to make the story engaging and easy to understand.

Building your story

It is imperative that your second paragraph builds on the story in your opening par. You must not switch to other people involved in the incident, change the story, or deliver lots of background information that doesn't move your piece forward. The job of the second paragraph is to amplify and explain.

Here is another example. You will see that the story in the intro is repeated in the second par, adding key information. Once again, the subject of paragraph one ("The wife…") is the same as the subject of paragraph two ("Maria Louise Hopes").

> The wife of a man found dead in the Rhondda has appeared in court charged with his murder.
>
> Maria Louise Hopes, 45, from Tonypandy, and her son Leon Port, 23, from Mountain Ash, have both been charged with the murder of 45-year-old Mark Hopes, who was found dead at a property in Brithweunydd Road, Trealaw.
>
> *WalesOnline*

In this instance, the story in paragraph two is the same as the story in paragraph one. The intro is easily understood and sells the story. The second paragraph builds on that and adds information, such as names, ages and locations to develop the story.

Par one	Par two becomes
"The wife":	Maria Louise Hopes, 45, from Tonypandy.
"a man":	45-year-old Mark Hopes
"found dead in Rhondda":	"at a property in Brithweunydd Road Trealaw"
"charged with his murder":	alongside her son Leon

Not all intros work this way, but there is an important principal and that is to stick with and extend the story in your introduction.

Get a quote high in your story

We know that "news is people" and quotes bring them into your stories. Quotes can offer human experience, colour and credibility to your report and they put the reader directly in touch with those involved.

Research from the analytics organisation Chartbeat has shown that articles with quotes higher in the story are more likely to be read. So while they do not make a good opening paragraph, you should aim to get a quote as high as possible. For the formula we are working on, that means a quote in the third or fourth par.

Just as the second par has to build on the intro, the quote that follows has to talk directly to that story and your selected angle. It must not take the story in an entirely different direction.

In the story about Jack Moore, above, the third paragraph delivers a quote from his mother that builds on the human interest angle.

> Firemen used airbags to raise the cabin before Jack was freed and taken to hospital, where he was treated for cuts and bruising and allowed home. His mother, Lisa, said: "He is a little shaken and bruised but apart from that he seems all right."
>
> *Telegraph*

The reader can empathise with the mother of a six-year-old who has undergone such an ordeal. A quote from one of the firemen telling us how they operated the airbags would not have had the same impact. A quote from one of them talking about how worried (or indeed unconcerned) Jack was during his rescue might have been a good alternative.

If you are looking for a potential first quote, then look for one that talks directly to the angle outlined in your opening paragraph.

A simple formula for news writing

We are trying to identify a simple approach that can be easily applied to any news story. Let's remind ourselves of the steps we need to take…

1. Identify why this story is news for your readers
2. Highlight the key facts required to tell that story
3. Construct your intro in one sentence of under 30 words
4. Build on that story in the second par
5. Get a strong quote in the third or fourth paragraph

How that works in practice

This example from *Wales Online* is clearly news. It is has happened locally, is surprising and involves conflict. The opening paragraph is simple and clear enough for anyone to understand. The second par builds on the story, adding the names of people and business involved to answer the question "is he OK?"

The third and fourth pars offer a quote, explaining the emotional impact of the attack.

> A shopkeeper had his front teeth knocked out when a neighbour's son punched him in the face following a "petty" dispute about an advertising board.
>
> David Crews, who runs Al Ponte deli in Cardiff with wife Karen, is still in pain from his injuries and has been told the dental treatment will take a year.
>
> "I've been in shock since it happened," said David, 63, who had to have three stitches to his mouth.
>
> "I've been extremely shaky. I never expected to be assaulted outside my shop."
>
> *Wales Online*

All four paragraphs are short and just one sentence long. Each one sticks to the same story but moves it forward, answering a key question for the reader. You can take a "squint test" with news stories like this. On a word document, it should look like news: short paragraphs of no more than two to three lines long. If you spot a large block of copy, or an excessively long paragraph, then you need to review your story.

Quotes from an eyewitness

Your first quote must build on the angle set out in the opening par. This story is about a fictional train accident – although it is based on a number of similar reports. It builds to a quote from one of the passengers that appears in the third paragraph. This gives us an impactful eyewitness account of what happened from inside the train.

> Four people have died and at least 34 were injured when a train derailed in the northern Indian state of Uttar Pradesh.
>
> Police said that they are still trying to rescue passengers trapped in the wreckage and that an estimated 20 people are unaccounted for.
>
> "It all happened so quickly," said passenger Nikhil Pandit. "I remember hearing the sound of glass breaking and shouts from fellow passengers. By the time I realised what had happened, the carriage had been badly smashed up."

Again, each paragraph is relatively short, clear and builds the story logically. The quote puts the reader directly in touch with someone who witnessed the crash.

Quotes from an expert

This story is about plans to overhaul transport in New York. It builds to a quote that offers opinion from someone with expertise and inside knowledge of this development. Corey Johnson, a representative of the city council, explains the rationale behind plans to "break car culture" in New York.

The intro is longer than the formula we are working to – it is from *The Guardian* and their intros could often be tighter. Do we need the two rather confusing figures relating to new pedestrian space and the term "landmark move"? Probably not, but the intro still works.

> New York is set to build more than 250 new bike lanes and add 1m sq ft (92,903 sq meters) of pedestrian space in a landmark move designed to "break the car culture" of the city.
>
> The city council passed legislation this week that will see $1.7bn invested in road infrastructure over 10 years in a move that it is hoped will transform city streets and dramatically improve safety for cyclists and pedestrians.
>
> The New York city council speaker, Corey Johnson, who introduced the "streets master plan" bill and is anticipated to run for mayor in 2021, said after the vote: "The way we plan our streets now makes no sense and New Yorkers pay the price every day, stuck on slow buses or risking their own safety cycling without protected bike lanes … I want to completely revolutionise how we share our street space, and that's what this bill does.
>
> "This is a roadmap to breaking the car culture in a thoughtful, comprehensive way, and I am so proud to pass this bill today."
>
> *The Guardian*

This quote allows the reader to hear directly from someone involved with the implementation of this plan and adds authority.

Building on stories about a speech

When a story is about what someone has said in a speech, or what has been discovered in research, then the quote needs to talk directly to the opening paragraph. Here, the story is the long-term health implications for people who play rugby. The source of the research in the opening par is just "researchers." You can be pretty sure that had this research come from either Oxford or Cambridge, then these universities would have been named checked in the intro.

The second par adds a key element to the story by explaining what action these scientists want governing bodies to take. The quote in par three reinforces the health concerns and explains why previous rule changes have not been sufficient. Hearing from an expert source adds authority to this story.

> Rugby may be seen as a sport for the fittest and toughest of players but the game's legacy could be a lifetime of health problems, according to researchers.
>
> Scientists are now calling on the sport's governing bodies to step up efforts to prevent injury and support players after retirement in the wake of their findings.
>
> Dr Karen Hind, from the Department of Sport and Exercise Sciences at Durham University, said: "It is clear from these findings that playing rugby union or rugby league is associated with lasting impacts in terms of injury and pain.
>
> "Although there have been initiatives and rule changes to try and make the game safer, the rates of injury across a player's entire career are still very high.
>
> "The game is now also faster and players are bigger than they used to be so the impacts are greater."
>
> *Independent*

Exercise 1: Analysing news stories

Go back to the local newspaper you used for Ex 1 in Chapter 2. See how many examples of news stories you can find that follow this formula. You will find plenty of exceptions, but this approach gives you a useful point of comparison to assess how effective they are.

How to use quotes: Direct quotes are important in your story. These appear within speech marks and they are the exact words that your interviewees used. They add authority and opinion, offer eyewitness accounts and put the reader directly in touch with people who matter. By using their exact words you are less likely to misrepresent what they said.

It is important that the reader knows who is speaking. In the story about the Cardiff shopkeeper, we have already been given his name, but the quote still comes with the attribution, "said David…." You should almost exclusively use the verb "said" in your copy and be consistent with the use of past (said) or present (says) tense.

> "I've been in shock since it happened," said David, 63, who had to have three stitches to his mouth.

"I've been extremely shaky. I never expected to be assaulted outside my shop. I can't believe it happened so quickly."

Wales Online

Attribution can come before, after or in the middle of the quote. If you haven't already been introduced to the speaker, then attribution should come before the quote, or (as with the example above) as early as possible within the quote. When we have a new interviewee, do not leave attribution to the end of a long quote, as this will confuse the reader. When you move from one interviewee to another it is vital you introduce the new speaker as early as possible.

Make sure you know how to punctuate around quotes. Different publications will have different house styles around the use of colons and double or single quotation marks, but the rules for punctuation do not change.

It's also worth noting that attribution can help to layer information. The attribution with this quote tells us that David is 63 years old and we find out about the treatment he required (stitches to his mouth). As you move through a story, weaving in information about interviewees like this can help you to write tightly, deliver important facts and keep the story moving forward.

Names and titles

The convention in journalism is full name (John/Joan Smith) for the first use, then either courtesy title (Mr/Mrs/Miss/Ms Smith) or surname or first name for the rest of the story. Each publication will have a different approach, and it is important to read their house style guide. (For more on this and similar points see the chapter on house style in *Subediting and Production for Journalists*, by Tim Holmes, Routledge.) Remember, be consistent: never follow "John Smith" by "Mr Smith," then "John." Variation for its own sake irritates the reader.

First, in general, use "said"/"says" to introduce and attribute quotes, though "told"/"tells" is a useful variation when we need to know both source and audience, as in "the minister told MPs." So do not write

Speaking at the meeting the speaker said …

but

The speaker told the meeting …

Always avoid variations like "claim," "admit," "state," "remark," "point out," "explain," "refute" – unless you intend the precise meaning conveyed by the word.

Do not use "he added" because you think the quote has been going on long enough and are too lazy to think up some other way of getting to the next bit. Keep "he added" for cases where there is a pause, an afterthought or a contrast as in:

He said it would probably rain – but he added: "We need it."

Exercise 2: First three pars

From the facts below plan and then write the first three pars of this news story to the formula we have outlined above. Select just one quote that you will deliver in par three to support the angle you feel is strongest.

Story outline

If you love pastries, sausage rolls and cakes with your morning coffee, then prepare yourself for some bad news. The popular bakery chain Crumbles is closing 47 of its least profitable stores around the UK. The business makes over £1 billion each year and it saw a 6.4% increase in the last financial year. But they expect a significant downturn in profits and say they need to reduce costs.

Job losses are inevitable with at least 650 redundancies across their business. This will include jobs at their head office and at outlets that aren't faced with closure. They say this is because sales have fallen 48% across the business in the last six months and up to 78% in some of its city centre stores, as more people work from home.

Workers will be consulted in the coming weeks with the first closures and redundancies likely to happen by the end of next month.

Company founder Brenda Wainwright said,

> Crumbles is a great British success story. We started from just one outlet in Chepstow and we've grown to be a major force on the high street. This year has been pretty tough on us. Businesses like ours need to see a rent and rate reduction if we are to remain viable.

CEO Thomas Bloxworth said,

> This is devastating news for our workers. We have made every possible effort to keep stores open by but sales figures make it impossible to avoid redundancies. We have to take this step today to ensure the long-term health of the business.

Financial officer Pauline Osbourne said,

> The Covid-19 lockdown has made this a tough year for all retail, especially those catering to commuters and city centre workers. Beyond that stores like John Lewis are struggling as are companies in the entertainment sector. Our business needs to evolve and we still have an ambitious plan for new shop opportunities.

First plan your story

Why is this news:
Who:
What:
When:
Where:
Why:
How:

You will find a suggested answer on page 242.

4
News structure and style

Different approaches to news

We have looked at one approach to the opening pars of a simple news article. This is a useful starting point, but not every story follows this formula. In this chapter, we will look at how to handle stories that make more than one point in the intro, and how to develop the structure of your news story and key elements of style.

We will also look at stories that don't take a "news-in-a-nutshell" approach to the intro. These aren't better or more advanced, and as we will see, a straight news intro can often be the most effective. But it is useful to understand other ways to selling key aspects of your story.

We can categorise these approaches under a number of headings...

Humorous and smart

Some intros use wit and style to promise a smarter or more interesting take on events.

The first example reports on a surprise 2-0 victory for Arsenal over Manchester City, but you don't get to hear about that until par four. Instead, it tells us that one player in particular has redeemed himself after a calamitous performance when the clubs last met. There's an insightful, conversational feel to the opening of this story.

> When football returned last month following the coronavirus lockdown, it appeared David Luiz did not quite get the memo.
>
> The Brazilian endured a horror show of an evening as Arsenal met Manchester City at the Etihad Stadium, coming off the bench only to spill

a Kevin De Bruyne pass into the path of Raheem Sterling, before later conceding a penalty and getting a straight red card.

Daily Mail

The next example uses wit to pull the reader in. Scientists have discovered a species of deep-water fish that can absorb up to 99.95% of the light to camouflage itself from predators. The writer shuns the straight "…according to latest research" approach to evoke a neat cultural reference.

> You might be able to apply black make-up, dye your hair a dusky tone and drape yourself in black leather, but you'll never be as goth as some species of deep-sea fish.
>
> *BBC Science Focus*

To cover the news of Tiger Wood's win at the 2019 Masters, sports writer Oliver Holt starts with an anecdote that reminds us of the golfer's turbulent career. It helps to put in context a win that could be his greatest ever achievement, according to Holt.

> Five years ago, when I was already plenty old enough to know better, I went to Orlando to chronicle the end of Tiger Woods' career.
>
> I visited some of the landmarks of his fall, like the Perkins restaurant at the corner of Conroy and Apopka Vineland where he began the affair with a waitress that led to the end of his marriage.
>
> *Daily Mail*

Scene setting

Intros can give the reader a ringside view of the action. This story starts with the moment that the Queen knights Captain Tom Moore. This centenarian was being recognised for his efforts to raise over £33 million, by completing laps of his garden with a walking frame.

> In the end, Sir Tom Moore didn't need to rise.
>
> On a day infused with emotion, Queen Elizabeth II tapped the blade of a sword once owned by her father on the slender shoulders of 100-year-old Tom Moore, making a hero of a nation a knight of the realm…
>
> *Associated Press*

This story about the recovery of F1 driver Michael Schumacher places the reader outside the gates of his home. We get few details but the promise is of a story afforded to a select audience.

Only close family and a handful of trusted friends are permitted through the high gates of Michael Schumacher's house on the banks of Lake Geneva.

And silence surrounds the German's condition since he hit his head while skiing in the French Alps six-and-a-half years ago.

Daily Mail

The narrative style

In the two examples below, the traditional news story gives way to the kind of narrative technique used in fiction. Both stories focus on a specific person and an important moment with an element of mystery to hook the reader.

The thud of something falling to the ground stopped Paul Hallett in his tracks as he tore apart the rafters of an old outside lavatory.

The handyman brushed off his hands and picked up a dusty wallet, half expecting to find nothing inside.

But picking through the contents one by one, Mr Hallett realised he had stumbled upon the details of a US Air Force chaplain stationed at a nearby RAF base in Suffolk 50 years earlier.

Daily Mail

Here is another that gives little detail of the drama about to unfold but is guaranteed to make the reader want to know more.

Choral scholar Gavin Rogers-Ball was dying for a cigarette. Stuck on a coach bringing the Wells Cathedral choir back from a performance in Germany, he had an idea – ask one of the boys to be sick and the adult members of the choir could step off the bus for a smoke.

It was a ruse that was to cost the alto dear.

The Guardian

Both stories begin with a dramatic moment – and name their main character. As with fiction, the trick is to get the reader involved with that person and what happens to them.

News stories about court cases and tribunals can often be handled in this way, and so can any light or humorous subject. But for the technique to work there must be a story worth telling.

The delayed drop

Here, the story is written in narrative style but the real news is kept back for effect. The change of direction is sometimes signalled by a "but":

A pint-sized Dirty Harry, aged 11, terrorised a school when he pulled out a Magnum revolver in the playground. Screaming children fled in panic as the boy, who could hardly hold the powerful handgun, pointed it at a teacher.

But headmaster Arthur Casson grabbed the boy and discovered that the gun – made famous by Clint Eastwood in the film Dirty Harry – was only a replica.

Mirror

The two pars above effectively tell us the whole story. The three opening pars below prompt far more questions than they answer and given the subject matter are guaranteed to get people reading on.

A naughty nurse called Janet promised kinky nights of magic to a married man who wrote her passionate love letters.

He was teased with sexy photographs, steamy suggestions and an offer to meet her at a hotel.

But soon he was being blackmailed . . . the girl of his dreams was really a man called Brian.

Mirror

As entertainment, the surprise factor of a well-told delayed-drop story is hard to beat.

Selling the story

Here the intro aims to sell this story to a specific audience. The report's forecast is that the internet will turn the world of banking upside down – that is where the straight news story starts. But the reporter has added an intro that dramatises the story and emphasises potential proximity ("friends or relations") and impact on readers ("turn their world upside down").

If you have friends or relations in High Street banking, tell them – warn them – to find another job. Within five years, the Internet is going to turn their world upside down.

This is the confident forecast in a 200-page report...

Daily Mail

Nostalgia is used in the next example: the straight news in par three follows an intro that reminds the reader of a pleasurable past spent buying clothing and listening to music.

They were the jeans that launched (or relaunched) a dozen pop songs.

Now Levis, the clothing manufacturer that used to turn everything it touched into gold, or even platinum, has fallen on harder times.

Yesterday the company announced that it is to cut its North American workforce by a third.

The Guardian

The risk with this kind of selling intro is that some readers may not have friends in banking, or feel particularly nostalgic about jeans and pop music. What is important here is knowing your readers and how they are likely to react.

Exercise 1: Analysing local news

Buy a copy of your local newspaper or head online to find examples of each of the news intro types above. Try to work out what element of the story the writer is trying to emphasise to engage the reader: human interest, storytelling, a different angle, or the proximity and potential impact on the reader.

News in a nutshell

There are alternatives to the traditional approach, but you will find that the news-in-a-nutshell is often the best, especially when you have a strong story. Here the same news is reported in three papers, from tabloid to broadsheet in a very similar way.

Each publication emphasises the human angle of the story and surprising objects used to perform a life-saving operation in midair. Note that the *Mail* and *The Sun* both start with doctors, which helps to deliver a tighter, more direct version of the story in active voice.

A woman who fell ill with a collapsed lung on a Boeing 747 had her life saved by two doctors who carried out an operation with a coathanger, a bottle of mineral water, brandy and a knife and fork.

The Guardian

Two British doctors carried out a life-saving operation aboard a jumbo jet – with a coat hanger.

Daily Mail

A doctor saved a mum's life in a mid-air operation – using a coathanger, pen top, brandy and half a plastic bottle.

The Sun

Avoid cluttered intros

The main cause of clutter in news stories is trying to say too much in the intro. This makes the opening par hard to read, and the story tricky to develop.

> Marketing junk food to children has to become socially unacceptable, a leading obesity expert will say today, warning that the food industry has done too little voluntarily to help avert what a major report this week will show is a 'far worse scenario than even our gloomiest predictions'.
>
> *The Guardian*

At 48 words, this is far longer than the concise intros we've been working on. The key problem is that the reporter wants to link two apparently unconnected statements on the same subject, which is fair enough in the story but not in the intro. The natural place to end the intro is after "will say today." That would deliver a clear and concise intro.

Instead, the sentence meanders on with the "warning" followed by the doom-laden "major report." But what's being asserted is not "warning" at all – "warning" here is journalese for saying or claiming. Then there's the word "voluntarily" – which adds nothing to "done too little"; there's "help" – which is unnecessary; there's "major" – journalese again (whoever heard of a "minor" report?); and there's the word "show," which implies endorsement of the report's findings instead of merely describing them.

Handling intros with two ideas

As far as possible, intros should be about one point not two, and certainly not several. Sometimes the double intro can work, but it needs to be developed carefully.

In the next example, the reporter has divided the intro into two separate pars. It's easier to read this way. The writer develops both stories in tandem and does that by first looking at story A (first female attorney general) and then story B (most diverse cabinet) in the following par.

This approach keeps each paragraph simple and easy to understand.

Intro A

Bill Clinton has completed his selection of the most diverse Cabinet in US history by appointing the country's first woman law chief.

Intro B

The President-elect also picked a fourth black and a second Hispanic to join his top team.

Extension of intro A

Zoe Baird, currently general counsel for the insurance company Aetna Life & Casualty, will be his Attorney General.

Extension of intro B

Black representative Mike Espy was named Mr Clinton's secretary for agriculture while former mayor of Denver Federico Pena, a Hispanic, will be responsible for transport issues.

Daily Mail

Developing structure with two points

Another approach is to develop one story over the opening pars before you return to the second story.

In this example, story A is that a little known golfer has won the Australian Masters in Melbourne. Story B is that Tiger Woods finished the day in fifth place, and it is the celebrity player that many readers really want to hear about. Just look at how much space is given to his quotes.

Intro (A + B)

Australian Lucas Parsons equalled the course record with a nine-under-par 64, but still could not quite take the spotlight away from Tiger Woods in the first round of the Australian Masters in Melbourne yesterday.

Extension of intro A

Parsons fired six birdies on the front nine before holing his second shot at the par four 13th for an eagle two – the highlight of the round. His approach shot landed on the green and bounced two metres beyond the flag, but then spun back into the hole.

Parsons now shares the Huntingdale course record with compatriot Mike Clayton and German Bernhard Langer.

Quotes supporting intro A

"My game has been getting better over recent months. This is a course I know and I can play well here," said Parsons. "I got off to a good start today and it just kept happening. I just went with the flow."

Extension of intro B

But Woods, who won the Bangkok Classic in Thailand on Sunday, his fourth tournament victory since turning professional last August, was still the centre of attention.

Development of B and quotes

He also enjoyed the long holes to finish at five-under-par 68 for a share of fifth place to remain in contention.

The 21-year-old big-hitting American birdied all four par fives on the par-73 course to the delight of a large gallery, even though he only used his driver once.

"I grinded my way around there and came in with a good score. Off the tee, it was probably one of my better ball-striking rounds in a while," Woods said.

"It was just the mental grind of playing a golf course that requires accuracy and so much precision off the tee. You don't really have a chance to relax.

"I haven't played my best golf today. I just made one birdie besides the par fives and that's not saying a whole lot."

Further information

Australian Peter O'Malley held second place with a 65. Former US Masters champion Larry Mize finished on five-under alongside Woods, while defending champion Craig Parry, of Australia, struggled to a 73.

Telegraph

Developing two stories at the same time can cause problems. You either have to make the reader hop about from A to B as the story unfolds, or develop story A fully before turning to story B. The problem here is that B can get forgotten before the reader reaches it.

The best intro is always the simplest: try to find one point for your intro rather than two. That may mean that you need to introduce important material not covered by the intro early in the story. But that is better than cluttering the first par and confusing the development of the story.

Introducing a second news angle

Here is an example of a news intro with a single point that is developed over the opening three pars. In this intro, McDonald's has won a libel trial, and the writer hints at a second story with the word "hollow." In the fourth par, we learn that this is not just because of the financial implications but because of criticisms of the company made by the judge.

Intro focus on story A

McDonald's won a hollow victory over two Green campaigners yesterday after the longest libel trial in history.

The hamburger corporation was awarded £60,000 damages over a leaflet which savaged its reputation, accusing it of putting profits before people, animal welfare and rain forests.

But the verdict cost more than £10 million in legal bills, which McDonald's will never recover from the penniless protesters who fought for three years in the High Court.

Introducing story B

David Morris and Helen Steel were also claiming victory last night after the judge backed two of their claims. In an 800-page judgment which took six months to prepare, Mr Justice Bell ruled that the company is cruel to animals and that its advertising takes advantage of susceptible young children.

Develop story A...

Mr Morris, 43, and 31-year-old Miss Steel are refusing to pay a penny of the damages. "They don't deserve any money," said Miss Steel, a part-time barmaid. "And in any case, we haven't got any."

Further information – background

The trial began in June 1994 and spanned 314 days in court, involving 180 witnesses and 40,000 pages of documents.

At its heart was the leaflet "What's Wrong with McDonald's?", produced by the tiny pressure group London Greenpeace, which is not connected to Greenpeace International. The defendants helped to distribute it in the 1980s.

McDonald's had issued similar libel writs many times before, and opponents had always backed down. But Mr Morris and Miss Steel, vegetarian anarchists from Tottenham, North London, were determined to fight.

The burger firm hired one of the most brilliant legal teams money can buy, headed by Richard Rampton QC. The defendants were forced to represent themselves because there is no legal aid for libel cases. Former postman Mr Morris, a single parent with an eight-year-old son, appeared in court in casual dress, usually unshaven. Miss Steel, the daughter of a retired company director from Farnham, Surrey, prepared for the case each morning while hanging from a strap on the Piccadilly Line tube.

Second extension of story A

Yesterday Mr Justice Bell ruled that they had libelled McDonald's by alleging that the corporation ripped down rain forests, contributed to Third

World starvation, created excessive waste and sold food which was closely linked with heart disease and cancer.

He said it was also libellous to claim that McDonald's was interested in recruiting only cheap labour and exploited disadvantaged groups, particularly women and black people, although the claim was "partly justified" because the firm pays low wages.

Developing story B

The judge also condemned as "most unfair" the practice of sending young staff home early if the restaurant was quiet and not paying them for the rest of their shift.

Critics of the company will also seize on his ruling that McDonald's "are culpably responsible for cruel practices in the rearing and slaughter of some of the animals which are used to produce their food".

After the hearing, McDonald's UK president Paul Preston said he had no wish to bankrupt Mr Morris and Miss Steel. "This was not a matter of costs, it was a matter of truth," he said.

But the case has been a public relations disaster for McDonald's, cast in the role of a hugely rich corporation using its financial muscle to suppress debate on important issues. Far from the leaflet being suppressed, two million copies have now been handed out around the world.

Daily Mail

Conflict

Conflict between people and organisations – in politics, business, court cases – often make news. If the issue is complicated, the intro should be an attempt to simplify it without distortion. As the story is developed it will become easier to deal with the complications.

This story is supposedly about complaints to the broadcasting regulatory body Ofcom that followed a TV interview. There is an element of quote and counter quote here – first the accusation from the MP – of a "diatribe" – and then the exchange between the two.

This is a model that can work well in stories where there is a disagreement between two organisations. Here, however, no one responds to the 281 complaints. The story here is simply retelling the on-air conflict for those who may have missed the original broadcast. A more newsworthy report would have offered quotes from both parties about the Ofcom complaint.

Piers Morgan has once again been hit with hundreds of complaints after "humiliating" an MP on Good Morning Britain.

Ofcom has been contacted by 281 people after watching Piers Morgan's interview with MP Andrew Bridgen, *The Sun* has reported.

Piers, 55, was left seething with rage after the backbencher accused him of having a "diatribe" against Prime Minister Boris Johnson.

The GMB presenter launched into a rant after asking the MP whether he was allowed to visit his two sons if he kept to the social distancing rules.

Andrew Bridgen had responded: "As far as I would be concerned, I do not speak for the Government, as long as you maintain social distancing in what you do."

However Piers hit out as he insisted it was "against the rules."

He raged: "You are a Conservative Member of Parliament, who thinks you know exactly what Boris Johnson has been saying, and you just told me to do something I'm not allowed to do.

"So this is the problem isn't it? There is no clarity. It's a load of flannel, talking about controlling the virus.

"You as a leading, high-profile Conservative politician haven't got a clue about what these rules actually mean, and you're an MP. You're part of this."

Mirror

News style

Bridges and links

In general, news does not need bridges to connect one par with the next. Transitional words and phrases like "also" – or the pompous equivalent "in addition" – are rarely necessary. When you start a new sentence or a new par, you are effectively saying to the reader, "also." That does not mean that these words and phrases are always wrong, but you should not strain to include them in traditional news.

Past, present or future tense?

Most news intros report what happened, so are written in the past tense. But some are written in the present tense. In this example it is because the investigation is ongoing...

An advert for Accurist watches featuring an ultra-thin model is being investigated by the Advertising Standards Authority.

The Guardian

News of the investigation makes a better intro than the fact that people have complained to the ASA: as well as being more immediate it takes the story a stage further.

Some intros combine the present tense for the latest stage in the story with the past tense for the facts that grab the attention:

> BT is tightening up its telephone security system after its confidential list of ex-directory numbers was penetrated – by a woman from Ruislip.
>
> *The Observer*

This intro uses "after" to link two stages of a story and the dash emphasises the element of surprise – that this huge organisation was apparently outwitted by a mere individual.

Speech-report intros are often written with the first part in the present tense and the second in the past:

> Copyright is freelances' work and they must never give it away, said Carol Lee, who is coordinating the NUJ campaign against the Guardian's new rights offensive.
>
> *Journalist*

Note that the first part of the intro is not a direct quote. Quotes are not used in news intros for two main reasons: as Harold Evans noted back in 1972,

> "Offices where intros are still set with drop caps usually ban quote intros because of the typographical complications. There is more against them than that. The reader has to do too much work. He has to find out who is speaking and he may prefer to move on."

When you write the intro for a speech report, take the speaker's main point and, if necessary, put it in your own words. The version you end up with may or may not be the speaker's actual words.

Some present-tense intros look forward to the future:

> Yule Catto, the chemicals group, is believed to be preparing a £250m bid for Holliday Chemical, its sector rival.
>
> *Sunday Times*

And some intros are actually written in the future tense:

> More than 1,000 travel agency shops will unite this week to become the UK's largest high street package holiday chain, using the new name Worldchoice.
>
> *The Observer*

Where possible, use the present or the future tense rather than the past and, if you're making a prediction, be as definite as you can safely be.

Quotes and questions

When you deliver a quote, you do not need to tell that reader that you asked a question or that an answer was delivered to you directly.

Your job as a journalist is to ask questions and to get answers. You don't need to tell people that this is what you have done. It is bad style in part because it suggests that on other occasions no interview has taken place – that your publication's stories are routinely based on unchecked press releases.

Journalese and jargon

Most of what is called journalese – whether downmarket ("axe" for "sack") or upmarket ("sustain injury" for "hurt") – is bad writing and you should avoid it. "Following" for "after" is certainly an example of this.

But certain code words can be useful – to maximise the amount of information you can convey to the reader. For example, if you are pretty confident – but not certain – that A will happen, you can write: "A is set to happen." You should always try to find out precisely what somebody's role is in something – but if you can't, it's usually better to write "B is involved with the project" rather than nothing at all.

The same advice covers phrases like "industry sources say" when your contacts will not give you identified quotes. Inform your reader – but keep the jargon under control.

Consistency

Be consistent. Don't change your tone in the middle of a story. Either write in the traditional style or use one of the variations; be serious or light – not both at the same time.

Particularly avoid the facetious remark dropped into a straightforward story. As the columnist Keith Waterhouse once put it:

The interpolation of a weak joke into a serious news story is so inappropriate that it can only be described as oafish.

Variation across a long story

One of the worst news-writing habits you can acquire is to avoid calling a spade a spade – or rather, having called it a spade in the intro, then a gardening tool, a digging device and a horticultural implement in the pars that follow.

This practice is based on two false assumptions: one, that the repetition of words like spade is always a bad idea; two, that attentive readers enjoy these variation words for their own sake.

Here's a good example of a narrative intro, about a fishmonger who missed the opportunity to sell on a lobster worth £20,000. Note how the writer attempts to avoid repeating the word "lobster" in the opening par.

> When Bernard Warner examined the lobster it did not strike him as being particularly odd. The crustacean looked paler than its rivals but it had arrived at Mr Warner's fishmonger shop in Doncaster as part of a routine delivery from the East coast, so there could not be anything unusual about it, could there?
>
> *The Guardian*

This intriguing story is weakened by the attempts at variation. Lobster becomes "crustacean" in par one, then an "animal" in par two, and "creature" in par four.

There can be times when variation is useful to avoid unintended repetition. Read your stories out loud and your ear should tell you when this is necessary. But remember that the plainer the word, the less noticeable it is when repeated. Don't worry about repeating words like "said" and "says."

Sometimes repetition tells you that the sentence itself is badly constructed – too long, too loose, too complicated. Here's an example with the repeated word in bold:

> A mother of three young **children**, jailed for two months after lying about a traffic accident, was yesterday reunited with her **children** after she was freed by three Appeal Court judges – but they reiterated the gravity of the offence and said the plight of her **children** had tipped the balance in favour of her release.
>
> *The Guardian*

About the only thing to be said in favour of this intro is that "children" does not become "offspring" in the second case and "progeny" or "issue" in the third. If you find yourself writing a sentence like this, don't replace the repeated words: rewrite to simplify the sentence.

Dealing with a running story

When a story runs from day to day it would irritate the reader to keep talking about "A man" in the intro. Also it would be pointless: most readers either read the paper regularly or follow the news in some other way. But it is essential that each news story as a whole should include necessary background for new readers.

News of the circus worker's injury has already been reported, here the latest development is a discovery about the background of the tiger.

> The tiger which bit a circus worker's arm off was the star of the famous Esso TV commercial.
>
> *London Evening Standard*

After this intro, the story gives an update on the victim's condition and repeats details of the accident.

Court reports are often running stories. Here, the trick is to write an intro that works for both sets of readers: it should be both vivid and informative.

> The 10-year-old girl alleged to have been raped by classmates in a primary school toilet said yesterday that she just wanted to be a "normal kid."
>
> *The Guardian*

In some cases phrases like "renewed calls" or "a second death" make the point that this is one more stage in a continuing drama:

> Another Catholic man was shot dead in Belfast last night just as the IRA issued a warning that the peace process in Northern Ireland was on borrowed time.
>
> *The Guardian*

Building a full news story

If you are struggling with the structure of the story, the best approach is often to ask yourself what the reader needs to know next. Keep it simple and this can deliver a logical development to your story. Let's look at how it works with this piece...

> **Man killed as L-drive car plunges off cliff**
>
> A man was feared dead last night after his car ran off a 150ft clifftop into rough seas when his girlfriend lost control while he was giving her a driving lesson.

How did she escape?

The woman, in her early 20s, scrambled from the Ford Fiesta as it crashed through a low stone wall at the edge of a car park at the Beacon, St Agnes, on the north Cornwall coast.

What happened to him?

Andrew Dunklin, 25, from St Agnes, was trapped in the vehicle as it rolled over the cliff. It is thought he was thrown through the windscreen into the sea. The car came to rest in 30ft of water and immediately began to break up.

What did she do?

The woman raised the alarm and coastguards launched a rescue operation which at its height involved a Navy helicopter, divers, two lifeboats and a cliff rescue team.

Insp Paul Whetter of Devon & Cornwall police said the woman had managed to get out just before the car went over the cliff.

What happened to her next?

She was treated for shock at the scene by paramedics before being taken to Treliske Hospital in Truro.

A neighbour looking after the missing man's mother at her home in the village said: "She has just lost her only son."

How did the search team operate?

The search operation was hampered by worsening weather and a Navy diver had to be pulled out of the sea. The St Agnes and St Ives inshore lifeboats could not get close to the spot.

"We sent our cliff man down to a point about 60ft above the waves, where the cliff became a sheer drop," said Mike North, sector manager with HM Coastguard. "He was able to keep an eye on the scene and spotted a lot of debris from the car.

"He saw some clothing and the inshore lifeboat was able to pick up the girl's bag floating in the water."

Why did they stop?

A spokesman for RNAS Culdrose added: "The first diver in the water said it was too dangerous for others to go in. He was being pounded by pieces of wreckage from the car which was being smashed on to the rocks at the bottom of the cliffs."

The search was called off at 5pm because the situation had become 'too dangerous' for rescue workers. It was to be resumed at first light today.

Why were the couple there?

Mr Dunklin is understood to have been giving his girlfriend a driving lesson on Beacon Road, a remote and little-used track near the cliffs. They may have driven into the gravel-surfaced car park to practise reversing or three-point turns.

Telegraph

Exercise 2: Analysing news structure

Find three news stories all over 500 words and answer the following questions.

- Why is this newsworthy for this readership?
- What facts appear in the intro?
- Where does the first quote appear?
- How is the story structured?
- What chain of questions does it answer?

5
Writing for the web

Gavin Allen

Digital journalism

Good writing remains good writing, whatever platform it appears on.

It doesn't matter if that writing is in a novel, a *New Yorker* longform, a *Buzzfeed* interactive, a Tweet or a GIF-overlay.

Post Covid-19, newspapers – already struggling to adapt to a digital world – are suffering in new and painful ways. You may think it's a straightforward transition from print to digital – readers swapping paper for website or app – but it doesn't work that way.

Digital doesn't yet have the answers to the financial crisis in journalism. It's struggling to find workable business models because not enough people are prepared to pay for news and advertisers now have unlimited websites to advertise on, not just a cabal of newspapers.

That's where you come in. You have the opportunity to help create the future of news.

Technology changes so fast that, in the space between me writing this and you reading it, some new piece of software may have been invented, or an idea been had that could change everything in the industry. Fingers crossed emoji here.

Digital journalism is a test-and-replace environment. The shelf life of a new idea is entirely meritocratic. If it works, it stays. If it's useless, it doesn't even get the honour of being tomorrow's fish and chip paper. Just you try wrapping fish and chips in HTML. It's really hard. The vinegar goes everywhere.

What you've already read in this book still applies. In some regards, digital journalism doesn't have to be different.

The *Financial Times* doesn't alter its editorial voice or content focus simply because the articles are online; they will not write about trending cat videos (unless that cat is wearing spectacles and a pin-striped shirt while analysing balance sheets).

However, writing for the web is different in some very important ways.

Among other things, you'll need to speak the language of social media as well as tabloid and broadsheet editorial. News organisations are so desperate to recruit new readers from younger demographics that sentences have become emojis, which means social media posts can be three words – "Oh My God" – or even three letters – "OMG." I'm not saying that you shouldn't aim to write perfect English and formal editorial, what I'm saying is that you need to be able to do both.

Knowing how and when to vary your language is a key element of "writing for the web."

What the web offers us is opportunity and variety.

We have the opportunity to hit an audience slap-bang in the belly of its desires and the variety of punches to do it. Anthony Joshua doesn't just come at you with one good right jab, he uses different types of punch, different angles, different hands and different combinations.

How does that apply in everyday journalism?

Consider football coverage. Do I want a Saturday goal described to me in print on Sunday or do I want to see video footage of it immediately? Do I want an interactive computer simulation of the goal that allows me to revolve 360 degrees around the ball to select my own camera angle or freeze frame? Do I want a funny audio clip of the commentator's strangulated oratory as it hits the net? Maybe I want all of them. In one place. Now.

The online journalist needs to be able to recognise which punch is required and know how and when to throw it. You need to be able to unleash combinations too.

Online journalism, done well, can be a velvet-lined rabbit hole, a choose-your-own-adventure warren of infomedia that swallows you down whole and burps you out in the wonderland of clarity and understanding.

We navigate that journey with the reader, not for the reader. Journalists are more contactable, approachable and engaged. We talk to our readers on a daily basis. We want to learn how to offer them more of what they want.

Digital journalism has the tools to lift content off the screen and into interactive life. It's not about throwing the kitchen sink at every online article, it's about understanding what digital elements will be most complementary to telling your story. It's about using the right tool for the right job, and to do that you need to understand the toolbox.

This chapter is not designed to be an exhaustive list of software and platforms with minutiae on how to use them. This is designed to help you frame what online journalism is and how to develop a mindset that will allow you to succeed in the field.

You need to understand that from the moment you set foot in the online landscape it will change continually under your feet. To maintain balance you'll need flexible ankles and a strong core.

Being open to change gives you a strong core.

Being an early adopter of technology will give you flexibility.

This state of perma-flux is a sword double edged by fear and possibility.

There is genuine fear that if some of the best brains in the industry haven't yet cracked this internet lark then the whole industry may just be on the precipice; the game may be up.

That means journalism is desperate for truly new ideas from minds untainted by past thinking. So your freedom to reimagine the boundaries and business of journalism is greater now than at any point in the industry's history.

So, if you have an idea, try it. If it's monetisable – even better.

Don't focus on the fear. Focus on the possibilities.

The basics

Everything you have read in the previous chapters still applies, but online peels the skin from print's muscular brevity to unveil the tendons beneath. Here are the things you need to remember:

Web readers are time-poor: Keep stories brief so they can cram news
Use short sentences: Readers scan stories, make it easy for them
Hyperlinks for depth: Give readers the option to click-through to separate full explanations instead of adding fat to sentences or stories
Don't presume knowledge: Online audiences are largely younger. They hate journalese and want terminology explained
Break up copy into smaller chunks: Use bullet points, cross-headings, images, fact boxes, etc.

Want proof?

Eye-tracking research by Jakob Nielsen (2006) discovered that people read on-line in an F-shape, first scanning across the headline and intro, then dropping down to the middle section and scanning horizontally before returning to the top and scanning vertically down the left side.

Among the report's actionable recommendations were the following:

- "The first two paragraphs must state the most important information… they'll probably read more of the first paragraph than the second."
- "Start subheads, paragraphs, and bullet points with information-carrying words that users will notice when scanning down the left side of your con-tent in the final stem of their F-behavior. They'll read the third word on a line much less often than the first two words."

Your intro and headline must contain key facts to seize interest in the first horizontal movement.

Bullet points or other eye-catching elements grab the second movement.

Cross-headings begin on the left to catch the third movement.

Key principle: serve the audience

You cut through the competition best by serving your audience.

Online news consumption is a growing market compared with print and TV partly because the industry is learning more quickly what the audience wants.

Customers today want up-to-date news via mobile phone while on a train or bus, or while walking. As print demand dies off, we instead deliver news digitally.

We create an article on a website that can be accessed via a device – usually a mobile phone; 69% of readers use mobiles to access news, according to the 2020 Reuters Institute Report.

However, the reader may see that article first on social media rather than by clicking directly on the news organisation's website – this is often referred to as "side-door access" to your article. They may get a push alert via an app, or an email newsletter. That customer will have chosen to sign up for that app, newsletter or social media page because they like your content. Those services offer a chance to create a relationship with readers.

If you create content that the readers like enough to "subscribe" to – and you offer them a clear path to that "subscription" – then you create a relationship.

I started my career in news as a paper boy delivering printed papers around the streets of the Rhondda Valley. The newsagent I worked for as a teenager used to be the reader's subscription point while I was the content delivery system.

Today the point of subscription might be sending your phone number to a WhatsApp Broadcast List, or registering for an email newsletter, or downloading an app. "Subscription" does not just mean paying a daily price for a daily service. It can also be these free agreements with a reader.

However, if you can understand and build relationships with your audience then you have a better chance of getting them to pay for a service they value; and that's what the industry needs to do – get paid for the content it supplies.

You might think news organisations have little idea who is reading their articles when almost all interaction is remote. This is not true.

Say hello to analytics

Metric: Something you can measure: a page view (PV), Likes, Shares, etc.

Analytics: Evaluating metrics to see what you can learn.

Before you begin writing an article, ask yourself these three questions:

- Who am I writing this article for?
- Where will that audience read this article?
- How will I serve it to them?

This simple approach means you will factor into your everyday workflow an effective way of serving the audience.

The workflow is cyclical. We take what we know about our audience and build it into the way we present our article. We use analytical tools to measure how well our article performed and then we ask what we could have done better. Finally, we add our new learning into our audience profile and we repeat the approach from a point of greater understanding.

We learn to serve the audience better using this strategy. You can also analyse how well that strategy works.

To analyse strategy, you'll need to decide what your key metrics are. What do you consider a marker for success? There are two main categories here:

Markers of audience size: Prize popular, high-clicking, short-tail articles that quickly deliver audience spikes. Bigger audiences help attract more advertising revenue, which online businesses need to survive. Dependence on this type of content will likely see audience size fluctuate between peaks and troughs. You should pay close attention to real-time metrics such as concurrent page views or unique users.

Examples: Significant breaking news, trending content or popular regular content, i.e., Liverpool FC or Beyoncé coverage, which carries a large in-built audience.

Markers of trust: Prize higher-quality reporting with long-tail value that shares well. It brings in returning customers and helps grow your brand. Reliance on this type of content will likely bring a more stable audience size. Pay less attention to real-time metrics and focus on dwell time, engagement, recirculation and social shares.

Examples: Investigations, news analysis and features, data journalism and quality columnists.

Getting started with analytics

With a newspaper or a magazine you learn retrospectively how many copies were sold (that's a metric) but you'll have no idea how many people read a particular article.

If a newspaper sells a million copies, then does each of its 200 articles of different sizes and subjects get read a million times each? Or are the splash and pages 3 and 5 best-read, while page 7 is marginally less well-read, and by the time you get to the centre-spread, it's anyone's guess who's still reading.

We're no longer in the business of guessing an article's value to the reader. Almost everything online can be measured; we check how many people clicked on an article, how long they spent reading it, whether they shared it on social media, whether they clicked on hyperlinks within that story, etc.

That's why analytics has become central to how online news works. It allows us to learn what our readers like and value – what we are missing or might improve.

Free analytics: Many social media platforms provide free analytics – Twitter Analytics, Facebook and Instagram Insights – so you can measure metrics such as engagements and page views.

Google Analytics can be applied to a blog or website to track key metrics.

Paid-for analytics: Many newsrooms use Chartbeat to determine the best-performing content. Chartbeat measures a website's traffic every five seconds so the information it offers is near-real-time. It even suggests ways to optimise your traffic. A similar option is Parse.ly, which has been used by the likes of Sky, Bloomberg, WSJ and NBC.

Custom analytics: This allows newsrooms to prioritise what matters to them. Publishers may not want to incur the cost of external analytics or give another company access to their internal data. However, it is a time-consuming and expensive approach.

At *The Mirror* we used the company's own creation, Hive Alpha, alongside Chartbeat and Google Analytics.

What is SEO?

SEO stands for Search Engine Optimisation – you are optimising your content for search engines to find. What would a reader type into Google if they were searching for your story? The answer to that question will provide you with your SEO keywords.

The likes of Google, Bing and Duck Duck Go read and rank the pages of the worldwide web.

That's a big job. What good SEO does is give search engines clear information to help them read and rank your article. When a reader googles a query – How far from the earth is the moon? – the search engine has already ranked its best answers to that question and serves them to the reader on a results page.

Good SEO is about more than just the headline...

SEO is a factor at multiple points of your article. The most powerful element will be the keywords in your headline, but your lead text (the standfirst) and intro will also have SEO value. Sub-headings are powerful for SEO too, while captions on photos or videos can also be ranked in their own right; Google has results page headings for photos, videos and even maps.

Hyperlinks also carry SEO weight. Search engines rate the quality of the other sources to which you direct readers and use that rating to help rank your article's authority against other similar articles.

News organisations may also use tags and topic pages to index their content. An article on the government's annual budget may be tagged with "Budget 2021" and "Chancellor of the Exchequer" and then indexed on the "Politics" topic page.

The headline is really important

To advance our SEO understanding we need to stop and think about writing good headlines.

Print headlines need to summarise a story in the space left by the page designer, which forces the sub-editor writing a headline to choose words to fill that space. In print, place names are rarely used and longer words are unusual.

Online headlines are different. SEO requirements mean specific place names, or individuals' names, are key to search discovery. Restrictions on word length have vanished online so it's ok to use Llanfairpwllgwyngyllgogerychwyrndrobwllllantysiliogogogoch if needed.

In that instance though, you'll discover no one actually types that name into Google. People in that area would search for "Llanfair PG." Knowing the correct search terms to use should be what dictates your word choices.

Online headlines tend to be shorter. Aim for 12–15 words for a full headline or 4–8 words for a mobile headline.

What makes a good web headline?

A good news headline needs to "tell and sell" the story:

- Make the reader want to read; don't be boring
- But be accurate and don't misrepresent the story by "overselling"
- Hone it for SEO with the story's key details

It's best to front-load SEO keywords in a headline.

This approach is most visible in the "Kicker" when two to five words followed by a colon precede the remaining headline. The "kicker" packs the SEO punch and allows the remaining headline to tell the story naturally.

Example: "Kicker Goes Here: Now I'm free from SEO chains to write what I want"

How might that look in real life?

I've just received a push alert on Princess Beatrice's marriage. The headline for that story reads,

> Princess Beatrice wedding: Royal in SECRET marriage to Edo - Queen attends
>
> *Daily Express*

The *Daily Express* has determined its key SEO phrase is "Princess Beatrice Wedding" and used that as a kicker to front-load the SEO.

Using SEO without ruining headlines

A journalist crystallises a news story in their intro.

> TENNIS star Andy Smash became the first British player to win Wimbledale for 77 years after finally defeating Serbia's Jock O'Vitch.

A print headline crystallises the intro.

> Andy is Wimbledale champ after Smashing Jock

The print headline above uses some key story elements – Who, What and Where. It also uses a pun. Importantly, in pursuit of brevity, it does not contain full names.

SEO crystallises the intro in a different way.

It takes those same key elements (Who, What and Where) but doesn't require the pun. It does require full names for search purposes.

In the above intro your SEO keywords are "Andy Smash," "Wimbledale" and "Jock O'Vitch."

Those SEO keywords are great for general discoverability but they don't tell you what this specific story is about.

They miss the What – he WON – which makes this a different story to "Andy Smash loses Wimbledale," which has been written before.

You need an SEO key phrase that unites these elements: "Andy Smash wins Wimbledale."

That strong, four-word SEO phrase works as a story-specific scannable mobile phone headline and a kicker in a longer headline.

Most websites use longer headlines than that, so to turn it into a full headline we have two approaches.

1. Use a kicker then add context
    "Andy Smash wins Wimbledale: Jock O'Vitch aced in straight-sets on Centre Court"
2. Pepper keywords throughout a headline in a natural sentence
    "Andy Smash wins Wimbledale in straight-sets defeat of Jock O'Vitch."

Both headlines contain all the key SEO terms, so why are they different?

Search engines give more importance to words at the front of a headline. In headline no.2, "Jock O'Vitch" is at the back. The search engine thinks, "That story is less focused on 'Jock O'Vitch' and more focused on 'Andy Smash'."

The equivalent *Serbia Today* headline might have read "Jock O'Vitch defeated as Andy Smash wins Wimbledale."

If a fan searches "Jock O'Vitch," they are less likely to see your article because you gave him less value in your headline. Google will serve up the *Serbia Today* headline because it is more focused on the reader's actual search query.

If a fan googles "Andy Smash," then the search engine is more likely to serve them your content because you gave that SEO term more value.

Front-load your key SEO terms.

Researching SEO for everyday coverage

There are some free and easy tools you can use.

A simple way to research SEO is to open Google and type in the beginning of a question.

Without pressing enter/return, type in "How to convert to"

As you type, Google automatically begins to suggest the most popular endings to your question.

The top three auto-replies today are...

'How to convert to Islam'
'How to convert to PDF'
'How to convert to Buddhism'

As the old joke goes, PDF is now the world's second biggest religion.

You asked Google a question and it did its best to answer you, even though you didn't even ask a full question. The more specific your question becomes, the more specific the answer a search engine can give you.

Another way to think about SEO then, is a question-and-answer exchange between the reader and the journalist.

Google Trends (trends.google.co.uk)

Google Trends (GT) allows you to examine a topic more closely. You can compare words or likely SEO search terms and GT will rank them for you according to popularity. It will offer a list of related search terms to help you to refine what questions readers have about that subject. You can narrow the search results by timeframe, country, language or category.

AnswerThePublic.com

This works much like a search engine but presents results differently. Enter a search term and the nifty AI algorithm fetches all the questions people have asked about that term. It offers three free daily searches or you can pay a fee for unlimited access.

SEO for breaking news

Picture the scene. It's 6am on your first day on the job in a professional newsroom. It's just you and the news editor.

A significant piece of news breaks and the news editor tells you to urgently research the best SEO to use while she begins creating the article. Speed is important here. You need to beat your red-top rival to the story.

What's the problem you face?

The news is brand new so no one has ever searched for that specific piece of news before. It has no search history.

Here's your story…

Ka-boom!

A tank has just exploded in Jesmond en route to a military parade.

Search terms take time to become visible on tools such as Google Trends. If you wait for that type of data to become available, you'll be way behind the curve.

You could scour social media to see what terms are being used in very early mentions of the incident and….

"Where are my SEO Keywords?" the News Ed politely bellows in your face.

What you need is a basic formula that works until accurate keywords become clear. Here's one:

Specific place/person name + specific event = basic SEO formula
Specific place/person name = Jesmond
Specific event type = tank explosion
Our strongest early SEO should be:
"Jesmond tank explosion"
A first headline might look like this:
"Tank explodes in Jesmond driving to military parade"

SEO terms change

Your basic formula solution will need refining as better SEO becomes clear. You'll need to update the headline to reflect that.

As the story develops you discover new details: the model of tank, exactly where it was and which parade it was heading to. Those details may be more important than the more generic ones you first identified.

It transpires that the tank in question is "Mephisto" – the only remaining WW1-era German A7V Sturmpanzerwagen tank on earth.

How might that change your SEO and your headline?

You'll likely find that "Mephisto" becomes a key word. It is known worldwide in certain circles. It trumps "Jesmond" as a key SEO term because the wider world cares more about "Mesphisto" than "Jesmond."

Your best SEO is now, "Mephisto tank explosion."

SEO goes out into the digital world fishing for as many readers as it can catch. You decide how big the net is.

If SEO is narrowly focused, it targets a niche of engaged readers. (The niche can be geographic or one of specialist subject interest.)

If SEO is broadly focused, it targets more but possibly less-engaged readers.

Exercise 1: Writing for SEO

Here's a profile of a fictional website and a story it may cover. Consider the audience profile and then answer the questions.

Your publication

Bodingshire Online (BO) is a digital-only publication generating around 37 million page views per month. It is tabloid in style and prizes video to accompany stories. The website has Facebook and Twitter accounts. BO prides itself on a reputation for social justice campaigning.

Area profile

Bodingshire is a largely working-class county with a population of 2.2 million people. The main industry is electronics with two large factories run by Japanese manufacturers on the outskirts of the city of Bodinger. Around 60% of Bodingshire Online's audience engages with coverage of local football club Holt Harriers, based in the suburb of Holt, which has around 40,000 fans on Twitter and 18,000 season ticket holders.

Press release from Holt Harriers FC

Holt Harriers striker Jackie Traction has donated £5,000 to the fund for striking staff at Bangyong Electronics.

Staff at the factory have been on strike for three weeks due to a pay dispute.

Jackie, 21, said, "I can't stand to see families going hungry. My grandad worked at the factory when I was young and now my dad is on strike there. Our family is ok but my goal is to help other local families."

Tweet from Traction's Twitter account

"I'm helping local people stand up to these money-grabbing capitalists paying slave-labour wages for an honest day's work from good folk. #Solidarity4strikers"

Official statement from Bangyong Electronics

"Bangyong Electonics provides more than 5,000 jobs in Bodingshire and it pays fair wages. We have made a fair offer to the striking workers but they have refused it. The rise would put our workers on equal wages to our neighbouring factory, Sianjing Electrics.

"If the people of Bodingshire no longer want our jobs then we will happily seek staff from the nearby county of Poppetton, who do want them."

Your task

1) Write a kicker-style headline in 15 words or less.
2) Write a headline in eight words or less to suit the BBC mobile site. (See sample answers on page 243)

Writing for social media

This isn't an exhaustive user guide to every platform, but a general approach to social media for journalists, with a "pocket guide" to the most important platforms and tips for success.

But before we start there is something really important to talk about...

Anti-social media

Social media is an unavoidable part of digital journalism. Unfortunately, it's sometimes a conductor for abuse.

If you are subjected to abuse or inappropriate material at any time:

* Don't deal with it alone: speak to an editor, colleague or your family.
* Don't engage with it: trolls want attention, don't give it to them.
* Put a stop to it: abuse can and will be stopped, sometimes by police.

Why journalists use social media

Social media breaks down into two key areas – the social we read and the social we write.

The social we read is used to source or inform stories.

The social we write is used to promote and disseminate stories.

Sourcing stories on social

Among the 16–34 age group, 98.5% of people own a smartphone, according to research from Statista (O'Dea 2020). Whenever news happens there is likely a camera within yards of the incident.

A witness films/snaps the incident, uploads the images to social media and gives you a front seat for the story. Whether you call that User Generated Content or Citizen Journalism, it's extremely powerful and has transformed everyday news coverage. There are two things to remember in this situation…

• Verify the material
• Seek permission to use it

Often these two things come together. The person who took the photo or shot the video and uploaded it to their social account is often the copyright holder – though not always. Contact the poster – reply to the social post as a starting point – to begin the verification process and hopefully gain permission to use the image in the same conversation.

Sometimes the poster will give you permission to use the image for free, sometimes they may ask for payment. Embedding the social media post itself may get you around the copyright issue initially, but without permission it becomes difficult to use the photo/video in the ways you'll need to use it – as a homepage banner image, for instance.

You need to know who took that photo and what your usage agreement with them is, but be very careful. Anyone can hide behind a social media account.

The person posting a piece of information may not be the person they claim to be. They may be posting blatant lies to deliberately mislead you. Some lies are easily knocked down with the most cursory of checks but in today's technologically advanced world there are also highly convincing fakes; doctored photographs and deepfake videos among them. Do not take these things at face value – investigate and verify.

You should also scour the content of photos or video before you embed them or use them to ensure they don't include graphic or inappropriate content.

Be very careful with the text too. You may think something posted on a verified social media account is fair game to use but defamation laws still apply.

Let's say one celeb tweets something defamatory about another celeb. If you report the content of that tweet – perhaps by embedding it – then you are liable for repeating that defamation. The first celeb can later claim that their account was hacked and that they did not post the defamation, thus leaving you as the sole provable perpetrator of the defamation because you put your byline on the article.

Take a look at the phenomenal 2019 #WagathaChristie row between Rebekah Vardy and Coleen Rooney, which ended up in a High Court defamation battle.

Disseminating stories on social

Like it or not, reporters are now the delivery person for their stories.

Just because a reader isn't clicking directly on your website homepage it doesn't mean you can't still knock on their digital door.

Which social platforms do I need to use?

Here are three better questions to ask:

- What is the audience for this story?
- What social media platform does that audience use?
- Do I have the right type of content for that platform?

Let's say you've written an article about the climate emergency school strikes inspired by Greta Thunberg. That content appeals to a key TikTok demographic (27% of its users are between 13 and 17 years old, according to Hootsuite stats (Sehl 2020)).

However, you don't have any suitable video with your article to use on TikTok. So, consider making a TikTok video as an addition to that story to attract the audience you seek. They can't click on a link (because there isn't one), but it can build brand awareness among that group.

You also need to match your needs with the most appropriate social platform because each has its own peculiarities.

A great image is best served by Instagram; long videos by YouTube or IGTV.

However, if you want to post a URL link to a story with the aim of driving readers back to your website, then Facebook and Twitter are the best options. Insta has a large audience, but it is very poor at driving traffic to your website due to its avoidance of link-posting.

What's the biggest social media platform?

The highest number of users according to Statista (Clement 2020) as of April 2020 is as follows:

Facebook: 2.49 billion
WhatsApp: 2 billion
YouTube: 2 billion
Instagram: 1 billion
TikTok: 800 million (and climbing fast)
Reddit: 430 million
Snapchat: 398 million
Pinterest: 366 million
Twitter: 326 million
*LinkedIn (not in this dataset) has north of 600 million users so sits between
    TikTok and Reddit.

The social media pocket guide

If you take one thing away from this section it should be this: include images in your social media posts.

That image may be a photo, it may be a video, or it may be a GIF, but people engage with images far more than just text.

According to research from Hubspot (2012), including a photo on a Facebook post adds up to 53% more likes and generates up to 104% more comments than text alone.

Videos in Facebook posts reach 35% more people than text alone.

GIFs on Facebook reach 14% more people than text alone.

Twitter

Tone: Newsy, witty, communal

Twitter's reputation is bigger than its audience. It has about 386 million users compared with Facebook's 2.49 billion.

Twitter gives a story a great head-start among a newsy audience, but it rarely delivers big numbers.

What it's good at: Sharing breaking stories fast, delivering link traffic, sourcing stories, engagement with a small but influential audience, scheduling story delivery.

What it's bad at: It's the worst echo chamber in journalism, you (STILL!) can't edit posted tweets and trolling is rife.

How to post well:

Use the formula: The average story post by a news organisation includes an image, text and URL link.

Use hashtags: Check trending topics to help readers discover your story; two to three hashtags max.

Don't always use the headline as your text: When you post a URL Twitter automatically brings up a preview card displaying your headline and associated image. Add value to your tweet by saying something that is not in the headline – a strong quote from the story often works well.

Strategise: You can tweet a story as many times as you like. You could write three tweets focusing on the views of three opposing politicians featured in the article – each will appeal to a different audience. Think about how you could appeal to different audiences with different words, hashtags and images.

Use "Threads": Link multiple tweets to tell an entire story.

Time it: Schedule tweets so that they're published at a time of your choosing, such as the moment a TV show starts.

Be natural: Build handles and hashtags into your sentence naturally, when possible, rather than sticking them at the end.

Use mentions: Include someone's Twitter username in a tweet. Get my attention by tweeting "Hey @gavinallen." I'll get a notification that you're speaking to me and I'll answer. I may like it or retweet you, showing your content to my audience too.

Use Twitter lists: Compile lists of experts on a subject, say "Sport," or "Celebrities."

"Borrow" other people's Twitter lists: Many are public, see what senior journalists are looking at.

Use Tweetdeck: Monitor your lists more easily.

Get your text right: You can't edit it afterwards.

Measure the returns: Twitter delivers traffic so analyse it.

*Twitter has a full user guide here: https://help.twitter.com/

Facebook

Tone: Familiar, friendly, colloquial, emotional

Facebook generally delivers the biggest audience share of any social media channel. For some publications it can be as much as a third of their overall traffic.

What it's good at: Attracting big audiences, link sharing, engaging readers, sourcing stories, broadcasting live.

What it's bad at: Attracting younger readers' attention, deleting fake news and harmful content.

How to post well:

Post a link to a story only once: Facebook's algo evaluates time and engagements, among other things. If you post an article and people have a conversation in the comments on that post, Facebook pushes it up users' feeds. If you repost the same article later, it splits your readers between two posts. Instead of having 100 people talking on one post and that being successful enough to rise up Facebook's feed, thus attracting more readers, you'll have 50 people on two posts, and neither is successful enough for Facebook to up-rank.

Keep your text short: People scroll-scan social, make your post scannable.

Don't repeat your headline: Facebook automatically pulls up the headline from your URL on a preview card. Don't waste words, add another angle to increase the story's appeal.

Use images: Facebook automatically pulls in the main photo from your article on a preview card. Make sure it works.

Use @ to engage wider audiences: If you are posting a story about the BBC including an @ to its official Facebook page (@bbc) might help it to be seen by some of the BBC's 2.7 million followers.

Be natural: Build @s into your sentence naturally.

Time it: Schedule a post to go live at a time of your choosing.

Instagram

Tone: Bright, fun, commercial

Instagram is a visual platform so you need great photos and video. You can also write significant length captions to give a feel for your publication's brand.

Insta is a much weaker platform for disseminating stories to increase web traffic. Its link-sharing options are limited (the "link in bio" option points people to only one place), so you'll need to be creative to succeed here. Determine what your metric for success is and then decide if Insta is the right place to do that. If it is, then spend time creating quality content. Insta is not a quick job, but Vice has 3.3 million followers (at the time of writing) so it can significantly grow your audience.

What it's good at: Brand awareness, attracting younger audiences, attracting big audiences, versatile formats (grid, stories, IGTV).

What it's bad at: Link-sharing to drive up website traffic

How to post well: Use the best images you can find.

Use lots of hashtags: Up to ten hashtags are normal on Insta.

Work hard on your captions: Compliment your image with a sample from your story.

Maximise the video options: The Grid (prominence), Stories (zeitgeist) and IGTV (length) each suit different video formats.

Overlay your images: Vibrant fonts and stickers add colour to increase visual appeal.

WhatsApp

Tone: Engaged, personal, punchy, informed

WhatsApp Broadcast Lists (WBL) are really growing in influence. WhatsApp is hard to strategise for. It's designed for private sharing and its messages are encrypted meaning it's hard to measure using Google Analytics. However, WhatsApp is owned by Facebook (as are Insta and Messenger) and therefore it has a significant impact on Facebook newsfeeds. Among the publications enjoying success here is WalesOnline, which grew a WBL of 3,360 subscribers during the 2019 Rugby World Cup. During the tournament, they sent 159 messages and received 190,000 page views. That works out as 56 page views per subscriber.

What it's good at: Growing targeted audience groups, engagement, sharing breaking news

What it's bad at: Clear analytics

Exercise 2: Analysing social media posts

Pick a news story from today's headlines on your favourite news outlet. Look at how that story was "sold" on different social platforms.

1) How does the Twitter or Insta post compare to the Facebook post?
2) Why did the publisher choose that platform for that piece of content?

Bibliography

Clement, J. (2020) *Global social networks ranked by number of users 2020* (Accessed 8 September 2020) <www.statista.com/statistics/272014/global-social-networks-ranked-by-number-of-users>

Hubspot. (2012) Photos on Facebook generate 53% more likes than the average post (Accessed 4 January 2021) <blog.hubspot.com/blog/tabid/6307/bid/33800/photos-on-facebook-generate-53-more-likes-than-the-average-post-new-data.aspx>

Nielsen, J. (2006) *F-Shaped pattern for reading web content. Nielsen Norman Group* (Accessed 8 September 2020) <www.nngroup.com/articles/f-shaped-pattern-reading-web-content-discovered>

O'Dea, S. (2020) *Smartphone ownership in the United Kingdom (UK) 2012–2020, by age.* (Accessed 8 September 2020) <www.statista.com/statistics/271851/smartphone-owners-in-the-united-kingdom-uk-by-age>

Reuters. (2020) *Reuters Institute Digital News Report* (Accessed 4 January 2021) <reutersinstitute.politics.ox.ac.uk/sites/default/files/2020–06/DNR_2020_FINAL.pdf>

Sehl, K. (2020) 20 *Important TikTok stats marketers need to know in 2020* (Accessed 8 September 2020)

<blog.hootsuite.com/tiktok-stats/#:~:text=TikTok%20has%20a%20reputation%20for, of%20the%20app's%20user%20base>

6
Developing feature ideas

What is a feature?

Take a pair of scissors to this week's Sunday paper and cut out all the news stories, TV guide, listings and adverts. What you are left with will largely come under the heading of "features." This is a broad term that covers everything from interviews and profile pieces to opinion, travel stories, obituaries, "How to…" articles, news analysis, reviews and beyond.

This variety is one of the great joys of being a feature writer. It allows you to explore a wide array of subjects and to flex your literary muscle in ways that are far harder for a news writer. News stories tend to focus on a single event (something has happened to, or has been done by someone or something) and often follow a familiar formula.

As we've already seen, the way that a murder is reported might be fairly similar in two different publications, that both need to cover the Who, What, How, When, Where and Why of the story.

Features looking into the issue of increasing murder rates in the UK for those two publications would be quite distinct. They would start in different places, draw on the expertise and experience of different people, follow a very different structure and focus on different aspects of the issue.

To succeed in this area of journalism, you need to be able to develop workable feature ideas. This is vital for anyone who wants to work as a freelancer, land their first job or progress quickly within an editorial team. The strength of your feature idea is a function of four key factors…

R: how well you understand your **R**eaders and the publication you are writing for

C: the currency of the **C**ontemporary issue you are looking at

V: the Value that your chosen angle offers the reader

S: the strength and originality of the Story you are going to tell

In this chapter, we are going to look at the first three of these factors: how to understand your Readers' needs; and how to identify an angle that is of Value to them on a Contemporary issue that they need to know about now.

We will look at how these factors help to shape the coverlines you see on the front of magazines, and how you can use them to construct the standfirst that often appears at the top of a feature. This is how an editor thinks about the articles they commission. So if you want to improve your chances of selling an idea, it helps if you can communicate on their terms.

Understanding your reader

The key to developing good feature ideas is to understand who you are writing for.

So, who reads this magazine?

Men's Health has been incredibly successful because it understands its readers.

If you answered: Male, ABC1 social class, aged 15–35, you are in the right area. In 2015–2016, the magazine said that 68% of readers were ABC1 and 60% were within this age group. Demographic information like this is important for any publication and it is particularly useful for sales teams trying to sell adverts into the magazine.

But "male, aged 15–35, ABC1" could be used to describe the readers of hundreds of publications and it tells us very little about the content that they want to read. (It's likely that the *Men's Health* demographic has changed slightly since then, but that isn't too important for our purposes.)

A better way to describe your readership is to think about them in terms of what they need from the publication. So picture the average *Men's Health* reader in your mind and decide what five hopes and fears you think best characterise them. When you've done that, turn the page for our suggestions.

Hopes

1. _____

2. _____

3. _____

4. _____

5. _____

Fears

1. _____

2. _____

3. _____

4. _____

5. _____

Men's Health readers

Hopes

1. Six-pack and muscles
2. To be healthy
3. Sexually successful
4. Career and financial success
5. Admiration of my peers

Fears

1. Getting old and fat
2. Being unhealthy
3. Lack of willpower
4. Have to give up fun, socialising, food and drink
5. Not enough time and money to get results

Search for the October 2005 UK issue of *Men's Health* online and you will see that all the coverlines correspond to these hopes and fears…

Lose your gut: and double your muscle (six-pack and muscles)
How to get away with an office fling (sexually successful)
17 Health foods you must avoid (be healthy)
Become an eBook millionaire (career success)
Get drunk, lose weight (Have to give up fun)
Gain the edge: With the sexiest new winter tech (admiration of your peers)
Burn Fat 24 hours a day (don't want to get fat)
Slash 2 kg with a bacon sandwich (willpower)

This isn't a fluke. Search for just "*Men's Health* cover" and you'll see this thinking applies to every issue and almost every single coverline.

First launched in the US in 1986 (and in the UK in 1995), this has been one of the most successful men's publications of the last 35 years. It is sold in 59 different countries and the US version recorded sales of over 1.8 million in 2012. While print sales are declining, it is still an impressive international brand that operates across print and digital platforms.

The key to its success is a phenomenal focus on reader needs.

Put yourself in the shoes of the reader for a moment (your name is Keith and you work in sales). Imagine it's your lunch hour and you are wandering into the newsagent's with £5 in your pocket. You're hungry and that money will buy you a sandwich and packet of crisps that will do nothing for your burgeoning waistline.

But before you head to the counter, you notice the cover of *Men's Health* with its promise to help you ditch some of that excess fat and replace it with a six-pack (in just six weeks). It also tells you how to beef up those arms, ask your boss for a pay rise, dress sharply and maybe even help start a conversation with Mandy in accounts.

That seems like quite a promise. So you put the sandwich back on the shelf and head to the till to invest your five pounds in some potentially life-enhancing reading.

To sell any publication (or just to get people clicking on your stories), you have to apply the same logic. You need to show that you have something that the reader needs or will be interested in. Vague and uninteresting ideas – even if they are roughly on topic – will not achieve this.

Covers are the purest expression of what a magazine is all about. In the words of publishing guru David Hepworth, a magazine cover has to appeal to a "moron in a hurry."

Keith (that's you in our role play above) isn't really a moron, but if we're going to get him to buy our magazine instead of that sandwich, then we have only a small window to make that happen. We need to give him a compelling reason to buy.

It's easy to identify the top five things that readers need from a specialist publication like *Men's Health*. When people have a hobby, they want to be better at it. When they have an interest in a subject, they want to be more knowledgeable about it. When they are part of a community, they may want to take a more active role, be able to talk confidently about the subject and gain the respect of their peers. When people buy publications related to their job, they want advice and information that will allow them to be more successful at work, to get a promotion or make more money.

It might be harder to describe the readers of *The Guardian* or *Mirror* in terms of hopes and fears, but coverlines and their equivalents still have to be clear on the value that each feature is offering.

It could be information and insight they didn't have before:

> How crime drives deforestation in Brazil's Amazon
>
> *Financial Times*

It could be offering to solve a problem or improve their life...

> Lambing Special: Easy-to-follow advice for a successful season
>> *Farmers Weekly*

...a story that's entertaining or gripping....

> The Body Wars of Instagram
>
> And the women killing themselves to compete
>> *Cosmopolitan*

...or one that promises to takes them somewhere new:

> 16 Amazing Voyages
>
> Sail, kayak and cruise to the ends of the Earth
>> *Wanderlust*

Even if your writing is freely available online, people will only invest their time in reading it if they can see that it has value. As a writer, get in the habit of asking yourself, "What does this do for my readers?" If you don't have a clear answer, then don't expect your readers to find one for you. They simply won't read it.

Exercise 1: Head to the newsagents

Spend a lunch hour in your local newsagent's and watch how people browse the shelves of magazines and newspapers. I used to do this as an aspiring features editor and it teaches you a huge amount about the challenge of selling ideas to potential readers.

Then look at one magazine from each of the following sections and try to identify who the **R**eader is and the **V**alue being offered in each of their coverlines.

Business: Travel: Sports: Women's Interest: Farming: Motoring: Photography: Crafts: Computers: Gardening

You can of course do this from the comfort of your computer screen, but there is value in watching real people interact with magazines. It helps you to focus on what is really important: your reader.

News-driven features

News stories report on events, while features often explore the wider issues and the people involved.

Let's assume you want to write a feature on obesity. Search Wikipedia and you will find lots of background information on this issue that will include biological causes and ways to manage the problem, as well as historical attitudes, and obesity in culture and the arts. While much of this information may be interesting, it is not journalism.

Journalism is concerned with the Contemporary: what is happening now.

In May 2019, Leeds became the first city in the UK to lower childhood obesity rates by helping parents set limits around sweets and junk food. This news could inspire a feature that looks at what other areas of the UK could learn from their experience. You would have to talk to young people and families affected by these issues, as well as medical experts, campaigners and politicians.

News events are an excellent way to generate feature ideas. Something new has happened or a change has taken place, and this gives us to reason to ask questions that will be of importance to your readers.

Remember your reader is time poor and has a host of distractions vying for their attention. They have two questions that need to be answered before they commit to reading this article: "Why should I read this now?" and "What will I get from it?"

This offers a useful formula for any feature…

Why Now? This is your newshook; the Contemporary element of your feature. It could be an event that has just happened, an emerging problem, a recent trend, a piece of research or a new scientific discovery. This is what gets your reader to commit to this feature now rather than bookmarking it for later.

So What? This is the question that you think your reader wants the answer to, even if they may not have realised it yet. It is the angle of your story that sets out the Value of your piece.

In our example about obesity rates in Leeds, we can see how that formula works…

Why Now? Leeds is the first city to see a drop in childhood obesity rates.

So What? What can the rest of the country learn from their example?

Put these two elements together and you have a potential sell-line or standfirst for a feature…

> Leeds is the first city to achieve a reduction in childhood obesity rates, so what can the rest of the UK learn from their example?

Readers who see this standfirst will immediately have a sense of whether they want to read it or not. It's about health, but it clearly isn't right for readers of *Men's Health*. It might appeal to parents and teachers, anyone interested in health care for young people, who will learn something useful from the results of the project in Leeds.

The importance of a standfirst

Your standfirst is a mission statement setting out the purpose of your feature. You can't sell your idea to a commissioning editor unless you are clear on what it is you are trying to achieve. And readers will only click on a story, or start reading it, if they understand the Value proposition (whether that's getting a six-pack, juicy insights on a celebrity, ways to improve their home and garden, or predictions on what the financial markets might do this year).

But the standfirst is even more important to you as a writer. You can't start to write a feature until you are clear on your purpose. A standfirst will help you to identify the people you need to interview and the research that will be required. It will help you to identify the best intro, a solid structure and the right quotes for your story.

Your standfirst may well change as you move from feature pitch, to research, to writing. You may identify a stronger angle as new information emerges. But you should start with an idea in mind and you should not begin to write until you are entirely clear on what it is you are trying to do. You cannot deliver a successful piece of writing unless you have that clarity.

Not all standfirsts conform to this formula. Some will have been changed by a sub-editor, who wants to sell the feature to a reader in a different way. Many have an implicit, rather than explicit, question in the standfirst. All good features will use a standfirst to clearly set out their Value to the reader.

Developing standfirsts from news stories

Can you spot the "Why Now?" and "So What?" elements in these feature standfirsts all taken from *The Times*? Some of the questions are implicit. What is the value of this story to readers?

1. As the Muppets returns to TV with a new show, Times writers explain their love affair with their favourite Jim Henson creations

2. As the Government declares war on obesity, the diabetes expert Professor Roy Taylor shares his proven weight-loss plan

3. He had been an MP for less than five years when he was given the second most powerful job in Britain. Who is behind the unprecedented rise of the new chancellor?

4. Five month's ago Sarah Cooper was trying to make it as a stand-up comedian. Now her Trump lip-synch videos have had millions of views – and attracted the attention of the democrats. Could she be their secret weapon in November?

5. Precious metals and minerals will drive a new Industrial Revolution that will be dominated by Beijing unless democracies unite

Using the newshook-and-question approach is a good way for new writers to start developing strong feature ideas. It will improve the focus and clarity of your writing. It will also make your research more efficient by helping you identify what you need to know and who you need to interview.

Forming your standfirst

A single newshook can potentially serve as the "Why Now?" for a number of different features, and different readerships.

Use the fictional story below to write a potential standfirst for each of the fictional publications.

Why Now?

A biker has been jailed after filming himself travelling at what is believed to be the highest speed ever clocked by a motorbike on British roads.

Adam Campion, 26, hit 187 mph on a stolen motorbike, pulled wheelies and weaved in and out of traffic in footage captured on a mobile phone, before colliding with a family car, carrying two children aged under three years old. Their mother believes it was the travel seats that kept her children safe.

So What?

It is your job to identify a potential angle for each of the publications below. The "Why Now?" will be the same (although it might be expressed differently), but the question you ask – "So What?" – will be different. It must be of interest and value to the readership of the title you are pitching to.

Motorbike Speed: For motorbike enthusiasts who love big bikes and riding fast
Police Weekly: For police teams and people involved in law enforcement
New Mum Magazine: Read by expectant mums and new parents
Absolute Actuary: For people who make money by selling insurance

Possible "So What?"

It's not difficult to match each of these questions to the four different groups above. You should be able to identify another five possible angles for each readership.

What are the best travel seats for very young children in your car?

What are the best ways to safely detain speeding drivers on our roads?

How can encouraging safe driving among your customers help boost your profits?

Where can you legally hit speeds of up to 190 mph on your bike? We reveal the top five locations.

The way you express the "Why Now?" in each standfirst will be different, emphasising the element that will be most important for the readership and your chosen feature angle…

New Mum Magazine…

A mum whose family walked away from a 187 mph crash believes it was…

Motorbike Speed

We are not condoning law breaking, but after a rider was convicted for hitting speeds of 187 mph, we want to know…

Exercise 2: Analyse feature standfirsts

Find at least ten features all from different publications. Can you identify these elements in each feature standfirst?

Why Now? Is there a news development, a seasonal link, new research, a new product, a prediction/warning, a change or trend that gives this feature a Contemporary newshook?

So What? What is the Value to the reader? Does it promise to solve a problem, make them more informed, tell them something they didn't know or simply offer an entertaining story?

Get inspired by other publications

When you've worked on a title for a couple of years, it is all too easy to get stuck in a rut and for feature ideas to start repeating themselves. One way to get out of this is to go back to the shelves of your local newsagents and look for coverlines on publications that are not in your sector. Look at the kind of features they are offering and try to find ways to adapt their feature approaches for your title.

While I was the editor of the outdoor magazine *Trail*, we had a lot of fun with this approach. It certainly got us thinking about the way we presented our subject matter. Who wouldn't enjoy the creative challenge of trying to adapt coverlines like "I'm haunted by my mother-in-law's ghost" and "Monster Truck head-to-head on the M1" to the subject of climbing mountains?

How to approach a commissioning editor

There is no one way to approach a commissioning editor, but it is important that you do your research. That means first reading recent issues to understand the kind of content they run. Then head online to see if they have contributor's guidelines. They may ask you to submit your proposal by email, but make sure you follow up with a phone call a few days later.

There is no point in pitching a 3,000-word travel feature on your trip to Peru, if a publication only runs 800-word pieces on European city destinations. Similarly, do not propose an interview feature with a leading scientist at the end of their career, if a publication only runs short news pieces on new scientific research. Pitching story ideas that are not appropriate to the publication is a rookie mistake and makes it clear you have not bothered to do the very basic of required research: actually reading the publication.

How to pitch your ideas

When you approach a commissioning editor, there are four questions that they will need answered…

1. **Will my readers want to read this story?** Your story has to be strong. Understanding the elements above is key to this. You need to have an interesting story and one that has a clear "Why now?" and "So what?". Does this feature offer something that will enhance their life, inform them about an issue of importance or simply offer a window into a world they haven't had access to? The story has to be strong enough to appear as a coverline on a magazine or to catch a reader's attention as they flick through a newspaper.
2. **Can this person write?** Show that you can deliver a well-written piece. Your proposal letter should be crisp and lively, get ideas across clearly, offer enough

information to interest the editor and to show that you have command of the key facts. Spelling mistakes, grammatical errors, poorly constructed sentences and woolly ideas are all likely to see your proposal binned.

3. **Do they understand my publication?** Show that the reader value you are offering matches the needs of their audience and that you know where this will fit into their publication. Don't offer a 3,000-word feature to a publication that only runs 500-word news pieces. Don't offer a feature on an issue that was covered in a recent edition, without a really fresh angle. Be clear on the section that you think it would be most appropriate for.

4. **Can they deliver?** How do you convince the editor that they can trust a new writer they haven't worked with before? Directing them to an online portfolio of work would certainly be useful (see Chapter 14). Evidence that you have already conducted research and that you are ready to write is important, especially if it shows an understanding of the issue and access to interviewees. This also makes it harder for the editor to hand your idea to another writer.

Writing a proposal

Your commissioning editor is busy, so you need to write tightly and get to the point. Answer all of the questions above and sell the value of the story. This should come across in the opening par. Do not bury it deep in the story by starting with an introduction to you.

Send your letter directly to the commissioning editor. This is unlikely to be the actual editor of a publication, so find the right person and make sure you have spelt their name correctly.

How to construct your proposal

Par one: What is your story? Don't start by introducing yourself, instead sell the story. Get to the "Why Now?" element of your feature and hook their interest with some sense of what your story is going to look at. If the subject is niche, then you'll need to explain it. If it is something that has already been well covered, then you'll need to show that you have identified a new and interesting development or angle as your point of focus.

Par two: What is your angle? What does your feature set out to achieve? Remember the editor will be looking for a story that will be of interest to their readers. Leave them in no doubt as to its value.

Par three: What research will you offer? A good feature needs to be authoritative and supported by solid research. Who will you be talking to and what will they contribute? Who do you have access to that others might not? What research have you already completed for this piece? What else do you expect to do to deliver an authoritative and engaging feature?

Par four: Can you deliver? Show you know where this fits into their publication, how it builds on previously published pieces and that you are clear on word counts and deadlines. Direct them to a portfolio of previously published work. Make sure that your writing is engaging and free of spelling and grammatical mistakes.

Dealing with rejection

There are few jobs where a complete novice can pitch for work in a professional environment. It doesn't work for brain surgeons, fork lift truck drivers, deep sea divers or builders, because too much is at stake. There is nothing to stop an aspiring feature writer firing off ideas to any title. With that ease of access comes the inevitable risk of rejection.

Your early feature proposals are almost guaranteed to get a "no" or indeed no response at all. And you should celebrate this. It means that you have joined the ranks of the thousands of other professional journalists who will also have faced rejection this week. It is part of the job and you have to get used to it.

Each rejection is a learning opportunity: a chance to look at your pitch and to ask yourself what you could have done differently. You only fail with your proposal if you do not learn something from it. If you're lucky, you might get some sort of feedback from the commissioning editor and you can always ask for this. It is more likely that you won't get any response at all and you will have to analyse your work for yourself. To do that, answer these questions as honestly as you can...

Did you spend enough time researching the publication before you sent your proposal?

Were you really clear on the reader value your piece offered?

Was your proposal well written?

Did you submit to the right person with the right name?

Was your proposal letter free from spelling mistakes and grammatical or factual errors?

Ideas, ideas, ideas...

As a feature writer, you are judged on your ability to come up with good ideas. If you wake up with the radio, any news story or talk show discussion should spark ideas. The same is true of newspapers, magazine articles, notices in shop windows, small ads and conversations you overhear on the bus. Keep a notebook: carry it with you and get in the habit of jotting down ideas.

If you are applying for a job on any publication, you should always go to an interview armed with feature ideas, as well as ways to improve their digital and print offerings. New recruits are a way of bringing a fresh perspective to the publication. So turn up with at least ten knock-out feature proposals that show the editor you are someone who understands the publication and its readers.

Exercise 3: Getting ready for interview

You are applying for a staff writer's job on *BBC Countryfile* magazine. They want you to bring five original feature ideas that could work for their autumn edition. Be ready to answer the following questions...

1) Who is the reader of this magazine?
2) How do your features meet these needs?
3) What would the coverlines say?
4) How would you construct each standfirst?

When you have done that, repeat the exercise for the publication that you would most like to work for.

Bibliography

Halliday, J. (2013) *GQ and Men's Health report biggest sales in PPA digital report*. Guardian (Accessed 8 September 2020). <www.theguardian.com/media/2013/feb/14/gq-mens-health-digital-sales-abc>

Men's Health. (2016). *Media Pack 2015–16* (Accessed 8 September 2020). <assets.menshealth.co.uk/main/assets/Media_Pack/MH_MEDIA_PACK_V15_FINAL.pdf?mtime=1432746860>

7
Starting your feature

A plan for features

News writing is classically illustrated with a triangle balanced precariously on its end. The message with this illustration is simple: put the key facts at the top and tell your story in the first paragraph.

Feature writers don't have it so easy. They set out to explore bigger issues and tell stories with greater complexity, that can't be condensed into a single sentence. But news and feature intros do have one thing in common: they both need to start with something sufficiently enticing to pull the reader into the story.

If you were looking for an illustration to think about feature intros, you might simply turn the pyramid the right way up. As we will see in this chapter, features

Feature intros

A feature
intro should
show the reader
something important

It cannot tell the whole story so
keep it simple: focus on one thing

An intro that involves people is often
more engaging and gives readers a way
to understand the issues

Develop the angle of your piece one paragraph at a time

often start with a sharp introduction that draws the reader's attention to just one person, one example or key idea that shows something of importance to your story.

This can't explain the whole issue that the feature is exploring, but it might aim to show one aspect of it. If we can get the reader interested in this, we can then lead them into the story to examine the question raised in the standfirst.

Your building materials

Before we look at what makes a good feature intro, it is important to understand the different building blocks that you have available to you as a writer. They include things that you SHOW the reader, things you TELL the reader and the QUOTES that you include from key sources.

Showing

Good writing helps readers to connect with your story: to experience the issues, to see the action and emotions, to better understand the characters in your feature and the way they react to people and challenges. Writers often say that showing is more powerful than telling, but what does that mean?

Good storytelling (as we will see in Chapter 9) is about giving the reader characters they can root for and showing us how these people overcome specific problems. We can TELL the reader how these characters react to a situation:

> When his car hit the truck he got very angry.

Or we can SHOW them:

> As the steam rose from crumpled bonnet, he hammered his head against the steering wheel, sounding the horn between a torrent of expletives.

Don't tell us that someone is tired; show the bags under their eyes, their drooping shoulders and their heavy movements. Don't tell us two people are good friends; show their tearful embrace as they meet in an airport after almost ten years apart. Showing allows the reader to deduce facts for themselves. It reveals important information and offers deeper engagement with the story.

Showing is a powerful way to connect readers to emotions and human experience. It can also give your reader a sense of the action unfolding in front of them. For a feature on riots in Hong Kong, you might want to describe the exact moment that a protest turned violent. For a feature on connecting kids to nature, you might want to show the reaction of children handling frogspawn for the first time.

Small, well-selected details about your interviewees – what they are wearing, what their home looks like, their reaction to challenging questions – can deliver valuable information. As a writer, you choose what to show your reader. You need to offer visual images that accompany the narrative, drawing the reader's attention to important aspects of your story. Don't tell the reader what to think. Show them what is important to your feature and let them draw their own conclusions. This is a far more engaging way to tell your story.

When you show, you need to think like a film director: one scene at a time, building the story in the way you want it to be told: revealing information that will have the impact you want. This chapter is concerned with the intro and, as we will see, SHOWING is often a good way to start a feature.

Telling

There are times when you need to deliver information in the form of data, report conclusions or facts that should be communicated quickly in your copy. Showing is an effective way to describe action, characters and location, to give a more engaging sense of the story. Facts and data can often support the point you are trying to make or offer background and context.

Let's go back to our children playing with frogspawn, with all the reactions that you might expect, from delight and awe to possible revulsion. That shows the reader something important about the learning potential of nature. Data will allow us to connect this anecdotal evidence to information about the wider population.

So we've seen these school kids getting excited by pond-dipping, but research might tell us how many kids get to have this experience. It might tell us the number of schools that feature nature in the curriculum; how many eight-year-olds can identify a newt, frog or dragonfly; and the proportion of time kids spend outdoors compared to their parents' or grandparents' generation.

We might SHOW the reader something important about a specific person, place or incident and then TELL them about the data and facts that offer supporting evidence, context and background information.

Quoting: Interviewees add authority to your feature. As we will see in Chapter 8, quotes can supply expert insight and analysis, eyewitness accounts, anecdote and opinion. Quotes add authority and engagement, allowing people to tell the story in their own words or putting the reader directly in touch with experts who best understand the issues.

In our story about learning in the outdoors, we might hear what the kids thought of the experience. We might hear from their teachers to find out how they are using nature in the classroom, from campaigners who are trying to promote this form of learning and academics who have been studying the benefits of this approach. Each of these voices offers a different perspective and helps to drive storytelling and add authority to your piece.

Research and attribution

These content types will be gathered in different ways. The data and other factual evidence may have been sourced through background research: from other people's studies, reports and findings. For these facts to be authoritative, you will need to attribute them to their source: such as a government report, a charity survey or an academic study.

If you are going to show the reader specific people, places or events, you probably want to have seen these unfold for yourself, although some details may have been sourced through interview or background research.

Quotes ideally need to come from interviews you have conducted directly, as these represent your exclusive content. They should offer specific answers to the questions that are important to your feature.

Your job is to tell a story that is engaging and authoritative. Using a mixture of these three building blocks is the best way to achieve that. A quote by itself is seldom enough, but supported by things that you SHOW and TELL the reader, you can construct an authoritative and engaging piece of writing.

How to start your feature

You should write your intro with the assumption that your reader has no prior knowledge and doesn't care about the subject matter.

That will be true for a surprisingly large proportion of them. Even if they do care, they are busy people with TV shows to watch, Candy Crush scores to improve, friends to catch up with and lives to lead. Your intro has the monumental task of getting them to put all that aside for a moment to focus on your story.

The intro has to move the reader from "I don't know and I don't care" to "this is interesting, I want to know more." One of the best ways is to SHOW them something of importance. It has to be simple enough to be understood and, to achieve that, it should focus on just one thing.

You might start with someone at the heart of your story, at a moment that illustrates one aspect of the issue you are writing about. We are naturally interested in other people and good storytelling always has people at its heart.

So with our story on reducing obesity rates in Leeds (Chapter 6), we might start with a young person in the city who has managed to get their weight in check. We might meet them in the doctor's surgery on their latest weigh-in to see if their body mass index (BMI) has finally dropped under 25 (the threshold for someone who is deemed overweight). We might show the reader their reaction to this news: the pride and relief their parents feel and that of the medical staff. It might look something like this…

> As Liam steps onto the scales, the room goes quiet. His mother and father glance nervously at their son, and the doctor who is busy adjusting the weights to get an accurate reading.
>
> "You've done it," she says, nodding. "That's another two kilos lost this week."
>
> Liam leaps from the scales punching the air, throws himself into the arms of his parents and begins to sob.

A news intro aims to tell the whole story in one sentence and under 30 words. A feature intro has a different job. We don't want to bewilder the reader or overload them with facts and background information. So, in this example, we haven't mentioned Leeds, the project or any of the debate about obesity. We have simply introduced the reader to one person who represents part of the project's success.

We have shown them one important moment in the life of a group of people involved in this issue. We have told the story in a narrative form. Its aim is to get the reader asking, "Why is he sobbing? I want to know more…"

They might want to know what Liam went through to get to this point and what impact obesity has had on his life. They might want to know what challenges he faced to overcome this problem. If they are asking some of these questions, then your intro has been successful, because your reader will look for answers in the next paragraph.

There are an infinite number of ways to start a feature like this. There are hundreds of young people like Liam who could all be our intro character. There are an equal number who will still be battling with their weight. Alternatively, we could start with a campaigner trying to tackle the interests of the food industry, a teacher running after-school PE classes or another helping kids and their parents take an interest in nutrition and fresh cooking. Each of these represents an aspect of the story and a potential way into our feature.

The intro should talk directly to issues identified in the standfirst and should start to reveal something of importance from the opening line. You need to be clear on what it is you want to show the reader and why it is important to your piece.

Exercise 1: Feature intro analysis

Answer these three questions for each of the following intros:

What does this intro show?
How does it aim to make the reader care?
What might the reader want to know next?

Intro 1: from a feature about the exploitation of refugees arriving in Europe

The wooden fishing boat, jam-packed with stick-figure people screaming and praying, was sinking fast. It was late October and the trawler's engine had failed en route from Libya to Italy. Freezing waves smashed over the bow and into the hold where 70 children – 50 of them unaccompanied – were crammed among 300 refugees and migrants. Darkness was falling and hopes fading when the Save the Children ship finally got to them.

Sunday Times

Intro 2: from a feature about the freeze on refugees heading to the USA

For Mohammed, an Iraqi civil engineer, the cruelest experience of his life was not when his father tortured him for being gay.

It was not when Islamic State extremists took over the 26-year-old's hometown in northern Iraq, forcing him to flee to Turkey. Or when he says he was almost raped at knife point and later laughed out of a Turkish police station when he tried to report the crime. Nor was it in January, when President Trump first tried — unsuccessfully — to bar refugees from entering America.

New York Times

Intro 3: a feature about "child warrior" Wasil Ahmad

All wars breed heroes, but some come in unexpected form. Wasil Ahmad was one of the unlikeliest. He was only eight years old when the war in Afghanistan, already a family affair, set him on a path for vengeance.

GQ Magazine

Intro 4: from a feature about tackling obesity in Mexico

Mexicans love their soda. Construction workers go to their jobs in the early morning clutching giant two-litre or even three-litre bottles. Babies in strollers suck on bottles filled with orange soda. In the highlands of Chiapas, Coca-Cola is considered to have magical powers and is used in religious rites.

The Guardian

Five types of feature intro

The job of a feature intro is to show the reader something that is important to your story. While the issue you are tackling may be large and complex, your intro needs to start with clarity and focus. Intros that involve people can be very effective, but this isn't the only approach. Read widely and you will find that many of feature intros fall into one of the following categories...

1 Throw the reader into the action

A narrative start can be very effective. The first example in the exercise above shows vulnerable people at a moment of peril and it highlights the risks they take to seek refuge in Europe. The fact that young unaccompanied children are onboard this storm-tossed boat adds to the sense of jeopardy and desperation. The writing here is bold and descriptive. It feels closer to a short story than a news report. There are few readers who wouldn't want to know how these people survived their ordeal.

Here is another example, this time about fly-tipping. The intro is visual and aims to get the reader wanting to know what is happening and who is throwing this litter into someone's garden.

> The TV comes over the garden wall first, in a graceful arc, rolling twice before coming to a stop, the screen miraculously unsmashed. Next come a tyre, a door frame, a drawer, miscellaneous pieces of wood and bits of hoarding.
>
> A young woman appears, voice raised in anger. "What are you doing?" she asks, filming events on a mobile phone.
>
> *The Guardian*

2 Start with someone who represents the issue

The fishing boat rescue has a number of people involved. The story of Mohammed, the Iraqi civil engineer, has just one. Introducing a character whose experiences represent part of the issue can be an effective way to get readers to care and start to understand.

Doing this gives your readers someone to root for, someone whose journey we will potentially follow through the course of the story.

This example is from a feature about an Ebola outbreak in the Congo. Again, it starts with a single character, six-year-old Bahati, in isolation, clutching a small toy. It conjures a strong visual image to bring the scene to life. His cheerful thumbs up contrasts with the heart-wrenching final line that leaves the reader needing to know more.

> Grinning broadly between dimpled cheeks, Bahati Kasereka clearly thought it was all a jolly wheeze. To his six-year-old eyes, the doctor hovering over him in a decontamination suit must have looked like an astronaut.
>
> The isolation unit in which he had just been placed perhaps resembled one of the tents he had heard about from his soldier father. Revelling in all the attention, Bahati whispered conspiratorially to a figurine of Sheriff Woody from Toy Story on the bed beside him.
>
> From time to time he raised his thumbs towards the strangers peering at him through the unit's thick plastic walls, as if to say he hadn't had this much fun for ages.
>
> Bahati may have just days to live. A few hours earlier, he had tested positive for Ebola at a nearby clinic.
>
> *Telegraph*

Here is another example, with an added element of celebrity to pull the reader in…

> Patrick Stewart was five years old when his father returned from the Second World War to wage his own war on his wife. On weekend nights, Stewart would lie in bed, alert, awaiting his father's return from the pub, ready for his rage, braced to throw himself between his parents to protect his mother.
>
> *The Guardian*

3 Bold, personal or opinionated statement

Bold or opinionated statements can also work well. If the writer is saying something the reader disagrees with, it might provoke them to read on. If it's something outrageous, they might want to know why it's being said.

Here's one from *The Guardian*'s Stuart Heritage. It's an entertaining take on the forthcoming election night and the whole feature sets out to entertain.

> Some people enjoy election night television, and that's because some people are sociopaths.
>
> *The Guardian*

Who isn't going to at least read the next line to find out why?

And that bold opening statement can potentially come from an interviewee:

> Rupert Everett is 100 per cent ready for death. "I wouldn't mind it happening straight after this interview," he says.
>
> *The Times Magazine*

4 Intriguing

A good intro can contain a mystery and promise an intriguing story. The two examples below achieve this in different ways. The first is the story of a "hitman for hire" scam on the internet. It starts with the writer describing the email that led them to this story. It sets up the question: who wanted him dead?

> I did not know Bryan Njoroge. I had never met him, talked to him, or encountered him online. In ordinary circumstances, I would have never heard of his death, more than 6,500 kilometres away. Yet in late June 2018, a message arrived in my inbox. Its subject read: "Suicide (or Murder)?" The email contained a link to a webpage showing unequivocally that someone wanted Bryan dead.
>
> *Wired*

The second example is about the demise of local radio in the States, but it uses a moment in the writer's research that promises a quirky and well told feature. It's another intro that uses first person, and the writer's own experiences form a significant part of the story.

> When I arrive at the radio station, Mark Lucke is standing in the doorway, looking out at the spitting, winter rain. He's slim and stoic, with sad, almost haunted, eyes. The first thing he asks is if I'd like to see "the dungeon." Who wouldn't?
>
> *The Guardian*

5 Bringing an interesting idea to light

Other intros can offer a unique perspective on a story or come at it from a thought-provoking angle. The intro below is about the fight to save giant sequoia trees in the United States. It muses on their longevity and blends classical history and modern culture to promise a smart piece of writing.

> Few living beings have experienced as much as the giant sequoias. With ancestors dating back to the Jurassic era, some of the trees that now grow along California's Sierra Nevada Mountains have been alive for thousands of years, bearing witness to most of human history – from the fall of the Roman empire to the rise of Beyoncé.
>
> *The Guardian*

Exercise 2: Building your own intro resource

Find at least three feature intro examples for each of these categories and try to assess how successful the writer has been. Cut and paste them into a word document and use this as a resource and an ideas prompt for your own features. Add to this document whenever you find an intro that you like, and you will create a valuable resource.

Building an intro to your strongest quote

Research from the analytics organisation Chartbeat tells us that features with a quote high in the bodycopy are more likely to be read to the end (Liqudis 2019). So if you are stuck for a way in, try to identify one of your strongest quotes and find a way to build to that.

The story below offers a good example of how that can work. Read the opening paragraphs and identify where the writer is TELLING, SHOWING and QUOTING.

The hidden jobless

Gerrard Shields watches with a wry smile when Liverpool stars such as Mohamed Salah and Roberto Firmino pass his home to reach the club's Melwood training ground. A team paid more than £2m a week between them, gathering in Lamborghini and Bentley sports cars, is an irony not lost on the unemployed 55-year-old.

"These players are on millions, coming and going in their flash cars. I'm on £158 a fortnight," he says, wearing a bright-red cycling jacket and black tracksuit bottoms at a jobs club run by his housing association up the road in West Derby. He pedalled to this CV training session, on a bike with a "Stop universal credit" sticker slapped to the frame.

"Tebbit would have loved this," he says, pointing at the bike propped up beside him. But then again, he adds, Thatcher's on-yer-bike employment secretary of the 1980s never had to get by on as little as he did on the Tory benefits scheme.

"I'm a living example of austerity," says Shields, who has been unemployed for more than 10 years and is a universal credit claimant. "It's all right for Boris Johnson and his likes; they live in a totally different world to people on housing estates. They just do not understand what it's like and they never will."

Official employment figures suggest people like Gerrard are in the minority. On the campaign trail, Johnson has repeatedly hammered home a key government statistic: unemployment has fallen to the lowest levels since the mid 1970s, at 3.8% or about 1.3 million people. More people are in work than ever before.

But a new study suggests otherwise. The Organisation for Economic Co-operation and Development and the Centre for Cities thinktank believes three million people are missing from the official jobless figures, implying the scale of unemployment issues in Britain is far larger than the official figures show. The UK's unemployment rate, the report claims, should be 13.2% or about 4.3 million people. It also suggested that austerity has bit-by-bit damaged people's chances of finding work.

The Institute for Fiscal Studies, the tax and spending thinktank, said this week the number of people on universal credit will almost triple in the next five years, with a significant risk families will be left without support. Labour says it would scrap universal credit. A spokesperson for the Department for Work and Pensions said more than 600 jobcentres have helped people to find work and that universal credit was supporting claimants.

Liverpool had the highest rate of hidden unemployment in the OECD/Centre for Cities study; with almost 20% of working-age adults out of work compared to an official rate in the city of 5.8%. The study used the central council authorities of Liverpool and Knowsley to define the city, excluding districts such as Sefton and Wirral.

The Guardian

Analysis

This feature starts by SHOWING the contrast between Gerrard Shield's life and that of Liverpool footballers. It moves into a QUOTE from Gerrard that runs over three paragraphs and that gives us a sense of his situation. Then the subsequent paragraphs TELL the readers the statistics that explain the scale of the problem and focus on the real issue of hidden unemployment.

Why are quotes so effective at increasing engagement? Journalism is about finding out new information to help your readers understand issues and events. Storytelling is at its strongest when you present that information through people. Effective feature writing often brings people who are involved in those issues to the top of the story.

We could have started the feature with information in paragraph eight: telling the reader that almost 20% of working-age adults are out of work in Liverpool. That's a shocking statistic, but it doesn't have the impact or engagement of telling the story through one person's experience.

It's also worth noting the details that the writer picks out: what Gerrard is wearing and the sticker on his bike that all help build a picture. The bike is important, because it offers a contrast to the sports cars driven by footballers. It also links to the reference about the former Conservative MP Norman Tebbit, who in 1981 made a speech urging the unemployed to get on their bikes and look for work.

The bridge

The job of your intro is to bring your reader's attention to one aspect of the problem that you are looking at. It needs to give them a reason to care about the issue and want to read on. As in the example above, you might do that through one person, but this story is about more than just Gerrard Shields. So after our intro we need a "bridge" to connect his story to a wider issue.

We normally want to tell the reader that the example in the intro is typical of a wider problem, but look at what happens in paragraph five:

> Official employment figures suggest people like Gerrard are in the minority…

This is the start of the bridge: the section of the feature that connects Gerrard's story to the problem of unemployment in Liverpool. But it seems that he isn't representative of the problem, so what's going on?

In paragraph six, we learn that these figures might mask the reality of the situation: creative accounting on the part of politicians is a key element of the story. There are far larger numbers of people just like Gerrard who aren't captured by official data.

The intro here gives us a human story to take us into the feature. It SHOWS us one person who helps the reader to understand at least part of the issue and gives them a reason to care. A bridge often TELLS the reader how this connects to the wider issues within our feature.

Exercise 3: Take me to the bridge

Go back to the intro examples you found for exercise two. For each of these, identify how the writer links the intro to the main theme of the feature. What does the intro show? How does the bridge use data or other evidence to connect this to the main body copy of the article?

Bibliography

Liqudis, N. (2019) *Real-time data, long-term reader engagement: Why publishers need more actionable insights* (Accessed 2020) <https://blog.chartbeat.com/2019/09/10/real-time-data-reader-engagement-for-publishers>

8
Structure and quotes

The power of the paragraph

Structure within a feature requires a coherent chain of ideas. For this to happen you need to understand the power of the paragraph.

"The paragraph, not the sentence, is the basic unit of writing – the place where coherence begins and words stand a chance of becoming more than mere words," says Stephen King in his book *On Writing, a Memoir of the Craft*.

A paragraph is a unit of thought. It may consist of one sentence or many, but it should be about just one thing: one topic or idea. Your standfirst sets out the aim of your feature, and every paragraph that follows has to progress your answer to the question it poses.

For many forms of writing, the opening line of a par is called the "topic sentence." This lets the reader know what the paragraph aims to do. In this chapter, we will see how it can be used to set up and get the most of the quotes you use.

Your intro and bridge work together to bring the reader into the story, but from there you need to explore the issues one idea (and therefore one paragraph) at a time. In this chapter, we are going to look at how to organise your thinking to find a workable chain of ideas. We will look at how to build story structure to make your feature logical, engaging and authoritative.

Identifying key ideas

Let's imagine you have been asked to write a feature on rising aggression towards cyclists. Riders in one race were recently injured after someone scattered tacks on the road, and there have been reports of wires strung across bike paths.

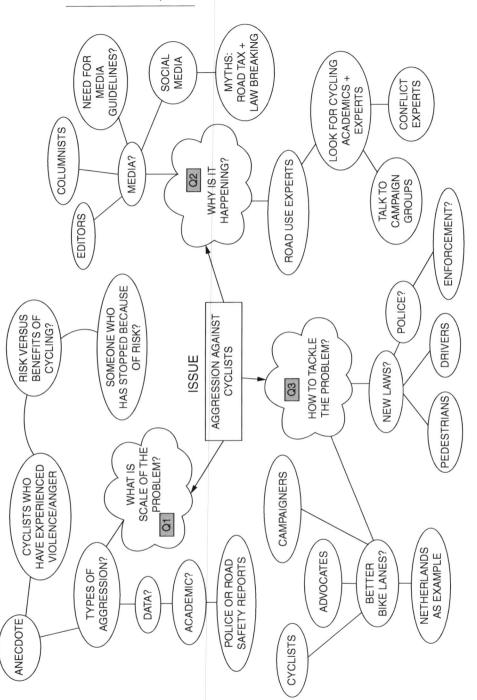

Mindmaps and additional background research can help you identify themes and potential sources.

This is the "Why Now?" to your feature.

You think your readers would be interested in knowing what is fuelling this anger and your working standfirst is as follows:

> Cycling is bigger than ever in the UK but it has provoked a poisonous back-lash. Recent incidents involving tacks scattered on roads and neck-high wire strung across cycle paths have taken the vilification of "Lycra louts" to a whole new level, so what is behind this fury?

You get the green light from your commissioning editor and you now need to conduct background research that helps you to identify the key people and organisations relevant to this issue. You will want to look for road users who have experienced this kind of conflict. You will need to find out where the current debate is heading, what campaigning groups are trying to achieve and the experts conducting research into this issue.

With this information, you can start to create a mindmap (see opposite) that will help you to visualise the key themes, causes, proposed solutions and people involved in the debate. Note that there are three key questions that will help structure the feature: What is the scale of the problem? Why is it happening? How should we tackle the problem?

Linking ideas

There will be many ways to write your feature, and you have to select one that is logical, engaging and authoritative. You need to look for ways to link ideas. Can you spot conflict between different groups? You can bring these together, because they will increase the sense of debate that will drive your feature forward. Where are people's experiences similar, or indeed very different? Bring these together, if they help develop to a narrative, driven by human interest.

Does one group blame another? Then move from accusation to response to move the story forward as it offers a right of reply. If we can spot these links within our research, we can start to find ways to structure and move your story logically from one point to the next.

Read the feature below from *Guardian* journalist Peter Walker to see how he delivered on the themes we have already outlined. You will notice that the question appears in his headline rather than the standfirst.

As you read, answer the questions below.

- How does the intro grab the reader's attention?
- Who is quoted in this story and what role does each interviewee play?

Sabotage and hatred: what have people got against cyclists?

Cycling is bigger than ever in the UK but it has provoked a poisonous backlash. Recent incidents involving tacks scattered on roads and neck-high wire strung across cycle paths have taken the vilification of "Lycra louts" to a whole new level

On 14 June 2015, Alec James was taking part in the Velothon Wales, a 90-mile mass bike ride on closed roads through countryside near Cardiff. The 28-year-old press officer, a keen cyclist, had invited along some London friends and was particularly proud to show them the region where he grew up.

Note one (see analysis below)

But his day ended early. "I was about 30 miles in, on a fast downhill stretch, and I saw one rider on my left go down," James says. "I moved to avoid him and started to slow. Then my front tyre blew out and I went over. I rolled with the bike for a good few yards, bashed my head, breaking the helmet. I was doing about 30mph. I got deep lacerations on my leg. I couldn't walk properly for a week."

After he struggled to his feet, James found a drawing pin in his front tyre, then saw a number of other tacks scattered on the road, at a point seemingly chosen to cause the most danger.

A fortnight before this, police in Brighton had issued a warning about wires strung between trees on a popular bike track through woodland, saying two such hazards had been spotted in as many days. A week earlier, in Dorset, a rider suffered cuts after hitting 15 strands of fishing line stretched across a cycle path in a country park.

In the same week, several riders taking part in Redhill Cycling Club's 70th anniversary road race, on back roads in the Surrey countryside, suffered punctures after drawing pins were scattered on the route. No one was hurt, but that was mainly down to luck, says Adrian Webb, the club's chairman: "You can guess how dangerous it can be if you have an 80-man peloton and someone punctures unexpectedly. These guys have got slick tyres pumped up very strongly for a race – there's every chance a tyre can explode. If a rider comes off, there could a mass pile-up."

Such incidents remain rare, and any such physical threat to cyclists is tiny when compared with the danger from other motor vehicles, especially lorries. One of the many paradoxical elements about cycling in Britain is that it is both far safer than many people think – numerous studies have shown it is many times more likely to lengthen a lifespan through increased exercise than shorten it – but notably more perilous than it could be.

Annual government road casualty figures for 2014, released last week, show the number of seriously injured riders rose 8.2% against the year before, a bigger increase than that in the number of cyclists. In London, in particular, the focus is on the danger posed by lorries, especially construction trucks. On 24 June, thousands of protesting cyclists brought the busy road junction at Bank to a halt after 26-year-old consultant Ying Tao was crushed by a tipper truck two days earlier. She was the eighth cyclist killed in the city in 2015, seven of whom died in incidents involving lorries, six of the victims women.

Another paradox is that even as cities such as London and Bristol are, finally, building segregated bike lanes, proven to be the best way to prevent such deaths, the tone of the debate around cycling has arguably become more polarised and poisonous than ever. Some campaigners worry that the sabotage incidents are linked to a public and media narrative in which cyclists are demonised equally as both anarchic lawbreakers and smug, humourless killjoys, sausage thighs squeezed into unsightly DayGlo Lycra.

Note five

The debate around cycling occasionally bears comparison with the treatment of so-called societal outgroups, according to Dr Ian Walker, a psychologist at Bath University. One of his experiments to research attitudes towards cyclists involved riding around his home town wearing a long brunette wig with an electronic distance gauge attached to his bike, to see whether drivers gave female cyclists more overtaking space than men. They did, even when the "woman" was 6ft tall and, for the drivers who happened to look in their rearview mirror, surprisingly hairy.

Note six

"What you see in discourses about cycling is the absolute classic 1960s and 1970s social psychology of prejudice," he explains. "It's exactly those things that used to be done about minority ethnic groups and so on – the over-generalisation of negative traits, under-representation of negative behaviours by one's own group, that kind of thing. It's just textbook prejudiced behaviour."

This is played out in the media, on television and radio and, most virulently, via social media and website comments. Under a Daily Mail story last week about Ying's death, the most-recommended reader comment until it was deleted read: "Why not ban cyclists? They don't pay road tax."

This is a particularly pervasive point, and one that ignores the fact that "road tax" – a car-based fund set aside for highway construction – was scrapped in 1937. Vehicle excise duty, its replacement, is based on emissions, meaning cyclists, if liable, would be zero-rated anyway.

Other comments under the piece surmised that such deaths happen because of rampant cyclist lawbreaking, notably jumping red lights. Again, this doesn't bear scrutiny. An analysis of police statistics found a failure to stop at a red light or stop sign was a factor in just 2% of serious adult cycling incidents; in contrast, drivers were deemed solely to blame about two-thirds of the time.

Lawbreaking is one of the difficulties of the debate for cyclists. The average person on a bike is arguably no more likely to break a law then their peer in a car. However, when they do so it's more obvious, less normalised. People notice a cyclist pedalling through a red light, whereas speeding – which 80% of drivers admit to doing regularly – is often ignored, despite the immeasurably greater human cost this causes.

Chris Boardman, the Olympic track cycling champion who is now policy adviser to British Cycling, recalls appearing on a recent episode of BBC Radio 4's You and Yours to discuss whether cyclists should be obliged to take out insurance, a discussion prompted in part by an incident where a pavement-riding cyclist struck a young child. This premise lacked context, Boardman argues: "When you put it into perspective, there's 36 people killed on pavements by cars, buses and lorries every year – that's just on pavements – versus about one every three years from a cyclist. It's ludicrous the programme was even on. Nobody seems to feel obliged to look at any facts."

Elsewhere over recent years, there has often not been any attempt at balance, even in generally sober parts of the media. Several years before anyone thought of stringing wire across Brighton woodland, Times columnist Matthew Parris half-jokingly advocated a similar idea in a piece titled: "What's smug and deserves to be decapitated?"

In November 2013, the Spectator ran as its cover story a long rant by Rod Liddle at cyclists, describing them as oversensitive lawbreakers who deliberately hold up traffic while wearing "pompous little pointy plastic hats." Even the Observer had an article in April of the same year by a regular columnist, Kevin McKenna, calling cyclists a scourge, complete with jokes about middle-class bike-riding fops and their "cous cous packed lunches".

BBC Radio Kent, meanwhile, ran a phone-in show about road safety last week under the banner: "Should cyclists be banned in cities?"

A recent twist on this narrative is the idea of a two-wheeled versus four-wheeled "war" on the roads, typically illustrated by dramatic cyclist helmet camera footage. "Many road rage incidents have been prompted by the ongoing war between motorists and cyclists," boomed a promotional tweet last week from ITV's This Morning programme. "Whose side are you on?"

Boardman is scathing about such hyperbole, not least because cyclists and drivers are very often the same people – British Cycling data shows 90% of its members also own cars.

"You've got 2% of vulnerable road users versus 98% in two tonnes of steel," Boardman says. "How can you possibly have a war? I think that's called a massacre. What could a cyclist possibly do to somebody in a car?"

He is, however, wary of connecting this media narrative with the idea of an increase in attacks and sabotage against cyclists: "There's about 250,000 assaults on the streets a year. If we're going to accuse other people of taking things out of context, we need to not do that. There are always going to be idiots and people who are evil or just plain stupid."

Others profess to see the hint of a connection, at least locally. Mark Strong, a transport consultant and cycling advocate in Brighton, says the debate about bikes in his home city has been increasingly toxic ahead of the wire-trap incidents, partly inflamed by the recently ousted Green-led council's introduction of new bike lanes and parking restrictions.

"There is an element of legitimisation towards dislike of cyclists from the attitudes of the press and politicians," he says. "It's almost an official endorsement to be anti-cyclist. And for everyone who thinks it's now OK to shout at a cyclist, at the tip of the bell curve there will be somebody who think it's OK to stretch wires across bike paths."

Note three

Rachel Aldred, a Westminster University sociologist who studies transport issues, argues that British cyclists suffer because, unlike in countries such as the Netherlands and Denmark, bikes are seen as frivolous, compared with the serious, adult business of driving. She says: "It's as if you're doing something you shouldn't be doing on the roads, almost like you're playing in the street and getting in the way of the traffic, like you're a child. There's also this dual way you can be stigmatised as a cyclist – it was historically seen as something for people with no choice, but now it's seen as something for people who have a choice. It's a leisure or play thing that they shouldn't be doing in this inappropriate place."

Note four

Aldred has also studied the environment cyclists face on the road, and her findings are alarming. In a pioneering paper published this month she finds cyclists experience on average one "very scary" incident involving another road user every week. Female riders suffer disproportionately more, thought to be because drivers are less patient with their slower average speeds.

Do toxic anti-cyclist comments in newspapers or on social media contribute to this road environment? It's impossible to prove. But some believe this is the case. "I'd be very surprised if that's not happening," says Walker. "It is acceptable to sit in a pub and say things like: 'Bloody cyclists, we should run them off the road.' Or to write things that are, literally, calling for murder. You can't do that with other groups."

Note two

In 2013, Walker led a study that saw a co-researcher sent on to the roads on a bike in seven different outfits, with a gauge measuring the space drivers gave him overtaking. Four outfits made him look like a cyclist of varying experience, while three had bright yellow waistcoats with written messages. One read: "Novice cyclist: please pass slowly." Another: "Polite: please slow down." And finally: "Police: camera cyclist."

The data for 5,700 overtakes showed just one garb made an appreciable difference to driver behaviour: the one saying "police." Here, the average passing distance was notably bigger, while the proportion of vehicles who passed very near the bike was significantly lower. In contrast, the tabard saying "polite" saw almost twice as many potentially dangerous passes.

The lesson seems clear: drivers are perfectly able to distinguish between different types of rider, and to read the message. But rather than adjusting their driving to the cyclist's apparent vulnerability, the only real trigger for them to take proper care is a possible legal sanction.

Will things change? Bike campaigners hope London's new network of segregated cycle "superhighways," now being built, will increase the number of riders, and act as an example to other cities. Cycling as everyday transport, and cyclists whose progress is separated from that of motor vehicles, will, they hope, drain the poison from the debate.

Note seven

Such tangled considerations remain far from the mind of James, now back at work and again on the bike, though with a pedal-shaped chunk out of his thigh from his high-speed fall in South Wales: "It was the worst bike crash I've had by far, and all the more upsetting as it was nothing that I did. Perversely, I was quite lucky with the injuries I had. If this kind of sabotage continues, someone will get killed."

Interviewee types

Interviews deliver quotes, which are the lifeblood of good journalism. Your initial mindmap gave you an idea of some of the potential sources for this piece. These quotes are your exclusive content. They drive storytelling, bring events to life and deliver expert insight and different viewpoints that help readers to understand the issue.

Interviewees fall into three broad groups: **Participants**, **Experts** and **People to be Held to Account**. When you are clear on the role that someone plays in a feature, it is easier to identify the questions you need to ask and then select the strongest quotes.

Participants

These are people who are involved in the story at some level. In this feature, they will include cyclists who have experienced conflict. The story above starts with Alec James – a participant – who has experienced aggression on the road. In Chapter 7, we suggested an engaging feature intro could start with someone who shows some element of the problem and build towards a quote.

In paragraph two, we get a quote from Alex that helps us to understand how the injury happened and how bad it was (Note one).

Participants help the reader to understand the problem from a human perspective rather than in the form of data and trends. The majority of intro examples in Chapter 7 involve participants in the story. They can tell us what it was like to face a particular challenge, offer an eyewitness account and explain the impact an incident like this has had on them. They may give the reader someone to empathise with.

Participants often play a key role at the top of a feature, when we are trying to get the reader to care about something and understand at least one aspect of the issue being discussed. Adrian Webb offers another participant viewpoint and Ying Tao's death humanises data that shows how vulnerable cyclists are in London.

Experts

The next person in this feature is Dr Ian Walker, a psychologist from Bath University who has researched the attitudes of drivers towards cyclists.

While the participant can offer their experience of an incident or event, the expert often takes a much wider view. These are people who can explain causes, link one person's experience to growing trends and identify potential solutions. Participants can tell us WHAT has happened, but experts can offer authoritative insight into WHY it is happening and HOW we can solve it.

It's worth noting that we don't hear from our first expert until paragraph eight. The opening seven pars set out the scale of aggression towards cyclists. We first need the reader to understand and care about the issue. Then they are ready to get deeper into the story and explore some of the underlying causes of the problem.

Other experts within this feature include Chris Boardman, former Olympic cycling champion and cycling campaigner, transport consultant Mark Strong and sociologist Dr Rachel Aldred. Each one brings a different perspective or area of expertise. Together they help the reader to understand the debate, the underlying causes of aggression and the ways that drivers react to cyclists on the road.

People to be held to account

One of the key jobs of journalism is to hold power to account, so who are the people who hold responsibility for this situation? Who has the power to make positive change? Is it a politician responsible for transport decisions or media outlets that run anti-cycling articles?

This is a story with conflict at its heart, and although the journalist hasn't spoken directly to people critical of cyclists, he has drawn on previous quotes to offer an alternative viewpoint. Their job within this feature is really that of participant. They are people who have expressed forms of anti-cycling rhetoric and their role here is to give the story some narrative direction.

Not every feature has to include all three groups of interviewee, but there could have been scope here – or in a follow-up feature – to talk to newspaper editors about the responsibility they have for running inflammatory stories of this nature.

In another feature, your experts or participants might have pointed the finger at certain groups or individuals they feel are responsible. You could then allow them to explain and justify their actions.

Good reporting is unbiased and impartial, and you will select your interviewees to give the reader a broad sense of the debate. You may not agree with all viewpoints, but you need to report those that are relevant to your feature. Your job is to present the facts and the debate and to let the reader make their own mind up.

Using quotes

When you have completed your interviews, you need to decide how you will use your research, but not all of it appears in the form of attributed quotes. Some of the information will simply be presented as facts.

Note two

Information on how Dr Ian Walker conducted his research could well have been discussed during an interview, but is not delivered in the form of a quote. The writer simply tells the reader how this research was conducted. It is not contentious and can be easily verified through Dr Walker's academic papers.

There are times when we need to be very clear on the source of information. This is especially important when we are dealing with opinions and facts that are a matter of debate. There are two ways to doing this: through direct and indirect quotes.

Direct quotes

We get our first quote in paragraph two from Alec James. He offers a vivid explanation of exactly what happened to him and it's hard not to wince at his description. This comes in the form of a direct quote that appears within speech marks.

Direct quotes are best used when they convey a powerful experience or when an expert can explain something better or more authoritatively than the writer. The more significant the interviewee, the more your reader wants to hear from them directly.

In paragraph two, we already have a good idea who is speaking, because they have been introduced in the opening par. The writer still gives us clear attribution after the first sentence (James says). You should always make sure the reader knows exactly who is speaking. Aim to get your attribution in either before the quote or after the first sentence, especially when you are moving to a new, or a different, interviewee within your story.

The promise with direct speech is that the words within speech marks were those used by the interviewee, so you should not change them. But people don't always talk in a way that works on the page. Some quotes may include hesitation, repetition: "ums" and "aahs" and "y'know what I means."

Sometimes these can be revealing and a useful part of your feature, but often they simply get in the way of the point that the quote wants to make. So it is acceptable to tidy up quotes. This may mean taking words away but never changing the meaning of what they are saying and never adding words that your interviewee didn't use.

You may need to add words for clarity: for example, the interviewee said "he," but you need to let people know they were talking about the Pope. So you put "[the Pope]" in square brackets to let the reader know something has been added.

If you need to take out elements from the middle of a long answer, then you use an ellipsis, which are a series of dots that show something has been omitted...

Always be clear on the point you want your quote to make, and don't let it go on any longer than that. Keep it tight and select only the element that you need for your story.

Setting up quotes

Your job as a writer is to keep the feature moving forward logically, always letting the reader know where the feature is heading. Don't just present the quote and expect the reader to decide what it means. Use the opening to your paragraph to set up the quote and to highlight the key point that it is going to make. You can also use this to explain complex terms or clarify any confusion there might be about exactly what is being said.

Note three

For example, when we get to Rachel Aldred in paragraph 20, the writer introduces the new expert to the story and her credentials. The writer also sets out the point that Rachel is making in her quote: that bikes are seen as frivolous. By doing this, we direct the reader to the key point we want them to take from that quote. You'll find the same thing happening with each of the quotes from different interviewees.

Attribution is important. It gives us a name and the person's qualification for being in this feature: the reason the reader should trust (or question) this piece of information. When we hear from Rachel again in par 23, the writer adds information relevant to the quote that follows. Not only is she a sociologist, but we learn that she has researched the kind of abuse that riders experience.

Note four

Aldred has also studied the environment cyclists face on the road, and her findings are alarming.

Just as with news, attribution like this can be a way to layer and weave information into your feature to deliver tight, informative writing.

Verb for attribution

Note that the verb used for attribution is almost always "says." In news, I prefer "said" and in features "says." This is because news generally tells us about something that has happened, but in features we are discussing live issues and delivering opinions that are relevant when they are published. You decide what works for you and your publication, but make sure you are consistent across the feature and that you comply with editorial house style.

Avoid using other verbs for attribution, such as exclaimed, cried, demanded or shouted. You may feel there is a need to avoid repetition and to bring some variety into your writing, but this is not the place to do this. If your quotes aren't sufficiently dynamic to deliver an engaging story, then you have a more fundamental problem with your research that you need to address.

If you are moving from one interviewee to another, then you need to let the reader know before the quote. Each paragraph should contain just one idea, and only one interviewee. If you are moving to a new source, then always start a new paragraph, and make sure the reader knows who they are going to hear from and has some idea of the point they are going to make.

Never finish one quote and then start another from a different interviewee immediately in the paragraph below. And never put attribution for a new interviewee, you haven't introduced, at the end of a long quote.

Reported speech

Direct speech needs to be presented between speech marks, but not all quotes are delivered in this way. The following line from par eight is an example of reported speech…

Note five

The debate around cycling occasionally bears comparison with the treatment of so-called societal outgroups, according to Dr Ian Walker, a psychologist at Bath University.

We know that this is something that Ian said to the journalist, because this opinion has been attributed to him. He may not have used these exact words but will have said something very similar. It is important that the journalist presents the precise meaning of the quote that they are attributing.

You use reported speech all the time when you are talking. Someone might have told you something and you want to tell someone else, for example…

Anne says to you: "I have got a new job in Paris. I love France and I'm moving there next month."

Two days later you meet Peter and you tell him: "Anne told me that she had got a new job in Paris and she is moving there next month."

You report the same meaning, but you'll notice that some of the words have changed. Instead of "I have got a new job in Paris," you tell Peter that "…she had got a new job in Paris." The subject (I/she) changes and so does the verb tense: from "have" to "had." You often see a tense change when we move from direct to reported speech, but not always. The verb tense stays the same for "is moving there next month" as this is something that will happen in the future. The same would be true if you were to tell Peter "Anne says she loves France." Again there is no need for a verb tense change, because it would be safe to assume that two days later this was still true.

You do this without thinking in speech.

Reported speech allows you to deliver quotes in a more succinct and snappy fashion: to get to the point and say what you need and to move the feature forward. You might want to use reported speech when a quote is long and technical but prefer direct speech when it delivers something sharper, more insightful, or helps to convey emotion, opinion or experience.

This piece of reported speech actually helps to set up the direct quote that does follow in paragraph nine.

Note six

The debate around cycling occasionally bears comparison with the treatment of so-called societal outgroups, according to Dr Ian Walker, a psychologist at Bath University.

"What you see in discourses about cycling is the absolute classic 1960s and 1970s social psychology of prejudice," he explains.

It's a rather academic quote and this set up helps to make it a little more digestible and easier for the reader to understand.

Reported speech is often a good way to deliver functional information, facts and data. You can change some words for clarification, so it might allow you to deliver technical or complicated information in a more accessible way. Equally, it might help you to improve the pacing of your story. There is a danger that you misrepresent something that they have told you, so extra care is required to properly represent the quote you were given.

Can you use too many quotes?

If you simply take the reader from one quote to the next, your feature can quickly lose pace. It will sound repetitive and formulaic. So be selective with the quotes you use. Mix them with SHOWING that brings people and places to life and TELLING that delivers evidence, background and insight.

Equally, mix quotes from different interviewee types and from people with different viewpoints or opinions to give your feature pace and direction.

Use quotes when your interviewee expresses something better than you could, to bring colour, authority, variety and life to your feature.

Bringing your interviewee to life

While you are interviewing you will be collecting anecdote, opinion and expert insight from your sources, but you need more than that for your feature. Your interviewees are more than a name or a job title that appears in their attribution. Give your reader a sense of what they look like, where they live, and how they behave, dress and talk.

If someone has been left with an injury after an incident, then a limp or bruising is going to be important information. If you meet them on the busy road where an accident took place, then help your reader to visualise it. If your interviewee has certain mannerisms or speech that reveal something important, then you need to bring this to life.

In this feature, we get just a few key bits of information of this nature. We hear about the slightly eccentric experiments that Dr Ian Walker conducts, and in the final paragraph we learn that Alec James is missing "a pedal-shaped chunk out of his thigh."

So while your dictaphone might be busily recording quotes, you need to be observing. You should interview with a pad and pen, making note of not only important answers but also detail that will bring your interviewees to life.

Mistakes to avoid

There are two structural mistakes that new writers often seem to fall into. The first of these delivers a potentially workable introduction that is followed by three to five paragraphs of often dreary background information that does not address the angle of the feature. This seems to say, "Here's all the stuff you need to know before we can get started on the feature I promised you."

It is unlikely that a reader will plough through this, because it is not the feature they were promised. Instead, you need to weave this information into the article, to deliver it selectively and exactly where it is required.

The second structural mistake builds a feature around people rather than ideas. It offers everything that Person A said, then Person B and then Person C. This means that differences in opinion aren't contrasted and that no clear narrative structure emerges within the feature.

Good features are structured around ideas, not people.

The outro

Note seven

A good outro needs to leave the reader with a sense of resolution. Do not use the final paragraph to summarise what the feature has covered or finish with your conclusions, unless you play a central role in the feature. And don't end a story that is dealing with complex issues with a glib line like "who knows what will happen next... only time will tell."

There are, however, some satisfying ways to conclude a feature...

1. **Bring it back to the intro:** If you start your feature with a participant in the story, then you can return to this person at the end. This is what happens in the cycling feature that brings us back to Alec James and gives him the final word.

2. **Forward-looking quote:** Just as strong quotes can make the opening section of a feature engaging, a well-selected quote can offer a good sense of resolution at the end of your piece. Alec James's quote talks about the impact that the crash had on him and outlines his worries about the future, if this kind of anti-cycling debate is allowed to continue. A forward-looking quote is a good way to finish a feature. It helps us to avoid the trap of ending with "only time will tell…" Instead, we finish with an informed view of what might happen next. A quote of this nature could come from one of our expert sources. They could highlight their concerns, discuss the best hope for change or identify the key policy they feel is required to solve the problem.

3. **Dramatic new information:** In some feature topics there may be new information that has just come to light that may change the debate around an issue. If this is really important, it should probably be in your main body-copy, but if it's just starting to enter the debate or if it's something new that you have uncovered in your research, it might offer an interesting way to conclude. Again, this might best be delivered as a strong, forward-looking quote from one of your sources in the story.

4. **Call to action:** For a feature that aims to inspire readers to take action, you might want to use the outro as an opportunity to get the reader to do just that. If your feature was talking about an environmental issue, then you might conclude with the one key action that the reader can take to be part of the solution. If the article was about climbing a mountain, running a marathon or growing spectacular garden veg, the final word might be added inspiration and a final piece of advice to help them act on what they have just read.

Exercise 1: Feature analysis

Find another feature on an issue that interests you and identify the key sources that the journalist has spoken to.

What role do they play in this feature (Expert, Participant, etc.)?
How are their quotes set up and delivered?
How are these quotes supported by things that the writers SHOWS and TELLS the reader?

9
Storytelling and travel writing

Telling stories

I remember sitting in a dark cinema in Plymouth in 1977, watching the opening crawl of the newly released *Star Wars*. My brother and I sat transfixed as storm troopers and a curiously asthmatic Darth Vader boarded a Rebel spaceship, furiously hunting for stolen plans to his Death Star.

Amidst the chaos of smoke and laser fire, two droids commandeer an escape pod and land on the desert planet of Tatooine. It is here that we meet Luke Skywalker, an orphan and reluctant farmhand who dreams of adventure. A fragment of message hidden in one of the droids leads him to Ben Kenobi, who convinces Luke to join him on a mission to save Princess Leia and destroy the Death Star.

To my seven-year-old eyes, it was bewilderingly futuristic, but in reality, it followed a classic fairytale formula: with a hero, wizard, princess, magic, strange beasts and an evil knight. I wanted to be Luke Skywalker. He was stuck on a dusty planet in the outer reaches of the galaxy, while I was trapped in a rural backwater of Dorset.

Stories across time and cultures follow a remarkably similar pattern, one that we can trace in *Star Wars*, *Harry Potter*, *the Hunger Games* or *The Wizard of Oz*. You'll find it also in the classical myths of Odysseus, Gilgamesh, the tales of the Buddha and the mesoamerican folklore of Quetzalcoatl.

They follow a pattern known as the Hero's Journey, charted by Joseph Campbell in his book *The Hero with a Thousand Faces*.

It presents us with a character given a call to adventure (the message in R2D2 or the letters from Hogwarts sent to Harry Potter). They journey into an unknown world, where they face a series of trials and tribulations. These challenges transform the central character who finally has to face their ultimate ordeal (Destroying the Death Star, defeating the Wicked Witch, or hunting the great white in Jaws), often risking everything to do so.

Great stories give us characters we care about, and we follow their adventures to find out how they overcome the challenges that stand between them and their goal. This is what drives books, films, TV shows and plays, and an understanding of the principles of storytelling is vital for any journalist.

What stories do to your brain

As Darth Vader first appeared on the screen, my heart started to beat faster and my breathing quickened. I squeezed the armrest of the chair and my seven-year-old brain released a small dose of cortisol. This is a chemical associated with our "fight or flight" response and it has evolved to help us react to threatening situations. Tension in stories produces a chemical reaction in the brain that captures our attention.

Luke Skywalker gave me someone to relate to. As I started to understand his situation and empathise with him and his companions, my brain released oxytocin. This chemical is connected to empathy and it is what gives you that warm feeling when you see someone you care about. It is involved in social bonding and it also increases our ability to recall details and events in a story.

When Luke finally destroyed the Death Star and returned for a celebratory end to the film, my brain released a small amount of dopamine, known as the "feel good" hormone. This was the ending I had been hoping for, and every brain in the cinema that night was rewarding its owner with a dose of this chemical.

Dr Paul Zak has pioneered research in this area. In one study, he showed one group a film about a father and son struggling with cancer. The audience all showed a spike in both cortisol and oxytocin. Tests on control group, who watched a film of the pair simply wandering around a zoo, did not show the same results.

Stories really are a form of Jedi mind control.

You don't need to understand the science to tell stories, but it can help you develop a strategy to capture and hold your reader's attention. You need to do much more than just present facts. You need to write with people at the heart of your reports; show the tension and challenges they face; and resolve your story with a satisfying (even if it's not a happy) ending.

Exercise 1: Watch a film

Treat yourself to a film this evening: one that you haven't seen before. As you watch, jot down your reaction to different parts of the story. How do you respond to moments of tension? Who do you empathise with most and why? How does the ending of the film leave you feeling? Where in your body do you experience those feelings? Understanding your own reactions will help you develop an appreciation of the challenges and approaches to good storytelling.

Travel features

Go back through all of the news and feature examples you have seen so far, and you will see how people facing challenges and threat can be used to pull a reader into a story: whether they are cyclists experiencing aggression, children at risk from Ebola or refugees on a sinking ship. As a journalist, you need an appreciation of storytelling. In this chapter, we are going to see how it applies to the world of travel writing.

Pick up a travel magazine or a Sunday supplement and you'll find news stories, product reviews, guides to cities in Europe and "10 of the best beaches/ski destinations/family break" round ups. But the classic travel feature is one where a journalist heads to a destination to write about their experience.

There are clear parallels with the Hero's Journey. The writer sets out with a mission to achieve or find something out, and this happens in a setting very different from their normal life.

Writing in the first person

There is seldom a reason to use first person in most features. If you're writing about road rage, obesity or hidden unemployment statistics, your experiences rarely qualify you as either a participant or an expert on the subject.

As a travel writer, however, you potentially become part of the feature. What you did will form a significant part of the narrative arc. What you saw and experienced will help the reader to understand what they might experience.

The "So What?" in the standfirst may well give the writer a mission to fulfil. The outcome is not guaranteed, which gives your story a sense of jeopardy. Challenges you faced will be key points in the story you tell, and readers will hopefully read to the end to find out what the outcome was.

Your reader doesn't care

One of the great problems with travel writing is that new writers see it as an opportunity to tell people about themselves ("Hey, look at me and the brilliant thing I did!").

As acclaimed travel writer Bill Bryson once said, "A basic error with travel writing is assuming everybody's interested. You have to work from exactly the opposite assumption: nobody is interested. Even your wife is not interested. You have to somehow make it so that they become interested."

Your writing shouldn't just say "Look at what I did!" Instead, it could say "This is what I did, and here's how you can do it too."

Your feature has to offer something of value, as well as a good story. This could be advice on how to tackle something similarly exciting or get the most out of a visit to this location. Armchair travellers, with no intention of booking a similar trip, should finish your piece with a sense of a well-told story, having learned something new.

Travel feature ideas

As with any other feature, your reader will ask two important questions: "Why should I read this now?" and "What is in it for me?"

There are some travel features that are seasonally driven. "Europe's most affordable ski destinations" is an article people might want to read in early Autumn, before they book a winter holiday. There are other features that are evergreen: content that people regularly search for online. This is an example that promises safari holiday advice from other readers.

> Going on safari is a dream trip for many, but making the most of that opportunity can be trickier than it sounds. We present your tips for ensuring every wildlife adventure is one to remember…
>
> *Wanderlust*

But for a large proportion of travel features it helps to have a strong newspeg. Your "Why Now?" might be the fact that a new flight has opened up, that visa restrictions have been lifted to a particular country or that a new travel trend is emerging.

Lonely Planet writer Oliver Berry takes inspiration from a range of sources for his features. "Some ideas come directly from PRs and travel contacts, but lots are based on areas and topics I've read about or researched," he says. "Having a new or original angle on a place is really important – what makes a place interesting, and why it's worth visiting now. Editors often look for topical hooks to hang a story on."

In this standfirst, the "Why Now?" is the end of the Ebola epidemic and the "So What?" looks at the motivations and experiences of travellers currently in Sierra Leone.

> As West Africa recovers from the Ebola epidemic we head to Sierra Leone's capital, Freetown, to find out what is bringing handfuls of intrepid travelers back to the country.
>
> *Wanderlust*

Other features may set the writer a mission. In the next example, the "Why Now?" is a new bus route and the social media frenzy around a destination in Norway. The "So What?" is the mission the writer has set themselves, to find out just what they can pack into a four-day trip to the area. This might be useful for readers thinking about an adventurous long weekend trip.

> Norway's trio of quirky rock formations have become social media sensations and are now linked by shuttle bus. So just how easy is it to complete this trekking trilogy (with obligatory selfie) in just four days?
>
> *Wanderlust*

Just like any other feature, travel pieces need a strong newspeg and clear value for the reader. Finding that combination is far more likely to get your pieces commissioned.

Travel feature intros

I wrote my first travel piece almost 30 years ago, after a three-month cycling trip around the Indian Himalayas. It took me five weeks to write and just one for the editor to send a rejection letter.

There was plenty that was wrong with the feature, but the intro was particularly problematic. It started with me getting on the plane in Heathrow with my bike, looking forward to meeting a girlfriend who was already in Delhi.

My readers' cortisol and oxytocin response to this intro would have been almost zero. Plenty of journeys start at an airport, so this was an entirely uninspired opening. And if you are the reader of a cycling magazine, why would you care that there was romantic motivation to my trip?

What readers wanted to know was how they could undertake a similar adventure.

Travel feature intros are tough, says Oliver Berry. "For me, starting and ending a story are the hardest parts," he explains. "Often I'll try to think of a surprising or unexpected experience to kick things off. I want to hook readers right from the start, so I look for incidents with real colour, a funny or weird quote. I'm a big fan of the unexpected: anything that makes them sit up and take notice.

I rewrote my story for Lonely Planet many years later, and this time I started with one of the most memorable moments. Two weeks into my journey I was sitting on top of a bus with my bike, driving along a mountain pass in Himachal Pradesh. Halfway through the bus ride, the handlebar was snagged on a live power cable and was left dangling above the road as the bus drove off. We were lucky no one was hurt.

Here is the new intro...

> You really had to admire the bus driver: the way he greeted my horror-stricken face, inverted in his windscreen, with such a sweet and engaging smile. Seconds earlier the handlebars had been snared by a low-slung power cable and the bike catapulted from the roof-rack of his bus. I'd watched in disbelief as it dangled above a rutted mountain pass while we continued our descent into the valley, sitting cross-legged on the roof.
>
> *Lonely Planet*

Throwing the reader into the action like this has its own Latin term, *In media res*, and it refers to stories that begin in the middle of the action. This approach breaks the need to start at the very beginning. You can still flash back to earlier events, before telling your story in a chronological way. This has the advantage of starting with something that is genuinely exciting or revealing: something that might provoke a reaction in the mind of your reader.

There are plenty of other ways to start a travel feature. You can arouse curiosity by bringing the reader's attention to a specific point of interest on your journey that will show them something of importance:

> Some 3000ft up in the sky, on the top of a mountain which is today the very symbol of the Lake District, there stands a plaque.
>
> It's not huge: a 2ft bronze oblong mounted onto the summit rocks of Great Gable. It's not ornate, save for the relief map of the surrounding mountains...
>
> *Country Walking*

This feature about a canoe trip through Canada combines comedy and curiosity by focusing on a particular type of peat bog found in Quebec:

> Muskeg is a delight unknown to many and it's not easy to identify. Step in it and it creates a farting noise, then engulfs your leg. If you're lucky you will

only sink up to your ankle, but often much more of you goes in. It consumes shoes, it rips off socks and sometimes you need help to get out. It's a dark tar-like substance, probably with a lot of beaver poo in it.

The Guardian

This one is about travelling to the UK's most remote pub and starts with a riff on the opening to the book of Genesis, that the reader might find intriguing.

In the beginning, there was the pub. And the people saw that the pub was good.

The pub was the Old Forge, and the Guinness Book of World Records declared it "the most remote pub on mainland Britain."

Outside Magazine

Or this from a feature about exploring London's Jimi Hendrix trail, which aims to evoke his unique guitar sound. I'm not sure how well it really works, but I love the idea. (If it doesn't mean anything to you, listen to the opening bars of *Voodoo Chile* on Spotify.)

A-wk-wk-wocka-wocka-wocka-wocka-chk. A-wk-wk-wocka-wocka-wocka-wocka-chk. Weow-da-wow-wow-wow-da-weow, weow-da-wow-weh. Weow-da-wow-wow-wow-da-weow, weow-da-wow-weh. Weow-da-wow-wow-wow-da-weow, weow-da-wow-weh. Weow-da-wow-wow-wow-da-weow, weow-da-wow-wow, we-waddar-wum. Whooomph….

Telegraph

Identifying key incidents

Every story needs a clear narrative arc, but with travel writing your task is made significantly easier. There is a chronology to your journey that will help you to structure your writing. The things that you saw and that you did happened in a certain order. This offers you a possible beginning, middle and an end. If your standfirst has set out a mission or something that you want to discover, then we want to find out if you succeeded somewhere near the end.

Travel writer and *Wanderlust* editor-at-large Phoebe Smith says she first identifies where she is going to start and finish her story. Then, she says, "it's simply a case of working out how to get from one to the other."

You clearly can't include everything that you did in your trip. So before you start writing you need to identify the key incidents that are important for the story you want to tell. These will often be moments of challenge, discovery or success in your journey.

Here is how I approached a travel piece for *Country Walking* magazine…

Why Now: It's almost autumn and that is the best time to hear tawny owls at night

So What: This feature will tell you how to do it for yourself with an exciting night-time walk

To research this piece, I spent an evening exploring woodland with wildlife expert Ian McGuire. I wanted to see owls, but that definitely wasn't guaranteed. The magazine's commissioning editor wanted practical advice and information on owl behaviour and conservation.

When I got home that night, I started to identify some of the key incidents that were important to my story. I needed to deliver a logical sequence of events to take me from someone who wanted to see an owl to someone who either succeeded (or failed) to do that.

These were the key points in my research that I knew were important, in the order that they happened...

1. Meeting the expert and his captive tawny owl
2. Looking for signs of field voles (a barn owl's prey) as we walked towards the woods
3. Calling for owls and going deeper into the woods
4. Hearing an owl in the tree above me
5. Seeing it fly above us
6. Trying to locate it in a tree
7. Finally catching sight of it

Here are the opening paragraphs of that feature. Read them and identify which of the key incidents above are included in this part of the feature...

> *Inject some adventure into your autumn walks with a nocturnal woodland safari that will sharpen the senses and get you up close to one of our most recognisable but elusive predators*
>
> The woodland floor is October crisp: a brittle blanket of russet, crimson and gold. There's just a hint of the fungi-rich odour that will compost leaves into a mid-winter sludge, but tonight they crackle and rasp with every footstep
>
> **Note one**
>
> Somewhere in the tree above sits a tawny owl, a hunter whose hearing is so finely evolved it can detect the delicate sound of a 25g bank vole in the leaf litter far below. I've barely eaten since lunch but I am still more than

3000 times that weight. There is no hope of muffling my boots as I move with pantomime stealth, imagining the fear that comes with being its prey.

And then it calls. Not the twit-twoo I was expecting, but something deeper, more flutey and descant. This haunting vibrato quavers into the cold night air with a simple message: "You are trespassing: this woodland is mine."

Owl expert Ian McGuire shines a light into the canopy, daubing pools of colour into empty monochrome branches. "That was beautiful," he says, "really deep and resonant. It's probably male: they tend to be the first out to defend their territory. Right now vocal challenges like this are going on up and down the country."

Note two

Autumn sees the young pushed out of their parental homes, and this is when territorial disputes reach their peak, so this is the best time to hear one. Once established in an area, most breeding pairs will never leave. "A tawny will invest a lot of time learning where to hunt in a woodland," explains Ian. "It knows where wet ground is, dry ground, where there are mouse nests, cover and fruit that attracts animals to feed. That knowledge is what allows them to survive. Losing it could spell disaster."

This wood is worth fighting for. It has rough grass ideal for small mammals, ancient trees with hollows for nesting, open woodland floor with banks and water.

There are five species of owl that breed regularly in Britain, but tawnies are our most common with an estimated 50,000 pairs across the UK. They prefer the broad-leaved, deciduous woodland we are walking through this evening, but they can also be found in coniferous forests, farm land, wooded urban gardens and even city parks. Head out on an autumn night and you may discover one surprisingly close to home.

Note three

We'd already been treated to a close up of Ian's own captive tawny, Jaz. As a licensed owner, Ian's now retired birds were used for educational visits, but Jaz is anything but tame. "Don't come in. She'd attack if you got close," he says as he opens the mesh door and approaches with a gloved hand. Tawny owls are notoriously aggressive. Wildlife photographer Eric Hosking famously lost an eye to one; an incident that inspired the title of his biography, An Eye for a Bird.

We watch as Jaz wraps the milky meniscus of one of her three eyelids across the glossy black pebble of her eyeball. Everything about this bird is tuned to hunt. Her soft wing feathers mean she can drop silently on her prey, and that nictitating membrane protects the eye from sharp mammalian claws.

She glides her head mechanically through its full 270 degrees of articulation, like a demonic ventriloquist's dummy. Exceptional night vision in tawny owls requires elongated, tubular eyeballs that don't move in their socket. Nature's solution? While we have seven neck bones, Jaz has 14, allowing her to rotate her head for all-round vision.

Note four

Light is already fading as we walk towards Overscourt Woods, a managed habitat that is home to tawny, barn and little owls. There are nest boxes in the trees, but the real secret to the success of this area can be found hidden under rough tussocks of grass.

Digging his fingers into a green thatch, Ian reveals a network of tiny pathways. "This worn line is probably used by a field vole and it's a sign that the area is rich in the barn owl's primary prey species," he says.

Country Walking

Analysis

Note one

The story starts at point 4 (hearing an owl in the tree above us). I wanted something that would conjure a sense of the atmosphere and excitement of hearing an owl deep in the woods at night. So I decided to use the *in media res* approach and start a few hours into our walk, in the darkness, when I realised that I was under the very tree where our owl was calling.

Note two

In paragraphs five, six and seven, the reader is still in the woods, but the focus here is on owl behaviour. So around the "live action" we are weaving the additional promise of the feature. As the story continues, it mixes our search for the owl with this kind of background information.

Note three

We stay in the woods until paragraph eight, when we move back in time to meet Ian and his captive owl, Jaz. There's no need to stick to a rigid chronological telling of your story, but you do need to signpost each new location and offer a visual anchor to give the reader a sense of place. Watching Jaz, the captive tawny owl, gives us another chance to talk about ecology and behaviour: a central part of this story.

Note four

The story now heads out to the first part of our walk as we set off in early evening, walking towards the wood and looking for signs of a barn owl's prey.

Again we need a visual anchor and to signal to the reader exactly where the feature is heading.

The rest of the story is told in a roughly chronological order: heading deeper into the woods, learning how to call to owls, and finally seeing our male tawny. Along the way, we learn about other species, hunting and conservation, and the role of owls in culture, religion and folklore.

The events of our evening give us a narrative arc and a structure to build our feature. But around this we weave advice on how to find owls and expert knowledge on their behaviour and conservation.

The outro

Every good story needs a satisfying ending. In the Hero's Journey, the main protagonist returns home, having faced great dangers and possibly even death. Bilbo comes back to Hobbiton; Harry Potter to the Dursleys' house and Katniss Everdeen returns to District 12 at the end of *The Hunger Games*. They return transformed in some way, with a gift or elixir, their allies rewarded and their enemies vanquished.

A sense of resolution is important for any story. As a travel writer, you may have given yourself a mission and there should be some sense of transformation. The experience might have changed your opinion or perspective on a place or the challenge you were set. It may have given you an idea of what you want to do next. This knowledge is the reward for your trip.

"Endings are hard," says Oliver Berry. "A great quote can be a nice way to end, or an experience that encapsulates something about the story you're trying to tell. I like to find something which suggests an ongoing experience: something which says the trip hasn't quite ended yet. If you're writing a chronological story it's easier to find an ending. If not, you need to be thinking about structure as you travel."

Signal to your reader that the end is coming and use this to reflect on your experience. If you are travelling with other people, they may have a perspective on the trip that you hadn't thought of yourself, and you could end with a quote that explains that. Equally a quote from a local or an expert might help you to clarify how you reflect on the experience.

The owl feature above ends with us walking out of the woods, hearing a male and female calling to each other, which suggests that we have found a breeding pair. It also refers back to the intro, rather like the cycling feature we read in Chapter 8…

And as we pick our way back through the woods half an hour later, we hear an orchestra of calls and responses that have nothing to do with us: the "hoot" and "ke-wick" that suggest a breeding pair. Good news for the owls of Overscourt Woods: bad news for anything rattling through the leaf litter.

Country Walking

Exercise 2: Analyse a travel feature

Find three travel articles and identify the key incidents that the writer uses to tell their story. How are these used to structure the piece of writing and what other information do they weave around this? How does the writer move you from one scene to the next? What is it about this story that holds (or fails to hold) your interest?

Quotes and dialogue

Travel is often about the people you meet and quotes allow you broaden the range of voices, experiences and expertise to reveal something important about the destination.

"For me, a place is nearly always better illustrated through the words of someone who lives there," says Oliver Berry. "They provide context and insight that flesh out the narrative of a story, and which often act as complement or counterpoint to your own personal view. A variety and diversity of subjects, and carefully chosen quotes, are what makes a good story really stand out from an average one."

In the owl feature above, quotes come from just one expert source. When I travelled to Cuba to learn to dance salsa for *Sunday Times Travel*, I was part of a group of eight other people from the UK. I was a complete beginner but others were already quite experienced and we all faced different highs and lows during our week in the city of Santiago de Cuba.

"I spend a lot of time in the salsa clubs around Edinburgh," says Orry Nowasad, a 41-year-old heating engineer. "But I've come here because I want to know how to lead and gain enough confidence to take charge."

We were all being taught by professional dancers, so they were some of our expert voices, who could help with technique and also help us understand more about Cuban music and dance. They were hugely knowledgeable and their quotes helped to bridge my lack of knowledge and tell the reader more about

Cuba. This was a quote from my instructor Odalys Armiñan, a professional dancer and local Communist Party official…

> "When I'm not out dancing, I work with my local youth groups," explains Odalys. "If one of them loses their ideology then it's my job to talk them through their problems."

I was also living in a house with a wonderful Cuban family. At breakfast one morning, my host Tita turned on the radio and got me to dance with her. She laughed raucously as I tried to show her what I'd learned so far. Her words really functioned as dialogue rather than quotes. They helped to conjure an important scene in my story, that revealed the sense of fun, love of music and spontaneity that I found everywhere in Cuba.

Watching a TV documentary on Fidel Castro later in the week, I included this quote from my host's 70-year-old mother that revealed something of the country I was exploring and different generational attitudes towards Cuban politics.

> "Everyone loves Fidel. The problems with this country are because the USA won't trade with us… not because of communism."

That story ended with all of the visiting students dancing to a live performance by the *Buena Vista Social Club* guitarist Eliades Ochoa. Each of us had made progress over the course of the week. We had experienced a transformation of our own, or at least shed enough of that British reserve to show off our new dance skills.

Dealing with cliché

There are a number of phrases that should be cause for concern for any travel writer. "Bustling markets"; "charming villages"; "stunning mountains"; "hidden gems"; "breathtaking or jaw-dropping" anything are all clichés that litter the world of travel features.

Oliver Berry keeps his own list of phrases that he will never use. "Having a style guide or 'banned' phrase list is really useful, such as 'somewhere is a country of contrasts'," he says. "There are hundreds of lazy words you see all the time in travel writing – bustling, vibrant, breathtaking. We have so many other words to choose from – so use them!"

These lack authenticity because they are borrowed phrases rather than your own words. They lack precision because they are generic rather than specific. Your writing should take the reader somewhere they haven't been before rather than to a scene that sounds like somewhere they have read about hundreds of times before.

When you find yourself using phrases like these it is time to stop and ask what it is that you really want to say. Identify the details that you could use to give a genuine sense of place.

So rather than saying that a village square is "quaint and like stepping back in time…" identify the details that will let the reader see this for themselves: the rain- and wind-eroded gargoyles, the sounds drifting from the local bar, the pensioners gathering on benches to talk in the shade. Be precise. Be clear on the details that matter. Then show rather than tell, to deliver stronger writing.

Don't tell us a market is "bustling and colourful." Describe the products on sale and focus on those that reveal something about the location, its culture and cuisine. Show us how people interact to bargain and haggle for produce. What about the buskers, children and animals?

The more you observe, the more you can reveal. So, as a writer, you need to train your eye to capture detail and then communicate that to your reader.

While showing is a good way to evoke a sense of place, telling will be important to deliver facts and detail that add to your story. So what can you find out about the history of the church and the village? What specialities are on offer here and how do they represent local culture and cuisine? What stories can you uncover that will give your reader a genuine sense of discovery? What information can you offer to transport your reader to this destination?

Dig for details that aren't well known, that tell an unexpected story and that deliver on the angle of your piece. The best way to do this is to talk to people locally. Some of this can then be delivered in the form of quotes and dialogue. These kinds of conversations may help you to find a better angle to your story or a richer sense of detail to weave into your piece.

Exercise 3: Observe and describe

Take a walk in a local park and spend at least an hour picking out the details that you could use to describe it. Make notes about the people and what they are doing here, the wildlife and plants, the sounds and smells. Before you go, research the park to find out something about its history. Look for signs on trees or park benches, litter or posters and notices that might give you a sense of what this place means to people locally. Then write a 300-word piece that brings this destination to life. Get someone to read it and then give you their honest feedback.

Think like a movie director

We started this chapter with *Star Wars*, and there's a lot to be said for thinking like a movie director when you write. Where do you want to start your story? What visual image do you want to conjure in the mind of your readers? Think cinematically and you can move the reader through your story to deliver a much better sense of pacing.

You may even want to storyboard your feature so you're clear on the scene you want to create. As you move through your article you can change focus, mixing your choice of shots.

Close-up works well for detail and narrative: the things that you will have seen as you were researching. Wide angle works better for setting, landscape and context of the location. Don't be afraid to zoom in from a big landscape to a small engraving on the side of a site of historical interest, if it's important to your story.

And if you think like a movie director, it will also encourage you to balance the fast-paced action with slower descriptive paragraphs that give your reader a sense of location. Mix shorter, punchier paragraphs with longer more descriptive sentences when you want the reader to linger on specific details. Build excitement and action, then let the reader slow down and take in the atmosphere of a destination.

Good storytelling is the closest you will come to mind control: putting images in other people's heads and causing their brains to release mood-altering chemicals and hormones. That's a pretty impressive super-power, and one worth working on.

Bibliography

Zak, P. (2015). 'Why inspiring stories make us react: the neuroscience of narrative', Cerebrum: the Dana forum on brain science, 2015, 2.

10

Interview features

The business of interviewing

Travel writing gives you a reason to bring yourself into a story, and to talk about your own experiences and opinions. But when you are writing an interview, that no longer holds true. Surely the focus must now be entirely on your interviewee?

"If it's a conventional interview, then you stay out," agrees music journalist and former Q editor-in-chief Paul Rees. "It's only when something extraordinary takes place that brings you into the story that this might change."

Flying to the States to interview musician John Mellencamp at his home, Paul was presented with just such a situation. The musician rolled up on a John Deer tractor and he walked towards Paul swinging a Victorian walking cane. "There was a sword sheathed inside," explains Paul. "As he got within 15ft, he pulled it out and flourished it within an inch of my nose and said: 'Right let's get on with it, fucker…' And then I was in the story. How could I not use that incident?"

Interviews often benefit from a clear "Why Now?" although, as we'll see, that isn't always so important. The newshook may be because an interviewee has written a book, featured in a new film or, for Paul's interviewees, released a new album.

"It's an unnatural relationship between interviewer and interviewee because they often want to sell something and you want more from it than just being told how great their new record or film is," says Paul. "You have to make sure you are in control. It is not a chat or an informal conversation and if you approach it like that you won't come away with what you need. Think of it more like a job interview. You are not their friend. It is a business arrangement."

In this chapter, we will look at how you get what you need from an interview and then how you use that material to write a well-crafted feature.

What makes a good interview?

The quality of a potential interviewee depends on the publication you are writing for. For music and film magazines, your "Why Now?" is likely to be a new film or album, but, as with this example, it needs to reveal something the reader doesn't yet know:

> After five decades in show business, Cher is funnier and more outspoken than ever. She talks about Miley Cyrus, America's lurch to the right – and whether Dalí really gave her a vibrator
>
> *The Guardian*

Interviews might also focus on people connected to news stories, to help readers understand recent events from a different perspective. The "Why Now?" is the event, the "So What?" a deeper understanding of the issues. Here's a story about a little-known environmental activist, who is trying to use the campaigning tactics of the right-wing National Rifle Association (NRA).

> "We Want to Be Like the NRA" – The Environmental Activist Using the Right's Tactics Against Them
>
> Jeremy Jones has found a way to get right-wingers aboard the climate crisis train.
>
> *Vice*

For business or special-interest publications, an interview might give the reader access to a thought leader. A "Why Now?" might be less important, but the "So What?" has to offer insight that is of value to anyone working in that industry. (We'll hear more from the journalist Jonathan Swift in Chapter 12.)

> Q&A: Polaris managing director Vivek Banga
>
> Polaris celebrated 25 years last year and also had a MD change with Vivek Banga taking the top spot. Banga catches up with Jonathan Swift about the future of e-trade and the role brokers can play.
>
> *Insurance Age*

Interview pieces can also focus on ordinary people who have done exceptional things. "It's important to have some kind of hook for a celebrity interview," says journalist Simon Hemelryk. "When other people are telling stories that are fascinating in their own right, a hook isn't really necessary, particularly if it hasn't been told before. It could be a member of the public with an extraordinary back story: someone who went from being bed-ridden to walking round Britain, or who started a successful business in prison.

Here's the example of an unknown priest with an interesting tale to tell:

> He left London to become a priest in an impoverished region of Central America, but Tom Hart is no ordinary man of the cloth.
>
> *Reader's Digest*

We are naturally inquisitive about other people. We're interested in what they have been up to and how they live their lives. As you progress as a feature writer, you will start to develop a sense of who makes a good story.

Pre-interview research

Background research and preparation are essential so that you go into an interview with a clear set of the questions you need to ask. "That list is like a road map with a beginning middle and end," says Paul. "It says to the interviewee that you know what you are doing. If you have an interviewer who is reticent or intent on giving very little away your questions allow you to set the agenda and to push them in certain directions."

These quotes will be your exclusive content and you need to prize information that is new, insightful and original above all else. Avoid asking questions that have been asked before, or for information that is already in the public domain. Identify an angle that demands new information.

If you are interviewing someone because they have just released a new book, film or album, then it's vital that you read, watch or listen to it. If they have a connection to a news event, then you need to understand and dig into the key issues. If the person has faced criticism from others, then you need to present these accusations to get their response. Research is vital so that you can ask questions that will elicit valuable answers.

Asking questions

The majority of your questions should be open-ended, so that they invite more than just a simple "yes" or "no." "You can't go far wrong with 'what happened?', 'why did you do that?', 'how did you feel?', 'what did you think at the time?'," says Simon. "Open- ended questions invite people to really describe events in detail."

Set expectations for the questions you are going to ask. That doesn't mean you are leading the interviewee towards those answers, but it will give you something to measure the quality of the response you do get and may help you listen out for interesting leads.

In the words of Tom Rosenstiel, journalist and executive director of the American Press Institute: "Write down what you think the story is before you go to report it, and after you're done reporting, if all you've come back with is exactly what you set out to find, you didn't do a very good job of reporting."

He was talking about how journalists should cover Donald Trump, but the same holds true with any story. Go with expectations but look for answers that are unexpected or that generate new, insightful information.

If you don't get the answer you need, then keep digging. "Don't be afraid to go back over anecdotes and make sure you know exactly when something happened, where it was, how old the characters were, who were the other people involved," says Simon. "These sorts of details really bring anecdotes alive."

Your background research may start to suggest possible angles for your feature, but it's likely that the real story will emerge during the interview. This makes it vital to really listen to what is being said. As a new writer, it can be all too easy to fixate on your prepared list of questions, whether the dictaphone is still recording, or worrying about how you are coming across. Your focus, however, needs to be on the interviewee and the answers they are giving.

"Don't be self-conscious about pressing for details," says Simon. "An interview for a human-interest piece isn't a conversation. It's about making sure you've got all the details necessary to make the written piece absorbing, surprising and memorable.

"There's no point just having a nice chat with someone if, when you transcribe it, you realise there's lot of important info missing from what could have been good stories."

Good storytelling requires people who face challenges in achieving their goal. So you need to make sure that these elements are all present in the interview you conduct.

Motivation may require some sense of who they are, what their childhood was like and what has made them the person they are today. The reader needs to know clearly what they want to achieve and why that is important to them.

What obstacles has this person had to overcome to get to where they are today? What problems still stand in their way and how do they plan to deal with them? What has been the emotional impact on them and their friends or family to date? How worried are they about problems they still have to deal with?

A well-told story requires a sense of resolution, so the reader will need to know how this person has changed or what they have learned so far on their journey. Get them to reflect on what they have been through, ask what it means for their life and what they plan to do next.

Setting up the interview

Try to find a location that is quiet enough for you to be heard and for the interview to be recorded. Avoid noisy cafes and pubs or find a quiet corner away from other people. Interviews for album and film releases often take place at a bland hotel, where you are part of a conveyor belt of journalists. If you can, try to meet somewhere that means something to your interviewee. Details from that location could reveal important information for your readers.

If you're using a dictaphone, make sure it works and that you have spare batteries, and a mobile phone as a backup. Always use a notepad and pen to jot down key details and the most important answers. Shorthand is exceptionally useful and speeds the process but takes time to learn.

Print your questions out on a sheet of A4 paper, with space in the margin to note down additional topics and questions that need to be followed up.

Your job is to turn up on time, so make sure you know how to get there. Have contact details for the person you are meeting and a mobile phone, in case they are late or need to be contacted.

How to interview

For acclaimed interview writer Lynn Barber, the art of interviewing could be boiled down to the following advice: "…be punctual, be polite and ask questions."

That's a good start, but there's clearly more to it than that.

Sometimes interviewees will take the interview off in unexpected directions. This may be because they aren't clear on who you are writing for or what your feature is about. So it is always a good idea to explain this at the start. On other occasions they may try to derail the interview because they don't want to give you the answers you need. Your job is to stay in control, be firm and get the answers that your readers need.

Don't try to impress an interviewee with what you know or share stories of your own. Your job is to get answers. Keep what you say to a minimum and make sure your interviewee is doing 90% of the talking.

Your lack of knowledge can often be your greatest asset, because it means you need to ask for information and your interviewee won't make assumptions about what you (and your readers) need to know.

Keep questions simple and ask them one at a time in a logical order. This will also help you when you transcribe your interview as key ideas will be grouped together.

Most of all you need to listen to what is being said. Be ready to dig for more information and to spot ideas and issues that are genuinely interesting.

Tough questions

When your interviewee has something to hide or doesn't want to answer a particular question, you need to find other ways to ask a question or return to a topic.

You may want to leave tougher questions towards the end of an interview, when you have the majority of answers you need and when you have potentially built some rapport. When you ask those questions, you do not need to be combative or confrontational, in the style of a TV interviewer. As a print journalist, it's the answer that is important, not the demonstration of conflict. Pitch these questions as a chance for the interviewee to put their side of the story:

"What would you say to people who have accused you of…"

Or explain that you are asking a question on behalf of your readers:

"People out there will want to know why you…"

As a journalist, you should be asking the questions that your readers want answered. One publication that took this to its logical conclusion was *Q Magazine*. Its monthly Cash for Questions feature asked its readers for the questions they wanted to put to the musician being interviewed the following month.

As editor of *Q*, Paul Rees says it taught him that his publication could get away with much more when it was readers asking the questions. "No one wants to say to a reader or fan 'I'm not answering that'," he says. "As an interviewer it taught us that pitching questions from a reader's perspective was often the best: the 'fans of yours would say…' approach."

Transcribing for structure

Transferring your interview from dictaphone to paper can take a long time. As you transcribe, identify those quotes that are going to be important to your story. If you ordered your questions logically, you should find that key themes are grouped together, which will help you structure your final piece.

This process can help you identify the best structure for your story. "Whenever you interview someone you have an idea of what the theme is or what you want to come out with.

But as I transcribe, I start moving things around trying to work out where ideas link best," says Paul.

Interview formats

There are a host of different formats for feature writing, and each one requires a different approach to get the most from your research.

Q&A

This is where the interview runs as a series of questions asked, and the answers that the interviewee gave. As a writer you need to do much more than simply transcribe your interview and hand it in. You need to be selective with the questions and answers you give. The questions that often appear in bold above the answer may not be the words you used. They do have to make sense to the reader and entice them to read.

Think of each question as a potential entry point for the reader. They may start with the second to last question that catches their eye, read that… then the final question and answer, before heading back to the top to read the whole thing.

Each publication will format this kind of article differently. Some will just start with the person's name and their credentials in potted form, and then launch straight into the Q&A format. So in this instance the opening questions have to make sure that the reader knows exactly who this is and why they are of interest.

Other features will start with a longer intro, possibly four to five paragraphs that offer an interesting way into this person's story. So here you will need to offer background and develop your angle. You might include a couple of direct quotes from your interviewee before you launch into the Q&A part of the story.

This format is deceptively difficult to do well, and everything hangs on the quality of the answers given. There is no SHOW or TELL. You can't bring in observational detail or stories that have appeared elsewhere, so you need to interview well and select your answers carefully.

You need to identify the most interesting and revealing answers and deliver them in a logical order. Make sure that, as you do this, you spread really strong answers across your feature to deliver a sense of pace.

Multiple interviews

You may also find stories that are built around multiple interviewees who all offer an interesting perspective on a topic or issue. Journalist Simon Hemelryk has commissioned plenty of articles of this nature, including one that ran the following standfirst:

> The immigration debate has fixated on hotspots such as Eastern Europe. So how do new arrivals from Tibet, Tristan da Cunha and other countries feel when they land on these shores?
>
> *Reader's Digest*

It then looked at the experiences of five immigrants from around the world all now settled in different parts of the UK. None of them were famous and their stories in isolation weren't particularly out of the ordinary. But together they offered a fascinating perspective on what life is like for migrants in an era of Brexit and populist politics.

Each story was written in the first person, as though the interviewee was talking directly to the reader. The writer would have chosen the strongest quotes and reordered them to deliver an engaging and accessible piece of writing.

Another piece Simon commissioned was written for *Saga*, a magazine for retirees in the UK, and it featured medical professionals who had decided to spend some of their retirement volunteering overseas. It featured three doctors who were working in places like Myanmar and Chad. Each story was written as a mini-interview, requiring its own intro and offering a mix of storytelling and quotes. The standfirst read…

> After a long career dedicated to easing suffering many people might sit back and think, "I've done my bit." But for some medics, ending full-time work is just the start as they embark on charitable adventures in deprived regions overseas.
>
> *Reader's Digest*

The story offered readers the chance to think about their own retirement, and together the interviewees offered a view of the challenges and rewards of volunteering overseas.

Continuous copy

If your interviewee's story is sufficiently interesting, then a long-form feature is likely to be the most satisfying for both reader and writer. This is where you get to tell a story, develop an angle and bring new information to the public's attention.

As with any story, you need a strong intro and a structure built around key incidents in this person's life that help the reader to understand their motivation, the challenges they have faced and exactly how this has changed them.

Exercise 1: Interview formats

Find three Q&A format interviews from different publications. How are these formatted? Do they have introductory paragraphs or just the name of the interviewee at the top? How are the questions ordered to give a logical structure? How easy is it for a reader to start reading at a random answer?

Where to start

Your intro needs to show the reader something interesting and of importance and make them want to read on.

As with travel writing, you can start by throwing the reader into the action. This could be a pivotal moment in that person's life that shows when something changed or when they were presented with a challenge or life-changing decision.

You may not have been there to witness the event, but you can still tell the story with a literary flourish or a movie director's eye to give the reader a sense of having witnessed it for themselves. Then, having given the reader something to hook onto, you might go back and tell their story in a more chronological fashion.

Here's a fantastic example:

> On April 12, 1987, Michael Morton sat down to write a letter. "Your Honor," he began, "I'm sure you remember me. I was convicted of murder, in your court, in February of this year." He wrote each word carefully, sitting cross-legged on the top bunk in his cell at the Wynne prison unit, in Huntsville. "I have been told that you are to decide if I am ever to see my son, Eric, again. I haven't seen him since the morning that I was convicted. I miss him terribly and I know that he has been asking about me."
>
> *Texas Monthly*

Just as you might start a travel feature by giving the reader a sense of the destination, you might start by focusing on your interviewee, especially if it reveals something new or interesting, as in the opening for this interview with the musician Stormzy.

> A battle cry resonates across the car park. A mob of school kids hurtles towards the stationary, blacked-out Audi A5 like iron filings to a magnet, their eyes wide and white. Greedy hands snake through the windows. "We can smell it! We can smell it! Give us some!" they yell, gleefully eyeing the joint as Stormzy, AKA 22-year-old south London grime sensation Michael Omari, takes a long drag with a cheeky, close-lipped smile. "I can't give you any of this, but I'll give you some Adidas trainers," he promises, easing his tall frame out of his car and wading into the sea of small bodies as he makes his way to the boot full of fresh "creps."
>
> GQ *Magazine*

Or it could be an imagined viewpoint that evokes an interesting scene and question about someone they don't yet know, as in this feature about a one-eyed Spanish matador, Juan Jose Padilla.

> What does the bull see as it charges the matador? What does the bull feel? This is an ancient mystery, but it seems like a safe bet that to this bull, Marques—ashy black, 5 years old, 1,100 pounds—the bullfighter is just a moving target, a shadow to catch and penetrate and rip apart. Not a man with a history, not Juan Jose Padilla, the Cyclone of Jerez, 38 years old, father of two, one of Spain's top matadors, taking on his last bull of the afternoon here at the Feria del Pilar, a hugely anticipated date on the bullfighting calendar.
>
> GQ *Magazine*

Avoid the intro that describes you waiting in a cafe for your interviewee to turn up. If you are going to play a part in the feature then there should be good reason. Someone brandishing a sword in your face (see above) could be sufficiently revealing to warrant being your way into a story.

Bringing your characters to life

All of the intros above start to bring their interviewee to life. They create a picture in the mind of the reader of a prisoner in their cell, a pop star on a London estate or a matador in the ring.

Quotes will be vital for your feature, but you also need to be able to observe and show the reader things that are important to your story. Where do they live or work? What are they wearing? How do they react to particular questions?

You shouldn't "overflower" your writing, says Paul, but focus on just two or three key points that are important to describe your character. You are putting the reader in the room, but your description should be economical and identify just the key things that you feel are important.

"The first time I interviewed Paul McCartney, I noticed he had a Beatles fridge magnet from Sgt Pepper and Linda's cookbook on the shelf," says Paul. "That was all you need. Identify two or three things: set the scene the rest of it will come."

If you move location with the interviewee, then you need to take the reader with you, identifying key points that create the scene. "The rest is what they are like as a person and how you interact with them," explains Paul.

Observation can be vital, because it can be almost impossible to get new information out of interviewees like McCartney. "He doesn't tell you anything new or anything he doesn't want you to know," says Paul. "If he saw I had loads of questions he'd take 20 mins to answer the first one, and then lean over and tap my paper and say: 'yeah no one ever gets through them all.'

"If you ask something difficult he'd say: 'When me and John were sitting on the bed together…' He knows there's no way you're going to stop Paul McCartney in the middle of a Beatles story.

"At that point it's not about what you ask. It's about what you see and what you perceive of that person. It becomes about being observant and taking in the world around you. There was so much about his world that was fascinating so you'd build up a story that way."

Key incidents in a person's story

If you are telling part of an interviewee's life, then you need to identify the key moments that reveal them as a person and the challenges they have faced. A lot of what they have been through will be boring, inconsequential or simply won't be relevant to the angle you have selected for your story.

We don't need to deliver this information in chronological order, but there needs to be a logical structure. You are unlikely to start with the moment of their birth, but you may need to go back to their childhood at some point to help the reader understand their background and motivation. You want to keep this information together in one place before you move on.

Think of the timeline and key incidents as the scaffolding for your story that gives it a logical shape. Around this you need to weave the background and issues that your feature requires.

When I interviewed Ravi Shankar for *Guitarist* magazine, I wanted to know about his youth as a classical Indian dancer, his relationship with his musical guru who taught him sitar and his experience of Woodstock, The Beatles and Hendrix. Readers of this publication are all musicians, so alongside his life story, I needed to weave insight into how Indian classical musicians approach improvisation and playing on a very different stringed instrument.

Quotes that reveal

Interview features obviously require quotes from your interviewee. These will deliver anecdote, explanation, opinion, emotion and justification. Quotes also allow you offer a sense of who this person is.

"I like to include unusual turns of phrase they use, odd words, expressions or witticisms," explains Simon Hemelryk. "Quotes should reveal something unexpected, witty or particularly honest. Avoid quotes that are a bit trite or obvious. Fill the piece with as many revealing, funny and moving anecdotes as possible. Things that readers will be dying to share with their friends and family."

Use direct quotes selectively. Don't let them drag on longer than is required. When you need to move the story forward, you can either use reported speech or summarise the story in your own words.

Direct quotes should bring incidents to life in a vivid or dramatic way, to explain emotional impact, opinion or change in perspective. So quote when you have something to reveal and tell when you want to communicate something quickly and efficiently.

Outro to your feature

Good stories require resolution. Your protagonist needs to leave the story changed in some way or with a different perspective on life and there should be a sense of reflection somewhere towards the end of the story.

This is an approach that feature writer Simon Hemelryk often uses. "I think it's generally best for the last fifth of the piece (roughly) to detail what the person thinks of what they've achieved, what others think about it, how the person thinks they've changed or learnt from their experiences and what their future hopes and plans are."

It is always a good idea to leave your interviewee with the final word, says Simon. So look for a strong quote and potentially one that both reflects on what they have been through and gives a sense of where they want to go next.

"I like to go out with something they've said. The person reading it is generally interested in your interviewee not you as the writer. So it's either a definitive quote about them or a genuinely surprising moment. If you can, end it on something they've said. Look for something that stops you in your tracks as you transcribe, that you know would send you back to the start to read the whole feature."

Exercise 2: Feature analysis

Read the story below about businesswoman Tracy Mackness that was published in *Reader's Digest*. As you do, answer the following questions…

1) How does the intro aim to grab the reader's attention?
2) What are the key moments in Tracy's life that are featured in this story?
3) Which of these show the challenges Tracy has faced?
4) Which show the things she has achieved?
5) How has Tracy's attitude to prison changed by the end of the story?
6) What are her hopes for the future?
7) Where do each of these elements appear in the story and why?

When you've worked through this story, do the same again with at least five other interview features.

Saving Tracy's Bacon

How One Lonely pig turned an Essex drug runner into an unlikely entrepreneur

It's 2001, there are two days until Christmas, and 47-year-old Tracy Mackness from Romford, Essex, is sitting in a prison cell.

She's just been sentenced to ten years for conspiracy to supply £4m-worth of cannabis. Her mother Caroline's cries on hearing the severity of the jail term are still ringing in Tracy's ears, but she's just stunned.

"I'd already done a few months on remand and honestly thought I'd be going home," she recalls.

A bleak decade lay ahead for Tracy – plenty of time for her to reflect on how her life had gone so badly off the rails.

"My dad Douglas ran fruit-and-veg shops, we had a farm with horses, and I always had pretty much what I wanted," Tracy remembers. "But he was always in and out of prison for everything from cattle rustling to hijacking lorries. When I was 14, he got put away for quite a long stretch. I developed a habit of going for flash, unreliable blokes with loads of cash, and that was part of my downfall. I was easily led, too."

Tracy got increasingly mixed up with Essex gangsters and drug dealers. "Then, when it came to the cannabis trial, the people I'd been arrested with made out that I was the main person responsible, which wasn't true. But I was known by the police, so the mud stuck."

Throw in a history of clinical depression, two failed suicide attempts and two divorces, and Tracy's post-prison prospects didn't look good.

Who could have foreseen that, by 2012, this former bad girl would be the founder and managing director of a thriving business, with a staff of 20 and a turnover of hundreds of thousands of pounds per year?

Step forward from the ashes of her former self, 47-year-old Tracy, proprietor of one of Britain's highest-profile independent sausage producers, The Giggly Pig Company.

Tracy supplies 75 flavours of banger to some 30 farmers' markets in the south of England (from Brixton to Haywards Heath), and several festivals, including the Hampton Court Flower Show and the East of England Garden Show. All the meat comes from 700 pigs on her two-and-a-half-acre farm, not so much nestling in the Cotswolds as jammed up against the Southend Arterial Road at Hornchurch, Essex.

So how did the transformation occur? Did Tracy find God? No, she met a pig called Ivy.

"After a couple of years at Holloway Prison and Highpoint in Suffolk, I'd managed to get myself transferred to an open prison called East Sutton Park in Kent. At the time, I was planning to set up my own fitness business when I got out. I'd volunteered as a gym orderly in jail and done an NVQ as an instructor. But on my first day working at East Sutton's farm, I turned the corner and suddenly there she was—this great, big, beautiful saddleback sow.

"Ivy and I both stood there and looked at each other. Both of us were in the same position, in a place we didn't want to be, and something just happened. I decided, I want to look after you—and that's what I proceeded to do. It was a complete change from my life before. I'd always been attracted to money, to men who were older and no good for me. Yet here I was, falling in love with a pig!"

And not just one pig, but the whole herd of 100 animals. Soon, Tracy was volunteering to spend all her working day with her trottered charges, and using all her spare time reading about them. "In prison, I was the butt of jokes from the other girls, who were lying around reading Bella or Cosmo, while I was there with my copies of Farmers Weekly," she recalls.

"At lunch, people didn't want me in the canteen because I was dirty from mucking out the sties, so I'd take my food back out and eat with the pigs. Mind you, I often got more sense out of my animals than I did from the humans!"

Keen to make up for her lack of schooling (zero O levels), Tracy took a total of 52 different courses while in prison. And as well as subjects such as "enhanced thinking skills" and "money management", she also opted for pig husbandry, and talked herself into any number of classes on butchery and sausage-making.

"I studied twice as hard as anyone else, and learned twice as much," she says. "It was a matter of knowing for certain that I wanted to run a pig-farming business, and trying to get as much knowledge as I could." Tracy even got a job in a butcher's near her mum's house on day release, four years into her sentence.

Just over two years later, Tracy was given parole. Then the hard work really began—she'd saved some £3,000 from what she'd earned at the butcher's and spent half of it on 30 pigs from the prison farm (including Ivy), housing them in a small field borrowed from a friend.

The pigs probably enjoyed better accommodation than Tracy. They had a nice, dry, wooden piggery while she lived alongside them in a leaky, un-heated mobile home, trying to survive on her remaining savings.

"Every morning, I'd get up about 3am and start work. It was so cold, I could see the breath in front of me. If I wanted a bath, I had to go to my mum's house. Prison was far more comfortable.

"Sometimes I'd just burst into tears, but I was determined not to give up. There were a lot of Doubting Thomases who'd known me before I went to prison, and who said I'd never stick to the farming, never carry it through."

But a couple of months later, Tracy had rented part of a local butchery with the help of a £15,000 loan from a friend and had started making sausages doing everything herself, from preparing the flavourings to grinding the meat. "I was confident I could make good products, but the key was finding somewhere to sell it. The people who ran the local farmers' markets were suspicious of me because of my past. I'm not your typical pig-breeding gen-tleman with wellington boots and a cap.

"Finally, after weeks of phone calls and pleading, I managed to get a stall in Romford Market, where my dad used to work. My friend Kim would cook the sausages, my mum would stand on the pavement, giving them out as samples, and I'd be on the stand taking the money and trying to drum up business.

"Gradually, we started doing more markets in more locations, and I was able to increase the production of sausages and the number of pigs. Often, it'd just be me and my mum, but soon we were doing so many markets that I started taking on other as-and-when staff to man the stalls. I began getting accepted by the other farmers and food producers, too. Hopefully, those who had no faith in me now have egg on their faces."

Tracy now has her own Giggly Pig shop in Harold Hill, Essex, and her bangers are always winning awards. They take in a range of ingredients, including olives, chestnuts, chunky bacon and jalapeño. There's even a Marmite flavour!

What's more, Tracy still rears the pigs, prepares the sausages, loads them into the vans, drives them to markets and sells them off the stall with her unique line of patter. "A happy pig is a tasty pig!", "Don't prick them, they don't like it!"

This on top of taking all the bookings, sourcing new livestock, doing the accounts and dispatching her sellers (18 at the last count) to her various pitches.

"I probably do more than I should," she agrees. "But I don't trust anyone. Some of the girls I was in prison with, you'd think butter wouldn't melt in their mouths, yet they'd been fiddling thousands of pounds off people's books. I like to know exactly what money is coming in, and exactly what's going out."

Her close control of her business has paid off. Within 18 months of setting up, she was able to pay off the £15,000 loan, and she now has a smarter mobile home. You only have to look at her face to see it's her pride and joy.

"My Jack Russells [Sausage, Mash, Gravy and Chops] now live in the old home. This new one is beautiful: it's got black marble tiles, a cream leather settee, central heating, and a walk-in wardrobe. It's not brand new; it belonged to a gypsy woman, who kept it really clean."

Indeed, with the purchase of a new pig trailer, there's nothing else that Tracy wants. She did become pregnant not long after leaving prison, but had a miscarriage, and although she has a live-in boyfriend, Barry, she acknowledges that her chance to have a family has gone.

As for ambitions, she says, "I've always liked the idea of running my own sausage- and-mash restaurant, though now's not the right time—people haven't got the money to go out much, at least not round here. Besides, there are business expenses: vans that need replacing; fences that the pigs have broken through.

"But do you want to know what my number-one ambition is? It's never to go back to prison. It's funny, though, because, looking back, it was the making of me. It's probably just as well I got a ten-year sentence. Two years in jail doesn't change you—it's not long enough."

Still, say her friends, though the newly entrepreneurial Tracy no longer gets into trouble with the law, she hasn't changed too much.

"Take the other day," says butcher Brian Perkin, who Tracy talked out of retirement to help with the sausages. "I walk into a pub up the road, the first day it's opened, and before I know what's happening, Tracy's got herself barred—and me."

"All I did was ask them how they could justify calling their meat 'locally produced'," Tracy protests. "And I was right, wasn't I? The only thing local about it was that they'd bought it at the super- market down the road!"

"You see?" smiles Brian, casting her an affectionate glance over trays of meat. "She's still the same old Tracy!"

And Ivy? She finally died last year after a relatively happy life breeding piglets on Tracy's farm.

Reader's Digest

Reference

Illing, S. (2020) *How Trump should change the way journalists understand "objectivity"*. Vox (Accessed 2020) <www.vox.com/policy-and-politics/2020/8/4/21306919/donald-trump-media-ethics-tom-rosenstiel>

11
Writing reviews

Harriett Gilbert

What is a review?

A *listing* is the straightforward provision of information: *Radio 2: 6.30 Zoë Ball*

A review, no matter how short, is different; it is a *critical assessment* of something that readers might be interested in watching, reading, listening to or buying.

You are already a reviewer. Each time you tell a friend how a movie you've seen drags towards the end, or enthuse about your singlespeed bike, you are in effect reviewing something. Perhaps you also blog about movies, makeup, music or some other passion, or post reviews on Amazon or Goodreads. If so, you presumably have strong opinions.

But, to review professionally, your opinions are only the start. You must also possess sufficient information to reinforce your opinions, knowledge of who your readers are, the skill to attract and hold their attention and, finally, an appreciation of the ethics of reviewing.

Although a review should be an enjoyable read in its own right – regardless of whether the reader has any intention of accessing whatever you're reviewing – at its most basic it is a consumer service: it helps readers decide which, among the crowd of new products and events, are worth their time, attention and money. A reviewer has influence and should exercise that influence responsibly.

What information needs to go into a review?

To know what information to include, first consider what *you* would need in order to access the art work, entertainment or product in question. For a one-night-only performance, for instance, you should let the reader know when and where the event will take place, plus the contact details for booking. It would also be helpful to give a range of prices. Conversely, if what you are reviewing is something your reader can buy at any time, in any number of outlets – a new book, a new mascara – then the price alone is probably sufficient. As in so many situations, put yourself in the reader's place.

Then, to the main action: helping the reader decide whether to bother with the product or event about which you're informing them.

The first thing is to describe whatever it is you're writing about, in more or less detail, depending on the word count. When space is tight you may be able to describe little more what something *is*:

> Scorsese's epic mafia picture is possibly his last on the subject: a fable of ageing, betrayal and murder based on the true story of mob killer Frank Sheeran, supposedly the man who pulled the trigger on Jimmy Hoffa.
> (From Andrew Pulver's review of *The Irishman* in *The Guide*)

With more words, however, you should aim for something more: to give a sensual impression of whatever you're reviewing – an impression of what it was like to experience. Here are excerpts from two more reviews of *The Irishman*:

> It's cinematic from the word go, opening with a single, sinuous tracking shot leading us down the corridor of a Catholic old folks' home – with its religious paraphernalia everywhere, you are already thinking about sin and redemption – until the camera settles on Frank (De Niro), now in his eighties.... This is not one of those furiously kinetic Scorsese films. Instead, it is leisurely and meandering and you sense that, as Frank looks back over his life, this is also Scorsese looking back over his career....
> (From Deborah Ross's review in *The Spectator*)

> Many of the key scenes play out in a velvety hush – at one point, De Niro and Pesci determine a man's fate merely with an exchange of looks. One beat. Two beats. The poor guy is as good as gone.
> (From Tom Shone's review in *The Sunday Times*)

Or see this from Sylvie Simmons's review in *Mojo* of Drive-By Truckers' album *The Unraveling*:

> The Truckers' twelfth studio album starts off with a solo piano – a simple, stripped-down succession of chords that make up the foundation of a very pretty song. Rosemary With A Bible And A Gun, it's called. It feels like a memory and sounds a bit like Bruce Springsteen. A girl driving down a highway, the wind in her hair, chasing the dream or escaping a nightmare, but getting out of Memphis either way... This allusive song pulls you into the album gently, and thus you're hit all the harder by track two, Armageddon's Back In Town – a scorching heavy rocker so full of adrenalized exhilaration that it might have been born on an arena stage on the band's lengthy last tour.

Or this from Dylan Jones's review of the Bentley Continental GTC in GQ:

> It is ridiculously fast, with whiplash acceleration. It goes from naught to 60 before you've properly decided to move at all... Also it has a beautiful, sexy interior, a roof that can be stowed or erected in in less than 20 seconds (this really is a seriously cool feature) and a display screen that flips from analogue to digital with such grace you wish it would never stop.

As in any journalistic feature, you're enabling the reader to imagine an experience they haven't actually had.

Exercise 1: Write a short review

Take a film, TV programme, album or book with which you are familiar and describe it for a reader first in two sentences, then – so as to give the reader a vivid sense of what it's like to experience – in two or three paragraphs.

Be clear on your opinion

From your description of what you're reviewing, the reader may well be able to guess what you think of it. But, besides description, a review should contain a clear statement of the writer's opinion. It's frustrating for a reader not to be sure whether, or how enthusiastically, you are recommending the product, art work or entertainment in question.

And don't be nervous about getting it wrong, looking stupid. As long as your opinion is genuine, informed and substantiated, it cannot be wrong.

I say "substantiated" because, as well making your opinion clear, you should also demonstrate how you've reached it. Except when the word count is really tight, it is not enough to declare baldly that such-and-such a book is "funny," for instance. You need to quote lines or summarise a passage illustrating said funniness. The reasons for this are several. First, an example is usually more vivid to read than a simple statement. Second, you enable your reader to check whether they share your sense of humour (or disgust, or whatever it may be). Third, in the search for a suitable example you may find yourself forced to modify or even change your assertion.

So: description; judgment; justification for your judgment.

One other thing that makes a review effective is providing your reader with important or interesting context:

> The widespread uptake of disc brakes has sent wheel manufacturers scuttling back to their drawing boards to reconsider how best to design wheels for modern riding. One outcome is that wheel rims are getting wider...
>
> (From a review of the latest Bontrager cycle wheels in *Cyclist* magazine)

> Back in the day, when the musical world celebrated Beethoven's 200th anniversary, his only opera, Fidelio, was an essential component of the Royal Opera's repertory. Between 1970 and 1976 the company mounted five revivals, most of them with mouthwatering casts, of a production by the conductor Otto Klemperer....
>
> (From Hugh Canning's review of Fidelio in *The Sunday Times*)

> Sebastian Barry won the Costa for Days Without End, in which two soldiers from the Union Army adopt a little girl from the Lakota tribe. Now the little girl has grown up and we get A Thousand Moons, her story.
>
> (From Melanie McDonagh's book review in the London *Evening Standard*)

And, finally, don't forget to name the creators whose work you've singled out. This may seem obvious if the creator is a famous chef, the lead singer in a band, the star of a show, the author of a book. But it also applies to backing singers, product designers, translators: if you've mentioned their work, name them.

And note that, for actors, there are two conventions, depending on the structure of the sentence. If, in the sentence, the actor is given more importance than the role, then you simply name him as you would any other artist whose work you were mentioning. If, however, it is the role that has most importance in the sentence, then the actor's name is usually inserted in brackets:

> In pre-revolutionary France, an artist named Marianne (Noémie Merlant) undertakes a treacherous sea voyage....
>
> (From Tom Shone's *Sunday Times* review of *Portrait of a Lady on Fire*)

How do you conduct your research?

Your primary research is to experience the art work, performance or product you're reviewing. You might think that should go without saying but a literary critic once gave a novel I had written an excellent review which was simply a reproduction of the blurb on the book's jacket. I also knew a film critic who would sleep through the larger part of a movie and, from seeing the beginning and the end, guess what must have happened in between. This approach is not recommended. Whatever you are reviewing, watch it, listen to it, read it, take it for a spin… in other words, *test it* for your reader.

Then, background research: most obviously, becoming familiar with previous work (if any) by the artist, entertainer, designer or company in question. This allows you to spot recurrent themes, obsessions, strengths and weaknesses and to assess the relationship of the new work to the old.

The amount of background research you need to do depends on three things. First is the ambitiousness of your review. A 1,000-word review of Steve McQueen's *12 Years a Slave* in which you are planning to discuss the issue of black representation in film will obviously need more preparatory research than a straightforward 200-word review.

Second is the amount of information available. About a new, young musician, information would probably be scant, whereas if you were going to review a Rolling Stones concert, for instance, you would need to become familiar not only with decades' worth of their work but with the accumulation of comment about it. (And, although it is impossible to know too much, it is worth remembering that knowledge works best as a foundation for what you write, not as rococo decoration incontinently splattered about. Its purpose is not to impress the readers with your brilliance but to ensure the solidity and soundness of your judgement.)

The internet, too, is obviously invaluable, although do remember to double-check everything you read there. For example, while an artist's own site is likely to have up-to-date information about tour dates, publications, film roles or whatever, it is most unlikely to contain information detrimental to the artist's reputation. Similarly, although Wikipedia is a go-to site for all kinds of information, its entries vary widely in terms of accuracy, detail and currency. And do bear in mind that, although you may use Wikipedia for background research, you should never quote from it in a story.

If you want to become a specialist reviewer, you might subscribe to an authoritative online service such as Oxford Reference (www.oxfordreference.com) or Oxford Music Online (www.oxfordmusiconline.com/public), which includes the magisterial Grove Music Online.

Note taking

In many cases, you will have one chance to watch or listen to the work you are reviewing. Even with recorded music, books or video games, for instance, although in theory you can return to the beginning as often as you like, in practice there may not be time for more than one go. So try to ensure that the notes you take are the right ones.

You should first note those *facts* that you will need when you start to write: that the novel's narrator is a 60-year-old lawyer, for example; or that the opera has been relocated to 1930s Berlin.

Sense impressions are also important: the look of a stage set; the way the actor playing Hamlet uses his voice; the lighting of a rock concert; the dominant colours of a movie . . . whatever strikes you, make sufficient notes to be able to recreate it in print. And do keep *all* your senses alert. A film, for instance, is more than its narrative. It is also a complex of composition, lighting, movement and noise. As well as dialogue, the sound track will almost certainly have music on it, not to mention the sighing of wind or the constant throbbing of helicopter blades. The camera may cling to the actors' faces in close-up, or keep its distance.

Similarly, a restaurant is more than its food. It is also the efficiency and/or pleasantness of the serving staff, the arrangement of the tables, the noise levels, the décor. Notice, *consciously* notice, all those things that are having an effect on you.

Where applicable, quotes are also useful. Write down those that are powerful in themselves and those that could be used to make a wider point.

Finally, note your reactions. If you smile, choke up, are frightened, are bored, write it down.

After all this, the next point to make is that you can take *too many* notes. Especially when reviewing a performance, if you spend all your time with your face in a notebook, you are liable to miss key moments. So, be selective: note only those things that make a special impression.

Some critics make no notes at all until a performance is over, on the not-unreasonable grounds that what they remember must be what most impressed them. If you trust your memory, try it. And, even if you have cautiously taken notes during the performance, it is still useful to write a quick sentence afterwards, to sum up your feelings: "Pretentious rubbish; I couldn't understand a word of it," for instance, or "Started slowly but, by the end, had me hooked." The reason for this is to prevent you, later, from writing yourself towards an untruthful opinion. For various reasons, including doubts about your judgement, this is easy to do.

How to take notes

Nicholas Barber, film critic and arts journalist

Tell people that you review films for a living, and it's surprising how many of them ask the same question: do you have one of those pens with a little torch built in? The answer is no, not any more – not after my fellow critics kept frowning at me and grumbling about light pollution. But whenever I'm watching a film, whether it's online, or in the offices of Sony or Universal in London, or at a festival in Cannes or Venice, I always have a pen and a notebook in my hands.

Most critics do. Some of us scrawl a couple of brief codewords which no one else can decipher; others fill sheaves of A4 with fully formed sentences. There is no right or wrong method, just as long as you jot down anything that could be useful afterwards. When were you scared silly or bored rigid? What didn't sit right with you? What jumped out at you? The wooden acting? The frantic editing? The action sequence which was lifted from another film you saw two years earlier? What you want are specific examples that might bolster your argument and convince your readers that you're not completely ignorant. And if you think of any clever analogies or sparkling jokes, so much the better.

I sometimes end up writing a review without referring to my notes at all, but, like snacks on a train journey, it's reassuring to know that they're there. And perhaps the process of scribbling a few observations gets my brain into reviewing mode, rather than watching-for-fun mode, so it doesn't matter if I read them or not. The one time it's essential to take notes is when an onscreen caption says "Paris, 1792." Later on, you'll have a vague memory that the film was set in Toulouse in 1812, so, whatever you do, get those places and dates on paper while you can.

How do you write for your reader?

A review is not written for the artists or manufacturers concerned, however much you might like their good opinion. Nor is it written for yourself. It is written for the reader of the publication for which you are writing.

I say "the reader" as if there were only one. What I mean by that is the archetypal reader that your publication's marketing department will have identified: a person with such and such an education; of such and such an age; with such and such political views and interests; and so on. And, in the same way as you modify your vocabulary and cultural references depending on whom you are talking to in real life, so you should modify your vocabulary and cultural references depending on this archetypal reader.

See, for example, how Jon Ronson's book about "social media fury," *So You've Been Publicly Shamed*, was reviewed in two very different publications. *Red* is a women's lifestyle magazine primarily concerned with fashion, beauty, relationships and celebrities. Its review of the book began like this:

> Jon Ronson is one of the funniest writers we have, as George Clooney will tell you (he bought the rights to Ronson's book The Men Who Stare At Goats and then starred in the film).

And that celebrity heart-throb endorsement makes up more than half of the 50-word review. In *The Guardian* the same book was given in the region of 2,000 words and, although the review also referred to *The Men Who Stare At Goats*, it did not mention George Clooney. Instead, it mentions the "Bilderberg Group" as though its readers will know, or be flattered by the assumption that they know, what the organisation is.

Similarly, when writing for the now defunct feminist magazine *Sibyl*, the literary critic Georgina Paul could talk of the "feminist reappropriation" of ancient Greek myth; her readers would have understood what she meant. Had she been writing for a local paper, the phrase would have needed to be explained or (preferably) replaced.

Readers of local papers are perhaps the hardest to target. You know where they live and should take that into account when reviewing things connected to the area, but, even more than with national papers, they tend to differ widely in age, income, education, cultural interests and politics. At least with most of the national press you know your readers' probable politics and incomes.

Magazines are more narrowly focused. They may, overtly or otherwise, be aimed at a particular sex or age group. There are magazines for people with such and such a hobby, job, cultural interest, religion, political affiliation. There are magazines aimed at people of a particular ethnic group or sexual orientation.

Their readers, of course, usually buy a whole range of publications. To take just one example, a black British woman estate agent might regularly read *Estates Gazette*, the *Daily Mail*, *Woman & Home* and *Pride*. Only in *Pride*, a magazine specifically aimed at black readers, would she expect a review of a gig by the Senegalese musician Cheikh Lo to open as Diana Evans's did:

> The Jazz Café is brimming with swaying "world music" fans, most of whom, it has to be said, are white. It's the same with most concerts by African stars. The question arises, why is it that black people don't listen to their own music?

Whether your publication's "reader" is a black person, schoolteacher, film buff, train spotter, gay, vegetarian, pensioner or clubber, your review should recognise that fact.

What is your angle/your story?

As with any piece of journalism, before you put finger to keyboard it helps to have an angle, a story – something you can sum up in a sentence: *This band used to be great but they've grown stale and tired*, for instance, or *The food in this restaurant may be Instagram friendly but it tastes vile and is overpriced* or *The colour-blind casting in this film makes such sense that after 30 seconds you no longer notice it….*

You have your story. Now, how to write it?

How do you write your introduction?

As with all journalism, the opening words should both snatch the reader's attention and relate, directly or obliquely, to the main point you intend to make.

If what you are reviewing is extraordinary in its own right, then why not simply announce it? Here, for instance, is the introduction to Alexandra Harris's *Guardian* review of *The Mirror & the Light*, the long-awaited third novel in Hilary Mantel's series about Thomas Cromwell:

> So the trilogy is complete….

In *The Oldie* magazine, Lucy Hughes-Hallett took a different approach to the same novel. She decided to drop the reader right into the action:

> Canterbury Cathedral. The dead of night. A few flickering lights. People huddled around an opened vault. In the dark immensity of the building, dogs are loose. The tomb of Thomas à Becket, murdered on this spot 400 years previously, is being opened on the orders of Thomas Cromwell. The dogs are to oblige the assembled monks to stay put and witness the desecration.

Similarly, in the *Observer*, Laura Cumming began her review of an art exhibition like this:

> Dusk at Ostend, and a black pall descends on the eerie lighthouse. The skyline is starting to fade, the shoreline dwindles to a glimmer. The town lies still, but out at sea the waves are heaving like a sleeper troubled by dangerous dreams. And this is where we are, where the picture puts us – out here in the drowning darkness. The Belgian artist Léon Spilliaert (1881–1946) was probably not more than 20 when he made this frightening image….

As long as the image is powerful or intriguing, your reader will wait for further explanation.

Another attention-grabbing opening is the teasing or provocative statement

> There is no foreplay with an I-Pace
> > (Dylan Jones reviewing an all-electric Jaguar in GQ)

> Wife swapping will be the main topic of conversation at dinner parties this month
> > (Charlie Higson reviewing Ang Lee's The Ice Storm in *Red*)

> A shark ate my penis. As excuses go, it's a pretty unusual one, but it's the excuse Samuel Bundy offered in 1860 before being arrested and imprisoned.
> > (Christina Patterson reviewing the book
> > Female Husbands in *The Sunday Times*)

Or you might start with an appropriate personal anecdote. Unlike a news reporter, whose experience and personality shouldn't be part of the story, yours inherently are:

> If I had to save one Paula Rego picture from a burning building, it might be The Blue Fairy Whispers to Pinocchio (1996)
> > (Lucy Davies reviewing the book *Paula Rego:*
> > *The Art of Story* in *The World of Interiors*)

> Misbehaviour is a film about the 1970 Miss World contest that was disrupted by "bloody women's libbers" – that's what my dad always called them, anyhow – throwing flour bombs and shouting "we're not cattle!" as Bob Hope fled the stage in a panic and our televisions temporarily blacked out
> > (Deborah Ross reviewing the film Misbehaviour in *The Spectator*)

Finally, you can always cut to the chase and open with your judgment:

> I love a good face oil, and this one is a doozy.
> > (The intro to an India Knight cosmetics review in
> > *The Sunday Times*)

How do you end your piece?

The end of a review is usually a summing-up of the critic's opinion. So, go back to what you decided was your story, your angle, and remind yourself of the overriding impression you want to leave with the reader: at its crudest, a thumbs up, a thumbs down, or a sort of half-hearted in-between shrug.

> I don't quite know how Swift does it – the book is light, perhaps slight, and the story is all told at one or two removes so that it reads as though it's happening in the next room. And yet it's a magical piece of writing: the work of a novelist on scintillating form.
>
> (How Barney Norris ends his review of Graham Swift's Here We Are in *The Guardian*)

> In truth, this is a barmy little sketch posing as a revolutionary satire.
>
> (The final sentence of Lloyd Evans's review of the play Radiant Vermin in *The Spectator*)

> This is not a novel to be tossed aside lightly. It should be thrown with great force.
>
> (Dorothy Parker)

How do you structure your piece?

You have written the opening paragraph. You know how you want to end. Then what?

First you need to make sure, if you haven't done so already, that you spell out what it is you are reviewing. A certain amount of mystery in the introduction can be intriguing, but don't draw it out for too long.

Then read through your notes and create two lists: one of those things you enjoyed or approved of (if anything); one of those things you *didn't* enjoy or approve of (if anything). Then select what you consider the most important and/or interesting points.

Think of these points as building blocks that need to be placed in an effective order. For instance, if your introduction gives the impression that you very much like the thing you're reviewing, you might then elaborate on what precisely it is you enjoy – let's say, in the case of an album, the pared-back guitar accompaniment; the singer's voice; some smart lyrics – then, more briefly, you might mention that one or two tracks don't really work (and why), before returning to a summing-up that encapsulates why you think that, in the main, the album is a success.

Or – to take two real examples – first, look at the structure of this short review by Amon Warmann in *Empire* of the movie *Sonic the Hedgehog*:

> Hollywood's track record with video-game adaptations is risible and Sonic the Hedgehog fails to move the dial in the right direction. This time the blue-furred speedster (Ben Schwartz) teams up with local cop Tom (James Marsden) to foil the plans of Dr Robotnik (Jim Carrey) to harness Sonic's powers for evil. Carrey chews the scenery at every opportunity and is almost worth the price of admission by himself. But frustratingly the central bromance between Sonic and Tim is undercooked, and while they're not without their charms, the super-speed sequences feel derivative of Quicksilver's big scene in X-Men: Days of Future Past The final moments make it clear that this is being eyed as a potential franchise, but on this evidence it's a threat, not a promise.

Here, then, an introduction that both provides a bit of context and lets the reader know immediately what Warmann thinks of the film. This is followed by a summary of the plot, then praise for Carrey's attention-grabbing performance (i.e., not *everything* about the film is awful), but then condemnation of the scripting of Sonic and Tom's relationship and of the super-speed sequences. The review ends by reiterating Warmann's negative opinion of the film.

Or see how Andrew Male structures this review in *Mojo* of *I Am Not a Dog on a Chain* by Morrissey, released when Morrissey was in widespread disfavour for political views he'd expressed:

> Bad men can make good art. T.S. Eliot was an anti-Semite and John Wayne a white supremacist. But people die, along with their crimes, and the art remains to survive on its own terms. That's one argument and possibly the only way to approach a new Morrissey album: will it exist beyond the life of its problematic author? Produced by Joe Chiccarelli, who's helmed his three previous LPs, this is a cloistered, time-haunted record that, lyrically, alternates between surrender and defiance. Beginning with the craggy rhythms of Jim Jim Falls – our hero considers suicide at an Australian waterfall – and ending on the choral exhaustion of My Hurling Days Are Done, it is a fittingly distressed late work from a scared and out-of-favour singer, the clichés of his art shored up as fragments of resistance. Removed from the living artist, it may one day be hailed as a great album.

Having chosen to introduce his review with topical context, Male then describes the sound and lyrics of two tracks that, presumably, stood out for him, before ending with a summing-up of his (tentative) approval of the album.

Besides the way those short reviews are structured, you might notice a couple of style points.

First, neither critic spells out "In my opinion," "I felt," etc., because it goes without saying that a review expresses the opinion of the journalist.

Second, note the care that both writers take over adjectives. Instead of such tired, vague adjectives as "terrible," "brilliant," "great," etc., they select words that convey more precisely the nature of their disapproval or approval: "risible"; "undercooked"; "time-haunted"; "craggy."

Exercise 2: Review analysis

Read two reviews of 500 words or more and break them down into building blocks of argument. What are the key points that the writer makes and what is their final conclusion?

Spoilers

At the end of Agatha Christie's theatrical whodunnit *The Mousetrap*, audiences are asked to keep the murderer's identity a secret so as not to spoil the suspense for those who have yet to see the play. Should critics generally refrain from revealing twists, surprises and denouements?

There are two schools of thought about this. The first holds that of course they should, that anything else would wreck the enjoyment of potential audiences and readers. The second holds that, since a review is not an advertising trailer, it is entirely legitimate to reveal whatever the critic likes – preferably giving the reader a Spoiler Alert. This is something you will need to decide for yourself. (When it comes to film reviews, however, the dilemma may soon become obsolete, with audiences ever more inclined to post plot-spoilers on social media even as they're watching.)

Knocking copy

In the same way that happiness and goodness tend to make for less interesting stories than anguish and evil, it can take more work to be interesting about something you like than about something you hate. A good insult springs from the fingers with such a satisfying elegance. Consider how gratified Mary McCarthy must have felt as she typed this condemnation of fellow writer Lillian Hellman:

Every word she writes is a lie, including "and" and "the."

Or what about this, from the nineteenth-century critic Eugene Field reviewing a production of *King Lear*:

> He played the King as though under momentary apprehension that someone else was about to play the Ace.

But merely because it is easier, and perhaps more fun, to knock than to praise, you do need to ask yourself whether the knocking is justified. Is whatever you're reviewing really quite as bad as you're suggesting? If it is, what is the reason for bringing it to readers' attention?

This does not mean that you should tiptoe around. If adverse comments are in order, go ahead. But do take care that your insults are appropriate and relevant. Insulting a performer's physical appearance, for instance, is relevant only if it has direct bearing on the work.

Bear in mind, too, that as a critic, *you are not immune to the libel laws.*

You do have a defence to the charge, which you share with columnists and satirists. It is known as "fair comment." According to this you may, paradoxically, be as *unfair* as you want, so long as whatever you write is your "honest opinion." But this is where things get dangerous.

First, opinion is not the same as fact. You would be perfectly entitled, for instance, to write that the crowd scenes in a production of Shakespeare's *Julius Caesar* gave the impression that Rome contained only three plebeians. But were you to write that the crowds were composed of three actors, when in fact they were composed of five, you would have no defence to libel.

Second, if your opinion is way over the top, it might be concluded that it could not be "honest." Libel suits against reviewers are rare, but a successful one was brought against a columnist whose comments on the size of an actress's bum were judged not only factually wrong but far too excessive to be "honest."

Third, you must not be motivated by malice. In 2011, the author Sarah Thornton was awarded £65,000 in damages for a *Daily Telegraph* review of her book *Seven Days in the Art World*. The reviewer, Lynn Barber, was found not only to have made an untrue assertion (she wrote that Thornton had never interviewed her, as claimed in the book, when in fact she had) but, second, to have been malicious: "spiteful," to quote the judge.

The fourth test of "honest opinion" is that you should be commenting on a matter of public interest. This should not usually worry you, since a product for sale, a published work or a public performance are obviously of public interest. But it does raise another, non-legal, question. Critics disagree about this, but to me it seems there is little point in slamming artists so obscure that, were it not for your reviewing their work, your readers would be blithely unaware of them. Would it not be better to leave them in obscurity?

How do different publications format their reviews?

Publications have a variety of formats for reviews. A film review in the specialist movie magazine *Empire*, for instance, gives a great deal of information at the top, including the names of the principal actors and director, a short precis of the plot, the release date and classification, and a star rating. Moreover, at the end of each review is a brief "Verdict" (presumably for time-poor readers). On the other hand, a magazine that's not primarily concerned with film, such as the *New Statesman*, will simply provide the film's title, classification and the name of the director.

Star ratings, positioned sometimes at the top, sometimes at the end of the review, are increasingly common. The one in *The Sunday Times* is even accompanied by a helpful code: 5 = KO; 4 = A-OK; 3 = OK; 2 = So-so; 1 = No-no.

Besides such obvious differences of format, it is worth noting quirks of style. In a review of Anne Enright's novel *Actress*, for example, after the first mention of her name the reviewer in the *Economist* refers to her as Ms Enright (as distinct from the terser, more usual Enright).

But to understand how to format your review is only one reason to become familiar with a publication for which you hope, or have been commissioned, to write. As described earlier, you must get to know your reader; you must acquire a sense of the publication's values; you should have read previous issues and registered what other contributors to the publication have said.

You cannot, as a journalist, write into a void.

Have you got what it takes to be a reviewer?

Arguably the most important thing you need to become a reviewer is a second income. Reviewing is very badly paid – although you do get to see a lot of movies / keep a lot of books / eat a lot of free meals…

Which leads to the second prerequisite. To enjoy reviewing and be good at it, you need to be seriously interested, to the point of nerdiness, in your subject. This includes researching its history, keeping an eye on current trends and, of course, directly experiencing as much of it as you can.

Third, you'll need ingenuity and persistence. To become the regular film critic for a national paper or glossy magazine takes time, experience and contacts. The same is true should you want to be a regular critic of any sort for a prestigious, well-paying media outlet. Such jobs are rarely available to young or inexperienced journalists.

Specialist knowledge or special experience can be a useful springboard. If, for instance, you know all there is to know about K-pop, you are in a stronger position than someone with only a casual, generalised interest in music. Similarly, if life has given you experience of accounting, snowboarding, being the child of alcoholic parents or whatever, you have a good case to put to a literary editor looking for the appropriate person to review a book on one of those subjects. Or, if you live out of London and know your way round the local music, theatre, dance, club or art scene, you could be useful to arts editors fed up with trying to persuade staff journalists to travel.

The crucial thing is to keep abreast of what is happening in your chosen field; by and large editors know about the immediate and the mainstream. Ask publishers to send you their catalogues. Keep in touch with your local theatres, music venues, clubs. Read specialist publications. Surf the internet. Hang out with people who work in the arts. And, if you get a job as a sub, editorial assistant or reporter, but would like to be writing reviews as well or instead, make frequent visits to the arts desk to enquire about what is coming up.

Finally, you need confidence in your opinions and, as importantly, the integrity to shift them only because you come to see that they are misguided, *not* because they are out-of-step with the views of the majority, not because they might upset the powerful, not because they might make you seem uncool. Your views, your take on things, are what matter – both to commissioning editors and to yourself. They are why people will want to employ you. They are what give you your individual voice. They are why you want to be a critic.

12

Making complex ideas accessible

Matt Swaine, Aidan O'Donnell and Nigel Stephenson

Business and science reporting

Certain areas of journalism, from business and technology to politics, economics, science and medicine, require writers to report on topics of real complexity. Very few of the students I teach have a background in these areas. Even as editor of BBC *Wildlife*, many of my writers had studied English and history, rather than zoology or a natural science, although as we will see this can sometimes be an advantage.

What's more, many of the journalists I have worked with will proudly confess a fear of numbers and data, elements that are vital to reporting on these topics. If you plan to make your living from writing, the onus is on you to develop the skills needed to report confidently on these issues.

New scientific discoveries and business developments are newsworthy. They influence our health, spending power, the state of the planet and the way we work and live. Being able to write about these issues effectively requires you to make complex ideas accessible to a wide audience.

In this chapter, we will hear from business and science journalists, to understand the approach they take.

We will start by looking at how to build your confidence with the numbers you encounter as you research a story. The secret, according to data journalism expert Dr Aidan O'Donnell, is to simply ask the right questions.

Numbers for journalism

Dr Aidan O'Donnell

Being a numerate journalist has very little to do with maths. It doesn't even have that much to do with numbers. It's about applying the same skills journalists use when dealing with sources and information: respectful scepticism, checking we have the story straight, understanding things before explaining them to audiences, asking the right questions of sources and placing our information in context.

The science writer Victor Cohn said that, for journalists, clear thinking is more important than calculations. He's right. When numbers are involved in mistakes in newsrooms, it's rarely because somebody couldn't do maths and more often because somebody (or more likely, several people) didn't stop to ask some basic questions.

So, what are the questions we need to ask – of our sources, and of ourselves – when we think we have a story? The following questions should keep you and your copy safe.

How did they get the numbers?

If somebody gives you a number, it means somebody has had to count something.

If I asked you to go out and count the number of "old people" you see while standing in the centre of town, who would you include, and why? Is it their retirement status, their grey hair, their ability to remember the moon landing of 1969, their pension, or just the fact that they're older than you?

During the 2020 Coronavirus pandemic the UK government twice got into trouble over counting things. When they announced that they'd carried out a high number of tests to check who had the disease, it turned out that "1000 tests" actually meant checking only 500 people, because each person underwent a nose test *and* a mouth test. When the government announced that a billion items of protective equipment had been delivered to health workers, it transpired that the number came in part from counting gloves as two items, not as a single pair of gloves.

Or look at the United States: you might be shocked to learn that, on average, there is a mass shooting every day!

Yet the numerate journalist will ask "How many people need to die for the incident to be classified as a 'mass shooting'? What exactly is a 'mass shooting'?" If you count any incident where at least two people are hit by a bullet, you will have many more "mass shootings" on your hands than if you decide a "mass shooting" is when, say, more than ten people are killed by gunfire.

Is that a big number?

The most useful question you can ask when faced with any number will be "Is that a big number?" It is the Swiss-army-knife of questions (originally promoted by Michael Blastland and Andrew Dilnot in *The Tiger That Isn't: Seeing through a world of numbers*, Profile, 2007). It simply means taking a number and putting it in context.

A tabloid newspaper screams "Standards plunge as hundreds of students fail exams," a press release from a local charity laments that the "Budget does nothing for the dozens of people sleeping rough on our city's streets" or the government declares "Extra two billion pounds for the NHS."

These are all important issues, but are these announcements news? If 200 students fail an exam is that more than last year? More than an average year? How many people are homeless in the city and are the numbers going up or down? How many more nurses can a region hire with two billion pounds?

This is not to suggest that a failed exam is not important to the student who sat it, that one person sleeping rough for a night is not a problem or that the government should not try to fund a health service. It simply means that until we know if our numbers are "big" or not, we are not yet in a position to report on the story.

Crucially, this question can also alert you to potential errors. Asking "Is that a big number?" is a good way to spot numbers that are way off, and that are so big or so small as to need checking. If you are about to report that the price of a barrel of oil has "dropped to $500," a quick check on whether this is a "big number" (or here, a "big drop") will set you straight.

Is something hidden behind this *percentage*?

"There's been a 50% increase in…" – that sounds like a "big increase" but is it? It just means there is half as many again. If, in a school district, two students failed the history exam last year, an increase to three students is not news.

One UK news organisation quoted a report that there had been a 50% increase in how many children were "experiencing emotional disorder" (from 2004 to 2017). But the actual rise – apparently moving from 4% of children in 2004, to 6% of children in 2017 – is less dramatic and may perhaps even be explained in part by an increase in reporting (see below: "Twice as many crimes, or twice as many crimes recorded?").

Percentages can help, however. The number of smokers in the world is increasing. But ask if the latest figures are a "big number" and you'll find that as the world's population keeps increasing, the number of smokers as a *percentage of global population*… is actually dropping. So numbers that may look like they're going up can actually be going down as a proportion.

Or is something hidden behind this average?

An average is a magical thing. It takes a big messy group and produces a single number that represents the group. That's where its power comes from (and its usefulness).

But it's vulnerable to being skewed by extremes and to the number of instances we are measuring. If a footballer has an average from last season of "one goal scored for every match played," it might be worth asking "how many matches did they play?." If the player was only on for two games, and managed a goal each time, the goal rate is less impressive than if they started every game in the season.

If average life expectancy in a country is 50, should we expect to meet very few people older than 50, or are we dealing with a place where a lot of babies and infants die? It could be either; we just don't know without extra information.

Risk

There's an increased risk of something! But what was the original risk?

The press is famously fond of stories like "Eating ice-cream more than once a week increases the risk of stroke by 50%."

Don't worry, it doesn't!

But even if it did, is this news? We don't actually know because we don't know what the original risk was. If there was a one in seven billion chance of having a stroke if you had a weekly ice-cream, and the risk has doubled – it's now just two in seven billion. So you can probably keep eating that Mr Whippy.

But if, for example, the risk of stroke for "ice-cream-eating middle-aged men who do no exercise" was one in ten, then a 50% increase in the risk probably is news. At least for those guys.

Is that twice as many crimes? Or twice as many crimes recorded?

If numbers of a particular crime are up this year is it because there is increased criminal activity? Or is it because more people, perhaps encouraged by media reports that this is a widespread phenomenon, are coming forward to report it? Or have people become resigned and stopped telling police at all ("Numbers of crime x reported have fallen").

Figures recorded are exactly that, the number of things that were noted down. So, are you looking at the number of crimes that took place, or just the number of crimes that were recorded?

Is this causation, or just correlation?

Every September children go back to school and the weather turns autumnal here in the northern hemisphere. If we didn't send the children back to school, maybe the weather would stay warm and summery?

This is clearly not the case. We know the weather is not changing *because* of the children.

And yet this link "Oh, whenever this thing increases, this other thing also increases" often encourages us to think "one must cause the other." The two things *are* sometimes related ("correlated"): the change in weather is related to children going back to school: not because one causes the other but because each is tied to a particular part of the calendar.

"The more mobile phone masts there are in an area, the higher the number of cases of cancer!" a campaign group announces in a press release. This sounds worrying, but it is never enough to observe "oh, x increases every time that y increases" – we need to investigate if one *causes* the other.

You can make the same observation but change it slightly: "The more post offices in the area, the higher the number of cases of cancer." This shows that you cannot assume they have a *causal* relationship – they do have a relationship but in these cases it's probably with a third element – the population: you often have more phone masts, post offices and sick people where the population is greater.

The mantra we have to remember is "Correlation is *not* [the same thing as] causation."

But why does the journalist care about this?

Because people like to make claims on this basis. The football manager observes, "Every time we put this player on, we score more goals. He's magic!" Maybe the substitute *is* the reason for the goals; or maybe when he goes on, a very bad player comes off which is actually what helps. Or maybe they always score in the last 15 minutes because they're a very fit team and the last quarter hour is when the substitute comes on.

Or a politician notes, "Since we came into power, crime rates have dropped."

The rest of the press conference may well be satisfied with the politician's observation, but the numerate journalist will ask herself, "well did their policies cause this, or is it just that the two things [this party in power, a drop in crime] happened at the same time?"

Writing about business

Numbers are clearly important to business journalism, but that does not mean you need a first degree in mathematics or economics, according to insurance journalist Jonathan Swift.

"I got a C in GCSE maths but have managed to get my head around balance sheets and year end results," says Jonathan. "When I started as a cub reporter on *Insurance Post* in 1998, my boss told me: 'Every story has an insurance angle'. I have written about topics from the insurance implications of Michael Jackson's death to manned space flight; cryptocurrency to issues around the legal cannabis market."

An understanding of the subject matter is important, but communication skills come first, according to financial journalist Nigel Stephenson. "We should never forget that we are journalists essentially telling stories," says Nigel. "Our skill is to find what's newsworthy in the financial world and to ask the right questions of authoritative sources.

"We approach business news just as we would any other topic. It has its specialist terminology and sometimes difficult concepts that we might have to explain, depending on our audience, but business reporting is no more complicated than reporting cricket. It can be learnt by anyone with a curious mind."

Finding the angle of your story

The first step in writing with clarity is to be clear on your story. The best way to do this is to ask what it means for your readers and why they should be interested.

"Business news affects us all," explains Nigel. "It is about what goes on in the economy, of which we are all a part. We all spend money; some save, borrow or invest. We work or run businesses, we pay taxes, we receive benefits.

"Identifying what a news story means first requires an understanding of your readership. Changes in interest rates or tax levels or even the profitability of our employer can directly affect our lives and livelihoods.

"Close to 1.3 million people in the UK work in finance and insurance and a lot of them read, and are willing to pay for, business news. Stories aimed at a general reader should include a reference to how the news in question can impact on their incomes, jobs, pensions, loan rates or holiday money."

Jonathan's editorial role now involves mentoring new writers. "We tell reporters not to get too bogged down with jargon and extraneous detail. Instead, when writing an article, to think about how they might explain it to their friends to make it interesting to a layperson, rather than a CEO or expert," he says.

While some of the ideas underpinning your story may be challenging, it is likely that the strongest news angle will be far simpler. "Most issues in business journalism are not that complex," says Nigel, "a company makes a profit or loss, unemployment goes up or down, Apple releases a new iPhone. The skill is in explaining to readers, whether specialist or general, why these events are important."

And within business and financial reporting, you are often following many of the same guides for news values: looking for conflict, human angles and even celebrity hooks for your story. "Even the world of business has its celebrities: from Jeff Bezos of Amazon, Mark Zuckerberg and Sheryl Sandberg of Facebook, Apple's Tim Cook and Virgin founder Richard Branson," says Nigel.

Dealing with jargon

As a business reporter, many of your sources will be experts: CEOs, business leaders, traders, financial analysts and economists. Words that they commonly use may be entirely unfamiliar to the average reader.

"Most business news, including in publications such as the *Financial Times* and the *Wall Street Journal*, is written for a general, but maybe 'financially literate', audience," says Nigel. "The journalist doesn't dumb down the subject or ignore its complexity but explains it. The most important thing is to avoid jargon.

"Sometimes journalists parrot the language of their sources, however obscure, as if doing so demonstrates they share their knowledge and expertise. Don't fall into that trap: do not write for your sources: write for your readers."

Ask the questions you need to understand the issue so that you can explain it clearly. "I tell journalists not to be afraid to ask someone to explain something again, and again if necessary," says Jonathan. "If a journalist has no idea what someone is telling them, how can they then explain it to our readers?"

Your lack of expertise, can actually be an advantage. "The best way to deal with jargon from an interviewee is to feign ignorance," says Nigel. "Ask the source how you can explain the topic to a general reader. Keep pushing until a useable quote emerges. Jargon comes naturally to some people whose work usually involves people with similar specialist knowledge. These specialists often do not realise they are using jargon and don't mind being prompted to simplify."

Making your writing accessible

You need to write your story with the first-time reader in mind, this group is particularly important if your publication wants to see circulation growth. Be ready to explain key terms so the story makes sense for an entry-level reader rather than expert.

"*The Economist* is famous for its helpful signposts in stories such as 'Goldman Sachs, a bank, …'. It might seem surprising that not every *Economist* reader knows Goldman Sachs is a bank," says Nigel. "When I worked in Russia in the early 1990s, even the concept of a share in a company was new and needed explanation in some local media.

"Avoid clever-sounding euphemisms. Economists can talk about 'negative growth' in an economy. What they mean is that it shrank, so say just that.

"And avoid quotes that are full of jargon. If they won't be understood, they will have little value to your readers. One approach is to put the information, properly explained, in indirect speech.

"This can cause problems if you are covering breaking news from a policymaker such as a central banker. If reporting in a time-sensitive situation, stick with the language used and keep the explanation for an update."

How to structure your story

The components of a good business story are the same as those of a general news story. Here is Nigel's approach, which closely resembles the model for news writing we set out in Chapter 3.

News intro: Your opening par should focus on the main news which, depending when in the news cycle the story is written, may be an event, or a number of particular significance. The analysis should start in the lead.

Par two: This paragraph should back up the lead with precise figures or detail.

Par three: A "nut graph" that delivers the "so what," explaining the significance of the news or the context that makes it newsworthy.

Par four: Somewhere high in the story you should aim for a quote that goes beyond information, that adds analysis or expert commentary. This may not be from the source of the news, i.e. the company announcing its financial results or the central bank cutting interest rates, but from an impartial expert evaluating what has happened.

Using the right numbers

Numbers are important in business but as a general rule, should be used sparingly in your writing. "The numbers you include should be those that matter to the story," says Nigel. "Layering is vital. Your story should compare what has happened with expectations – a prime factor in market reaction. Company result statements can be a sea of figures and, while some financial news readers will pore over them, all readers want to be directed to the most important number.

"That's why it's important to know what the market is expecting and what these experts think is likely to be most important news. In a piece about a listed company's results, the company's profit or loss, its revenue and any share price reaction are essential."

Big numbers can be hard to grasp. If company A made a profit of $x last year, how does that compare with the year before? Without the comparison, we do not know if the company has had a good year or a bad one.

Even more important in financial journalism is comparing a company's profit or an economic indicator with market expectations. If a company announces a profit in line with what market participants were expecting, chances are its shares will not move. If the profit was better or worse than forecast, chances are they will.

"For example, if the US economy adds 200,000 new jobs that number may not mean a great deal to your readers," says Nigel. "Explain the relative increase as a percentage growth and make the figure relatable: tell them that it is the equivalent of the population of Aberdeen.

"When Apple's market value hit \$2 trillion, that's about the size of the Italian economy. One year BT made a huge profit and one UK news organisation helped readers to understand the figures by saying it equated to £136 per second."

How professional reporters deal with jargon

Covering the world of business and finance, journalists encounter unfamiliar concepts that an outsider might struggle to understand. It is their job to explain these terms and their significance.

"You've probably never heard of an 'inverted yield curve', which is often seen as a signal of impending recession. It doesn't happen that often but it's worth a story, even if it's just one indicator that a contraction in the economy might be imminent," says Nigel.

When Larry Elliott covered a story about inverted bond yields in August 2019, he started by explaining that a sell off of shares was sparked by the news that investors would now get more for a two-year bond than a ten-year bond.

The next paragraph explained clearly why that caused problems for investors…

> This is unusual because for the most part investors demand a higher yield on 10-year bonds because there is more uncertainty over what could happen in the next decade than in the next two; higher risk equals a higher return.
> *The Observer*

The following paragraph explained that this was often seen as a signal for impending recession…

> It indicates that investors are more concerned about short-term growth prospects than about inflation risks in the longer term and, historically, it is often the moment the recession warning light turns red.
> *The Observer*

By starting simply, each paragraph moves the idea forward, slowly building complexity.

Here is Colby Smith of the *FT*, reporting on the same issue from January 2020:

> The US Treasury yield curve, whose movements are watched by traders for harbingers of recession, has become inverted again as the intensifying coronavirus outbreak revived fears of a global growth slowdown.
> *Financial Times*

The *FT* story is for a more economically literate audience, but it still included a helpful graphic showing the difference between the two yields dipping below zero, i.e. inverting.

And finally, the BBC's Andrew Walker, on the same story, aimed at a much wider audience.

> Financial markets have flashed a warning sign about the economic outlook for the UK and the US.
>
> It is known in the jargon as an "inverted yield curve."
>
> It means that it is cheaper for those countries' governments to borrow for 10 years than for two.
>
> It is an unusual development and it often comes before a recession or at least a significant slowdown in economic growth.
>
> BBC Online

Again, it's a simple explanation of an inversion and why the reader should care. Notice there is no mention of bonds or interest rates.

These are all examples of how it should be done. Introduce the idea, explain it without jargon and say why it matters. The nut graph ("This is important because…") is key.

Exercise 1: Analysing financial news

Find five current business and economic news stories from a range of publications, from papers aimed at a financially literate audience, such as the FT, to those intended for a more general audience, such as BBC news. How is each story structured? What technical terms require explanation? How is this information layered? What numbers are used in each story? Who is quoted in each piece and what information does this add to the story?

Reporting science

Scientific research can impact the lives of millions of people. New medical discoveries offer hope for patients, innovative technology can change the way we live and work, while studies from the sub-atomic to the outer reaches of space help us to unlock the mysteries of the universe.

"Science explains the world around us. Everything we do, use or think can be explained by science. It is vital to understand the complex world that we live in," says science journalist Jheni Osman.

There's never been a better time to be writing about science and the environment, according to award-winning wildlife writer Ben Hoare. "There's a huge public hunger for trustworthy stories about everything from climate change and the extinction crisis to pandemics," says Ben. "Expertise is key – readers crave insight from scientists and conservationists on the front line."

As with business reporting, a background in science can have value, but the ability to communicate ideas is key. "Some of the best reporting comes from journalists with a non-science background," says Jheni. This is because they report on complex topics in a way that can be understood by the average person.

Be clear on your story

The components of a good science story are the same as any other piece of journalism. News value will often depend on a story's impact on readers, and factors such as conflict and celebrity can also be important. You need to be able to explain your story in a single sentence and know that it has something to capture your readers' attention.

"I always think about how I'd explain the story to friends," says Jheni. "The tricky thing about reporting science stories is that scientific discovery is a gradual process – very rarely are there 'eureka moments' – and so often it's the quirky and sensationalist science stories that get commissioned."

There is no shortage of potential stories out there with an estimated 2.5 million new scientific papers published each year, university press departments firing out press releases and conferences taking place around the world.

Your job as a journalist is to identify those that are important to your readers. We all value our health, so stories that help us to understand what we can do now to live better into old age are a good example.

This is a section of a scientific paper that was the source for the story that follows.

> Healthy cognitive ageing is a societal and public health priority. Cerebrovascular risk factors increase the likelihood of dementia in older people but their impact on cognitive ageing in younger, healthy brains is less clear.
>
> *Nature Communications*

This has been written for scientists and it uses words and phrases that would mean very little to most people. This is how *The Guardian* reported it…

> High blood pressure and diabetes bring about brain changes that impair thinking and memory, research suggests.

Doctors examined brain scans and medical data from 22,000 volunteers enrolled in the UK Biobank project and found significant structural changes in the grey and white matter among those with diabetes and high blood pressure.

The Guardian

Note the opening paragraph of this news story is a single sentence of 16 words long, contains no jargon but clearly communicates the element of the research that is most important to readers.

Dealing with jargon

In order to get stories that are free of jargon, you need to question technical terminology as you interview. "Scientists sometimes use jargon because for them it is everyday language," says Jheni. "I tend to stop them and ask what it means and if they can give an analogy. Even if I know what a phrase means, I will ask them to define it for the reader."

Making these terms accessible to your readers is paramount, agrees Ben. "Jargon, nerd words and acronyms have their place and can be valuable in your article, but I ask the interviewee to define them for me as the layperson – even if I already know what they mean," he explains. "I find this process leads to greater clarity."

Certain words that might seem familiar have a different meaning for scientists and members of the public, according to science writer Carl Zimmer. Scientists might talk about a "positive trend" and your readers might think this is a good thing, when it means an upward trend. When scientists talk about "uncertainty" they do not mean ignorance but the range within their findings. If your mate Dave has a theory, it's just an idea. When we talk about Darwin's Theory of Natural Selection, it is accepted scientific understanding.

So ask for explanations as you interview to ensure that you really do understand the story.

There are plenty of scientists who care about quantum communication and who will read the abstract to this scientific paper with great interest.

Quantum communication is rapidly gaining popularity due to its high security and technological maturity. However, most implementations are limited to just two communicating parties (users). Quantum communication networks aim to connect a multitude of users. Here, we present a fully connected quantum communication network on a city-wide scale without active switching or trusted nodes.

Quantum Communications Hub

Even readers of *New Scientist* probably aren't that bothered about quantum communications. They almost definitely own a computer, use the internet and care about online security. So this jargon-free report on the same piece of research might catch their attention.

> A more secure internet could be around the corner thanks to the reported largest-ever quantum network of its kind.
>
> Quantum communication systems are more secure than regular networks, because they rely on the quantum properties of photons…
>
> New Scientist

You should aim to bring this kind of simplicity and clarity to any story that you write.

Using numbers in science reporting

Do you know what "21 millions of tonnes of tiny plastic fragments" looks like? This is how much waste scientists have calculated is floating in the Atlantic Ocean, but I can't picture it or fully appreciate the scale of the problem.

It's enough waste to fill 1,000 container ships, according to a *BBC Science* story, and this gives me a way to visualise and begin to understand the data.

What about 586 billion tonnes of water? That's the amount of ice that scientists say was lost in Greenland in 2019. Like me, you probably have no idea of what that looks like, so this story begins…

> High temperatures saw Greenland lose enough ice to cover the US state of California in more than four feet of water in 2019….
>
> Independent

I get that California is big and I know four feet would be over my waist. The article goes on to say that the total loss is "equivalent to 212.8 million olympic-sized swimming pools over the course of 2019, or seven for every second of the year."

From the sub-atomic to the science that explores the universe, science deals with numbers that are outside the understanding of the average reader. Comparisons like these can give the reader a way to visualise and understand the data.

Using analogies

Analogies with more familiar ideas can be helpful when you are trying to explain complicated scientific concepts.

Astrophysicist Stephen Hughes from Queensland University of Technology uses baking to explain the universe. "Astrophysicists often use the 'raisin loaf' analogy to explain the expansion of the universe," says Stephen, in *The Conversation*. "The dough represents space and the raisins galaxies. Imagine sitting on a raisin in the middle of the dough as it bakes in the oven. As the loaf expands we would see every other raisin move away from us."

It's a way to think about the expansion of the universe and how every galaxy is moving away from our own Milky Way, he explains.

Roy Peter Clark, senior scholar at the Poynter Institute, says one of the best analogies he has seen in science writing was used to explain how earthquakes work. The writer, Kathryn Schulz, asked the readers to put their hands face down with the middle fingers touching.

> Your right hand represents the North American tectonic plate, which bears on its back, among other things, our entire continent, from One World Trade Center to the Space Needle, in Seattle. Your left hand represents an oceanic plate called Juan de Fuca, ninety thousand square miles in size. The place where they meet is the Cascadia subduction zone. Now slide your left hand under your right one. That is what the Juan de Fuca plate is doing: slipping steadily beneath North America.
>
> *Poynter Institute*

As with the use of big numbers, good analogies can provide a way to think about complicated ideas, but they need to be used wisely. Analogies have their limits and can be used badly. There's only so far you can go with a loaf of bread if you want to understand the universe.

Help scientists to help you

If you are interviewing a scientist responsible for a piece of research, then their aim often aligns with yours: to communicate their research to the widest possible audience. There are some important ways that you can work together and the first of these is to read their original paper in full, not just the abstract or press release.

Ideally you get to talk to the lead researcher: let them know exactly who your readers are so they can pitch their explanation and answers accordingly. "Over time, I've learned that it's best to say quickly when you don't understand something, rather than pretending you do and ploughing on in the assumption you can just check online later," says Ben. "I like to read back what I've understood to be the key points of the story, so my interviewee has a chance to correct me and offer a different steer.

"I'll also finish up by asking if they think anything is missing from my analysis. This back-and-forth approach tends to be productive, often resulting in an entirely new angle for the piece."

Developing a good contact book of expert sources will be vital if you aim to succeed in this area. For that to happen, trust is vital. You need to develop a reputation as someone who gets their facts right. Make sure your stories link to the original research papers, to allow those readers to find out more and to show that you have sourced your story effectively.

Stories with punch

Some science stories want to emphasise the potential impact it will have on the lives of your readers. Others will simply relish the incredible advances in our knowledge of ourselves and the universe we live in.

Here's a fascinating intro that tells us something about the way we have all learned to grieve:

> Bronze age Britons remembered the dead by keeping and curating bits of their bodies, and even turning them into instruments and ornaments, according to new research…
>
> *The Guardian*

This story is actually about the development of new super-tough materials, but it starts with the dynamic species that inspired the research.

> They may be little more than 10cm long but mantis shrimp pack a serious punch – they are able to whip out their club-like forelimbs at 23 metres per second and smash them into their prey with the force of a rifle bullet.
>
> *BBC Science Focus*

Not everyone will get excited about discoveries in the world of palaeontology, but give it a popular cultural reference and it might grab more readers.

> The enormity of a prehistoric mega-shark made famous in Hollywood films has finally been revealed by researchers.
>
> *BBC Online*

Exercise 2: Analysing science news

Find three science news stories online that offer links to the original research paper within the story. Read the abstract of the research paper and compare this to the opening paragraph of the news story. What is the angle that the journalist has taken and where does that appear in the abstract? How has the journalist dealt with jargon in their piece? Who is quoted and what do they add to the story?

Seven-point plan for clear writing

Let's boil all of this down into a simple guide to making even the most complex ideas accessible to the general reader.

1. **What is your story?** If you can't explain it in a single sentence then you aren't ready to write. What does it mean for your readers and why should they sit up and take notice? How would you explain it to friends?
2. **Keep it simple, engaging and conversational:** Avoid jargon in quotes from experts and your own writing. Be conversational and write to engage your readers, not to impress the experts you interviewed.
3. **Use numbers well:** Identify the numbers that really matter to your story. Make them meaningful and use comparisons that can help readers to understand what they mean.
4. **Explain key concepts:** Whether it's an inverted bond yield or the expansion of the universe, start simply and explain your terms clearly. Find ways to relate these concepts to things your readers will understand.
5. **Get the facts right:** Numbers, facts and detail matter in any piece of journalism. Read papers carefully, check the facts that you use and ask your expert sources to verify your understanding.
6. **Build your story:** Layer the information so that you take the reader into the story, explaining key concepts at the top of your piece. Each paragraph should contain one key idea and link to the par before it.
7. **Use boxouts, infographics and links:** Boxouts and infographics can be used to help readers understand the issues. Linking your story to source research gives your story authority and allows readers to find out more.

Bibliography

Blastland, M. and Dilnot, A. (2007). *The Tiger that Isn't. Seeing through a world of numbers*, Profile.

Boon, S. (2017). *21st century science overload* (Accessed 8 September 2020) <blog.cdnsciencepub.com/21st-century-science-overload>

Clark, R.P. (2016) *This may be the best analogy in the history of journalism* (Accessed 8 September 2020) <www.poynter.org/reporting-editing/2016/this-is-maybe-the-best-analogy-in-the-history-of-journalism>

Hughes, S. (2016) *Kitchen science: Gastrophysics brings the universe into your kitchen* (Accessed 8 September 2020) <theconversation.com/kitchen-science-gastrophysics-brings-the-universe-into-your-kitchen-58147>

Siddarth, J. et al. (2020) 'A *trusted node–free eight-user metropolitan quantum communication network*', Science Advances, Vol. 6, no. 36 (Accessed 8 September 2020) <www.quantumcommshub.net/research/a-trusted-node-free-eight-user-metropolitan-quantum-communication-network>

Veldsman, M., Tai, X., Nichols, T. et al. (2020). '*Cerebrovascular risk factors impact frontoparietal network integrity and executive function in healthy ageing*', Nature Communication, Vol. 11, 4340 (Accessed 8 September 2020). <doi.org/10.1038/s41467-020-18201-5>

Zimmer, C. *Science writing guidelines and guidance* (Accessed 8 September 2020) <carlzimmer.com/science-writing-guidelines-and-guidance/>

13
Boxouts, design and multimedia

Thinking your feature onto the page

Find a print magazine on any subject. Thumb through the issue until you spot a feature that catches your interest. It can be anything you like: celebrity gossip, travel story, new tractor review in *Farmer's Weekly*, news driven story in *Time*, interview in GQ or a "How to…" article in *Garden Answers*.

Then identify the element of the feature that first caught your attention. Was it a picture and the caption below? Was it the main image, then the headline and standfirst? Was it an arresting quote that appeared in large font somewhere in the middle of the page, or a boxout that offered background, potted facts or useful advice?

I'm willing to bet that it wasn't the intro paragraph and the same is likely to be true of anyone else who read that feature.

As a writer, this might seem slightly depressing. You will have invested hours crafting an engaging intro that leads into a beautifully structured story. You will have written that on a word processing document, where it's perfectly logical to start at the top of the page with the headline, standfirst and then the intro.

But the reader experiences the feature in an entirely different way. When they see it laid out on a page they have a number of ways to get into your story. And it's far more likely to be a picture, a boxout or pull quote that catches their attention and finally funnels them towards the intro.

So as you write your feature on a word document, you have to be able to visualise it in its final laid out version as you plan and then write your piece.

"Writers really need to think about how people engage with magazines," says Richard Ecclestone, art editor on BBC *Wildlife*. "Readers tend to flip through from the back so it's really important that any publication offers entry points to the story, from the back of the feature to the front. These could be boxouts, pull quotes and images that grab the reader's attention."

In this chapter, we are going to look at how you plan your feature to deliver a strong package of content, and how you write boxouts and multimedia content. We will also look at basic page furniture such as captions, crossheads and pull quotes, which you may be required to write.

Sketching out your story

I have worked with some brilliant art editors, and every feature we commissioned started with a thumbnail plan: a basic pencil sketch of how the feature might look on the page. That sketch is a way for "words people" and "pictures people" to communicate.

"We will thumbnail out stories as much as possible in the office, especially when it's something we are commissioning from scratch," explains Richard. "Sketching out is a good way to start the design process, to identify images we need, decide where boxouts will sit and how long they should be."

I encourage all new writers to get into the habit of visualising their feature in this way. When you are clear on a word count for different elements of the feature, you can research and write far more efficiently. It encourages you to use different types of boxout to deliver a stronger package of content that will appeal to a wider readership.

I wrote the owl feature in Chapter 9 for *Country Walking* magazine, as a freelancer. Research involved a night in the woods with the magazine's photographer, Tom Bailey, and this sketch meant we were both clear on the images we wanted.

When it came time to write, the design team sent me a contact sheet of photos that Tom had taken. I specifically wrote about moments from our "owl prowl" that could be supported visually in the final feature.

My thumbnail plan looked a little like this...

Turn the page and you'll see how the final feature turned out. Not quite the same, but not at all far off...

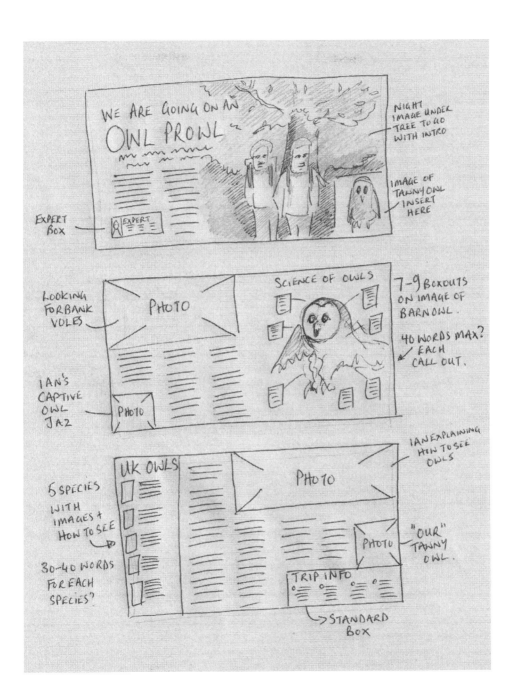

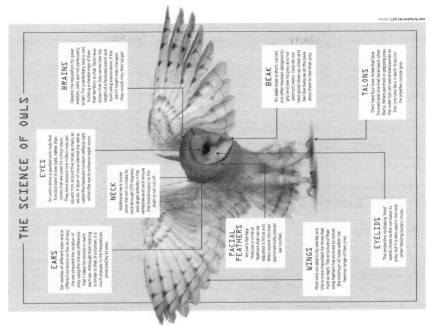

PHOTO: LIFE ON WHITE/ALAMY 85

OCTOBER 2020 COUNTRY WALKING

THE SCIENCE OF OWLS

EARS
Ear cavities of different sizes and at different locations on the skull help the owl pinpoint the location of prey using the minute difference that it takes for sound to reach each ear. Although their hearing is similar to that of a human, it is much sharper in the frequencies produced by its prey.

EYES
An owl's retina is packed with rods that function best in low light, rather than cones that are used for colour vision. They have around one million rods per square mm, around five times as many as we do. A layer of tissue behind the retina, called the tapetum lucidum reflects light within the eye to enhance night vision.

BRAINS
Despite the reputation for great wisdom, owls are not particularly smart. For a sedentary tawny owl, building a mental map of their territory is vital. Tests have shown that they remember the height of a favoured perch and hunt using sound alone. If the perch height was changed, they would miss their target.

NECK
Additional neck bones allow the owl to rotate its neck through 270 degrees, and larger arteries in the vertebrae and neck ensure that blood supply to the brain is not cut off.

BEAK
An owls beak is short, curved and often hooked, designed to grip and tear. They are not obstruct vision. Owls do not have good close-up vision and hair-like features on the beak allow them to feel their prey.

FACIAL FEATHERS
An owl's flat face features a circle of feathers that can be adjusted to focus and direct sound into their asymmetrically placed ear cavities.

WINGS
Most owls are able to fly silently and this is more important for those that hunt at night. The structure of their wing feathers has evolved to deliver the minimum of noise within the hearing range of their prey.

EYELIDS
The protective nictitating 'third' eyelid closes as the owl blinks. It is used to keep the eye moist and protect the eye from prey, but it is also used in the nest when feeding hungry chicks.

TALONS
Owls have four toes: three that face forward and one that faces back when flying. When perched or gripping prey, the outer toe can swivel backwards so that two toes face in each direction for a better circular grip.

We'd already been treated to a close-up of Ian's own captive tawny, Jaz. As a licensed owner, Ian is now retired birds were used for educational visits, but Jaz is anything but tame. "Don't come in. She'll attack if you got close," he says as he opens the mesh door and approaches with a gloved hand. Tawny owls are notoriously aggressive. Wildlife photographer Eric Hosking famously lost an eye to one: an incident that inspired the title of his biography, *An Eye for a Bird*.

We watch as Jaz wraps the milky meniscus of one of her three eyelids across the glossy black pebble of her eyeball. Everything about this bird is tuned to hunt. Her soft wing feathers mean she can drop silently on her prey, and that nictitating membrane protects the eye from sharp mammalian claws. She glides her head mechanically through its full 270 degrees of articulation, like a demonic ventriloquist's dummy. Exceptional night vision in tawny owls requires elongated, tubular eyeballs that don't move in their socket. Nature's solution? While we have seven neck bones, Jaz has 14, allowing her to rotate her head for all-round vision.

Light is already fading as we walk towards Overscourt Woods, a managed habitat that is home to tawny, barn and little owls. There are nest boxes in the trees, but the real secret to the success of this area can be found hidden under rough tussocks of grass.

Digging his fingers into a green thatch, Ian reveals a network of tiny pathways. "This vole runway is probably used by a field vole and it's a sign that the area is rich in

"...as night seeps between the trees, we wander deeper into the woods"

the barn owl's primary prey species," he says. "Barn owls have relatively poor eyesight. They rely on hearing to locate field voles and the feathery of their facial disk have evolved to reflect sound towards their asymmetrical ears, which are offset and different sizes to help pinpoint prey as they fly."

Barn owls are one of the world's most widely distributed owl species, but in the UK they are at the edge of their range. Softer wing feathers that have evolved for silent flight are easily waterlogged, so they can't fly when it's raining, they struggle to hear when it's windy or hunt when there's snow covering the ground. Young, inexperienced owls are particularly vulnerable and it is thought that up to 85% of fledglings will perish by the following spring. Road collisions, drowning in cattle troughs and poisoning from rodenticides all contribute to fatalities, but barn owls numbers have recovered from a low in the 1970s and are now thought to number around 10,000 pairs in the UK.

While barn owls can be seen flying slowly over open fields, the shorter, broader wings of a tawny owl are built for manoeuvrability between trees. These perch hunters will wait to drop silently on their prey, mainly small mammals, but also amphibians, insects and even fish.

If we want to see owls tonight, we need the same patience, so as night seeps between the trees, we wander deeper into the woods. ▶

AFTER DARK
As night falls, the woods become a different, magical place to walk.

Plan your trip

WALK HERE
Overscourt Wood is a 207-acre area of relatively new woodland to the east of Bristol and south of the village of Pucklechurch. It's an ideal place to explore as an evening wander on fairly short loops. If you're looking for owls, aim for woodland fringes and then let your ears lead you.

GETTING HERE
There is a small car park just outside Overscourt Woods that will take between five and 10 cars.

WHERE TO STAY
The Langley Arms (thelangleyarms.co.uk
0117 957 3512) is a 17th-century farmhouse located a short drive away in Bristol and offers B&B accommodation, doubles from £75pn

WHERE TO EAT
The Bull at Hinton (thebullathinton.co.uk
0117 937 2332) is about four miles from Overscourt Woods with a good selection of beers and local food; vegetarians well catered for.

MORE INFORMATION
See visitbristol.co.uk

PHOTOS: ALAMY; SHUTTERSTOCK

"If this is one of an established pair, then their down-covered chicks could be fledging by the end of May," says Ian, as this beautiful but surprisingly dumpy little bird looks us with its gaze. "This time next year they'll be heading out to find territory of their own."

And as we pick our way back through the woods half an hour later, we hear an orchestra of calls and responses that have nothing to do with us: the hoot and ke-wick that suggest a breeding pair. Good news for the owls of Overscourt Woods had news for anything rattling through the leaf litter.

ancestors, owls would have been a common sight. For the ancient Greeks they represented wisdom; for the Aztecs a harbinger of death; for Hindus, African and native American tribes they hold spiritual significance. Shakespeare used an owl in *Julius Caesar* to signify bad luck and its hoot is the go-to sound effect for added drama on any B-movie or TV crime series.

Nature writers Mark Cocker and Richard Mabey, in their book *Birds Britannica*, said that 'an owl somehow resembles a human if humans ever had bird form'. And sure enough, when we finally spot it nestling against the trunk of a tree, with its forward-looking eyes and cryptic woodland suit of browns and whites, it all too easy to

WHAT'S FOR SUPPER?
As the sun goes down, a tawny owl comes out to hunt for small mammals like mice and voles.

PHOTO: LAUBOMIR NOVAK/SHUTTERSTOCK

Long-eared owl
There are thought to be around 3,500 breeding pairs in the UK, joined in winter by birds from Scandinavia. A mainly nocturnal hunter of countryside woodland, it is very poor and it got West disease Britain owls. Its ear tufts stood up when it is perched and its deeper orange eyes help distinguish it from short-eared owls.

ON THE FRINGE
Matt and Ian study the treetops at the edge of Overscourt Wood for any shadowy glimpse of an owl.

He is convinced this is a male. "Female owls are 25% larger than the males and they've been known to attack and kill young owls encroaching on their territory," he whispers. "We hear the hoot and we wait for the contact call – a sharp ke-wick – that might indicate a breeding pair. If the does have a mate, they could lay a typical clutch of two or three eggs in late winter or early spring, that will hatch after a month's incubation.

Ian calls out again with his near perfect tawny impression and an insistent warbling fires back:
Hoo-weet, woo-weet, woo-weet.

And then we spot it: the broad, stubby outline of an owl flying past metres above us, and I whirl on my heels trying to see where it lands. For our

WOODLAND PERCH
You need the patience of a hunting owl to spot one, so you might want to sit down.

"When I bring people out to see owls, I get them to sit with their back against a trunk and listen quietly," says Ian. "Focus on an area of empty sky through the canopy and you may well see them silhouetted as they fly through the trees."

Tawny owls reached their peak in Britain in the late Mesolithic era, after the glaciers had retreated and woodland returned. Numbers at this time are estimated at around 160,000 pairs. Specialist nocturnal hunters, they have large eyes that account for 3% of their body weight and a retina that is packed with light-sensitive rods.

But our ancestors evolved to hunt out here too and our eyesight compares surprisingly well. The structure of a tawny owl's eye is designed to produce a large, bright image, but their success as hunters relies on a mix of vision, hearing and local knowledge. Our ability to see at night is an ancestral heirloom we've largely forgotten; a genetic Picasso hidden in the attic of your DNA. In an era of beam torches, backlit screens and Netflix, we seldom sit quietly outdoors at night and explore what our senses can really do.

As dusk deepens, shapes and textures appear out of the gloom. There's a whiff of fox in the air, breeze moving through branches and a robin's alarm call in the distance. Above, the tree canopy are like the frames of an ancient yurt, and between the latticed branches, we finally see a shadow flying overhead.

"That's a tawny owl," says Ian, leaping up.
"Won't be much else flying around now."

We follow its flight, feeling our way between the trees. I try to keep my footing on uneven terrain, while tree roots claw at my boots. As Ian hoots we zig-zag, following its response. Suddenly there is a full-blown conversation and I find myself unable to distinguish between Ian and the owl above me.

Barn owl
Often seen quartering over open fields, this long-winged owl hunts in flight over wetlands, and populations are much these times at Yorkshire and East Anglia. While underneath led a golden buff on the top, it is instantly recognisable. It is not particularly vocal but the males screech can be heard during the breeding season.

Tawny owl
This owl is nocturnal hunters that are widespread across Britain but not found on Ireland. The oldest recorded was over 23 years old, but these typically live between four years old, and is in a nested breeding. Young are budged out of their parents' territory in autumn but often then their own within just a few kilometres.

Short-eared owl
You might see this owl hunting over rough grassland or coastal marshes and it is one of our most active during the day. It breeds much further than a tawny owl and numbers of these found on the west coast of Britain are thought to originate from Scandinavia. While you may not spot its ear tufts, its yellow eyes can help you with identification.

Britain's owls

Little owl
This charismatic species is often seen running along the ground in pursuit of insect prey. It is a non-native thought to have been introduced to the UK in the 1870s. The smallest of our owls, it is an active owl, and diet is woodpecker-like flight. They can be seen across England and Wales in open countryside farmland and orchards with holes that offer nesting cavities.

"Focus on an area of empty sky through the canopy and you may well see them silhouetted as they fly."

Boxouts

Boxouts are a key part of many features, and they are likely to have been part of the proposal that you first pitched to the commissioning editor.

Each of these is a potential entry point into your article. They may well be the last thing you write on a word processing document, but they could be the first thing that your reader engages with.

Each boxout should have clear value and offer an interesting way into the feature. They should be visually strong and aim to appeal to different types of reader.

Think about each boxout as a question that your reader might ask. That makes it much easier for you to decide what content you need and your sketch will suggest a potential word count.

On the plan for the owl feature, the three boxouts asked and answered different questions...

How are owls adapted to hunt?
What owls can I see in the UK?
How do I do the walk that I've just read about?

There are plenty of other questions that I considered as boxout ideas:

How does owl behaviour change during the year?
Where are the best places to see owls in the UK?
What kit do you need for a night owl prowl?
What are the challenges for owl conservation?
How well are owls doing in the UK?
How do I find and dissect an owl pellet?

Boxouts are not the place to dump extra information that you don't know what to do with. You need to challenge yourself to deliver content that really adds value. The best way to do that is to identify the questions your reader needs answered.

Formats for boxouts

There are a range of different approaches that you can take to boxouts to make them visually engaging. Some might be just blocks of copy, others might appear as lists, or broken down into steps. Others might be annotated to an image or be based around key numbers and facts.

Annotated images

A boxout gives the writer and the designer a chance to enhance the visual appeal of a feature. Annotated images can be really effective way of achieving this and this was the approach we took with the boxout that asked "How are owls adapted to hunt?"

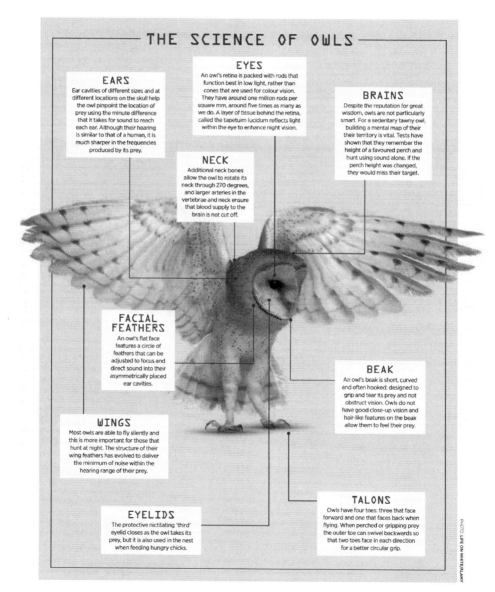

THE SCIENCE OF OWLS

EYES
An owl's retina is packed with rods that function best in low light, rather than cones that are used for colour vision. They have around one million rods per square mm, around five times as many as we do. A layer of tissue behind the retina, called the tapetum lucidum reflects light within the eye to enhance night vision.

EARS
Ear cavities of different sizes and at different locations on the skull help the owl pinpoint the location of prey using the minute difference that it takes for sound to reach each ear. Although their hearing is similar to that of a human, it is much sharper in the frequencies produced by its prey.

BRAINS
Despite the reputation for great wisdom, owls are not particularly smart. For a sedentary tawny owl, building a mental map of their territory is vital. Tests have shown that they remember the height of a favoured perch and hunt using sound alone. If the perch height was changed, they would miss their target.

NECK
Additional neck bones allow the owl to rotate its neck through 270 degrees, and larger arteries in the vertebrae and neck ensure that blood supply to the brain is not cut off.

FACIAL FEATHERS
An owl's flat face features a circle of feathers that can be adjusted to focus and direct sound into their asymmetrically placed ear cavities.

BEAK
An owl's beak is short, curved and often hooked: designed to grip and tear its prey and not obstruct vision. Owls do not have good close-up vision and hair-like features on the beak allow them to feel their prey.

WINGS
Most owls are able to fly silently and this is more important for those that hunt at night. The structure of their wing feathers has evolved to deliver the minimum of noise within the hearing range of their prey.

EYELIDS
The protective nictitating 'third' eyelid closes as the owl takes its prey, but it is also used in the nest when feeding hungry chicks.

TALONS
Owls have four toes: three that face forward and one that faces back when flying. When perched or gripping prey the outer toe can swivel backwards so that two toes face in each direction for a better circular grip.

PHOTO: LIFE ON WHITE/ALAMY

The title didn't say that, but the value it offers is still clear. Owls have incredible hearing and eyesight, feathers on their wings are adapted for silent flight and those on their face can direct sound towards their ears. I mentioned some of this within the feature, but this boxout gave me the opportunity to go into this in more depth.

It also allowed us to use a rather beautiful image of a barn owl and then to annotate different parts of the body to explain a little about owls' unique adaptations.

The reader doesn't have to have read the main feature to understand this. It is visually strong, easy to scan and read and I would guess that a good number of readers would have started with this element of the feature.

My initial sketch gave me a good idea of the number of boxes required and a rough word count for each one. I wanted to make sure there was a spread of information, with something to say about adaptions for hunting from their talons to their brains.

For a previous feature on owls, this time for *BBC Wildlife*, I had a boxout about how to build a nestbox. Again this was annotated to an image to explain the specific design requirements to help owls and their chicks to breed safely and avoid predation.

Digging around in magazines I've worked on, I can see annotated boxouts for "How to camp wild in the mountains"; "How do I perfect my swimming stroke?"; "How do I cycle up hills fast?": and "How do I grow the perfect wildlife garden?" They use annotated images of campers, swimmers, a cyclist and a garden to deliver that information.

Lists

The other key boxout in this feature is a list of the five species of owl that live in the UK. Each element features an image of an owl and short copy that tells the reader something about that species, how to identify them and where to see them.

Again, you don't have to have read the main feature and it's highly likely that a number of readers will have started with this boxout. It's easy to scan, offers a different element of visual interest and a way of showing other species not mentioned in the main feature.

Let's imagine we are writing about running your first marathon. There are a host of questions that we could use to formulate boxout ideas and a number of them would be well suited to a list.

The reader might ask, "What do I need to know to run my first marathon?"

You might answer that question by interviewing someone who has run a marathon before and deliver it as a list titled "Five things I learned by running a marathon."

Alternatively, you could offer a boxout that asks, "What are the seven rookie mistakes that any first-time marathon runner should avoid?": or "What are the five best races for first timers?"; or "What is the essential kit every new marathon runner needs?" All of these could be delivered in an easily scannable list.

It isn't only practical stories that work well in this format. This approach allows you to come at the issue from another interesting angle, ask a question that isn't addressed fully in the main copy and deepen the readers' understanding of the issue. They don't all have to have a number next to them. Here are some boxouts that I've found attached to various features online (the last was one of mine)…

Five key moments that brought Trump to power
Five classic horror movie cliches
Five footballers to watch next season
Five musicians who loved ukulele

Running copy

Let's go back to our example about tackling your first marathon. You may have an interview with a first-time runner that you feel would work well as a boxout. For a reader who is worried about attempting to do the same thing, there is plenty of value they could get from their advice.

On your visual thumbnail of the feature, you might decide it needs their picture at the top (ideally in running kit or from the big day) with their name and the race they undertook. The main copy of the boxout could read like a mini-interview, of 150 words, delivering a mix of inspiration, a sense of the challenge and the key lessons they learned.

While it may be much shorter than a standard interview, it is worth approaching it in the same way. It still needs a clear structure and an engaging intro. You need to start at a point in the race, or their training that is going to engage the reader. You've only got 150 words, so you need to get straight to the stuff that will be of value to your readers.

You might decide to write this all in first person, as though it has come directly from the interviewee. To do this you need a really strong set of quotes that deliver what you want in a coherent and engaging way. If that's not the case, then it might be easier to run it as a more standard interview where you use just three or four strong direct quotes.

Timeline

Some features require explanation, context and historical background. When a chronological sequence of events is important, information can work well on a timeline. This could run along the bottom of a spread and would have the added benefit of visually pulling two separate pages together.

For a feature on the war in Syria, it might answer the following question: "How did the conflict begin?" It would then offer the key moments that have led to the current situation and give readers some of the context and background that they require to understand the current situation. It could also appear as a list with key dates acting as bullet points in the copy.

For a story on the Black Lives Matter campaign, we might run a timeline that looks at significant moments in the fight against racism in the UK: the Notting Hill Race Riots (1958), Bristol Bus Boycotts (1963) and the murder of Stephen Lawrence and the follow-up Macpherson Report (1999). It would offer a clear visual indication of the struggle for equality and missed opportunities for change.

The owl feature above might have asked the following question: "How does owl behaviour change during the year?" That could have been answered with a calendar timeline that starts with finding territories and pairing in Autumn to breeding and laying eggs in March, hatching in April and the chicks fledging around the end of May.

Timelines offer another visually interesting way of delivering information and can be very effective depending on the question that your boxout sets out to ask.

Statistical information

In Chapter 12 we talked about the value of helping readers to visualise big numbers through your writing. So ice melt in Greenland was expressed in terms of millions of swimming pools that it would fill in a year. Plastic waste in the Atlantic was expressed in terms of the numbers of container ships it would fill.

You can put visual images in the mind of your reader through your writing, and you can supplement this with key statistics and images that help to underline your point and set out the scale of the issue you are writing about.

A boxout might ask the following question: "How bad is plastic pollution in the oceans?" This could be a way to set out the problem. We could show the number of container vessels required to hold all the plastic in the ocean, the fact that one in three fish caught for human consumption contains plastic, that waste has been found at a depth of 11 km in the oceans, that every person on the planet uses 150 plastic bags a year and that 88% of the sea's surface is polluted by this kind of waste. These statistics would offer a compelling and visually strong way into your feature.

Exercise 1: Boxout inspiration

Find a special interest magazine and look for an example of each of the boxout types above. What value does each one offer? Can you express that as a question? How effective is each one as a potential entry point for readers?

Page furniture

It's worth also being aware of other elements of page furniture that need to be written for a feature. Some of these you might be asked to write, others might be produced by a sub-editor or production team. You will find plenty of information on these in the book *Subediting and Production for Journalists* (2020, Routledge) by Tim Holmes.

Captions for photos

We've spent a lot of time thinking about the main bodycopy of news and features, and the importance of strong introductions. But if images are likely to be the thing that grabs your reader's attention, then it follows that the words that appear below them could be some of the most important in your feature.

Every image in your story, whether it is print or digital, news or feature, needs to have a caption. Ideally they should tell the reader who or what they are looking at and either sell the feature or amplify key elements of the story. If you are on the editorial team, it is likely that you will write those captions directly onto the final layout of your features. If you are a freelancer, or someone working away from the office, you might be sent a PDF and be asked to send captions via email.

Each caption has a dual role. Most importantly, it is an entry point for those people who haven't read the feature to encourage them to do so. They also have to work for people who are in the middle of the feature, to reinforce key points of the story and encourage them to read on.

Do not assume knowledge of names, occupations or locations that may be in the main feature. The imperative here is to sell key elements of the feature, to entice people to engage with your story and reinforce elements of the feature.

Pull quotes

Pull quotes are added at the design stage. They help to break up copy, and to deliver a more visually interesting layout and another potential entry point. Like captions, pull quotes have a dual role. They need to entice the new reader to engage with a feature and they need to encourage someone in the middle of that story to keep reading.

The most important element for a pull quote is that it works in isolation. We don't necessarily need to know who said it, but the quote has to be sufficiently strong for it to work with no additional context.

There are two pull quotes used in the owl feature. One aims to sell the adventure of walking at night in woodland.

As night seeps between the trees we wander deeper into the woods…

The other shows that there is practical advice within this feature.

Focus on an area of empty sky through the canopy and you may well see them silhouetted as they fly.

As you are writing your feature, it is a good idea to identify potential pull quotes. You can highlight these at the bottom of your word document and make sure they are clearly identified to the design team. Including this in your final manuscript marks you out as a professional: someone thinking about complete package.

Headlines

You should also offer possible headline options for your story, says BBC *Wildlife*'s Richard Ecclestone. "It's great to see headline suggestions," he says. "I really like to see two or three ideas to help the design team get a sense of what the feature should be doing."

A good headline needs to connect with the reader. It needs to get their attention, sell the feature and capture the tone of the story.

For a visually strong feature, you should aim to write with the opening image in mind. "The headline and opening image is vital," says Louise Parker, art editor on *Trail* magazine. "They need to work together and capture a feeling immediately."

If the reader's eye is likely to fall first on the opening image, then it is best if it is reinforced by the headline. So in your notes to the designer on the page you might want to identify the specific image that you would use and then the headline that will go with it.

Crossheads

Crossheads are the words that appear in bold, larger font in the middle of the bodycopy of the main feature. They are like mini-headlines, often just two to three words long and they have an important role to play in breaking up dense copy.

As a writer, you should not put these into the written feature that you submit. They are a design element that is added at the production stage by the layout team.

Putting them in a word document encourages writers to break the narrative flow of their copy. You often end up with something that reads like a series of boxouts rather than a cohesive story.

Crossheads are even more important online where copy needs to be broken up, but even here you need to put them in as you lay out the feature on the page, so that they are balanced neatly with pictures and multimedia elements to deliver the most visually appealing end product.

Multimedia content

Every writer is now a multimedia journalist. Online offers scope for a range of additional content: including video, interactive graphics, embedded tweets, maps, timelines and infographics. Every week, it seems that there is a new way to present information and tell stories.

Your thinking around multimedia should be the same as written boxouts. Don't start by saying "We need a video here." Instead, think about the questions your reader needs answered and the additional value can you provide. Think about function rather than format and you are far more likely to deliver content that will engage, be shared, be retweeted and attract attention in a digital space.

And that is the really exciting part of multimedia content. While boxouts for print features require the reader to be holding the publication, multimedia can be broken down into chunks and shared far and wide around the web. One piece of multimedia can be posted on Facebook, Twitter, TikTok, Instagram and via WhatsApp groups. Each of these would be an entry point to your feature, but the potential audience is enormous.

That makes it even more important for multimedia content to function as discrete packages of content that work in isolation from the feature. First, identify the question your multimedia is going to answer (How are owls adapted to hunt?) and then the format that you will use (video, interactive image, infographic, etc.). Here are some categories to help you think about the function that a piece of multimedia can perform.

Help me to understand the issue or the background to this story

If your feature is dealing with a complex subject matter, it might be useful to offer background or explanation as part of your multimedia mix.

Science is a complex subject that may fascinate many people, but the majority of readers do not have expertise in any particular area. Let's say we're writing about a recent discovery about the rate at which the universe is expanding. A boxout or multimedia piece of content could help us answer the following question: "How did the universe begin?"

Functionally that's a good question that I'd want to know the answer to. We could deliver that as a written boxout, or as a Q&A interview with an expert, in written, video or audio format. Equally, we could deliver it as an explainer video: a short three-minute piece that potentially uses images and captions to answer that question. Type "How did the universe begin?" and "video explainer" into Google and you'll find plenty of examples.

And creating this kind of content is surprisingly easy. I visited Kolkata, India, to teach multimedia content creation to journalists in 2019. We ran an exercise to plan explainer videos, sketching them out with pen and paper. In the 40 minutes that the exercise took, senior journalist Sambit Pal (now a journalism lecturer) hadn't bothered to sketch it out. He'd edited the entire 90 second video on his smart phone using the free app Splice. Download it to experiment and see what you can achieve.

Get me closer to the story

Good storytelling is vital to engage an audience. One of your multimedia elements might aim to get the reader closer to the story by giving them an insight into the experience of other participants. We've already done this with a written boxout: "What I learned running my first marathon." This could easily be delivered in video or audio format.

Multimedia offers plenty of ways to get even closer to a story. Let's say we are running a feature on the challenges facing Syrian refugees in Turkey. A number of them hope to make it to parts of Europe and we could run a piece of multimedia that asks "How hard is it for Syrian refugees to get to the UK?" We could deliver that as a written interview, an audio recording or video.

One of my recent students produced exactly this piece of work. He and his family had travelled from Syria to the UK and he recorded their journey on his mobile phone. Some of this footage was used for a documentary that won best postgraduate director at the Royal Television Society awards.

What does this story mean for me?

Publications have always found ways to personalise boxout elements ("Take this quiz to find out which member of Take That is your perfect partner"). Multimedia allows us to take this to a whole new level.

I'm writing this during the Covid-19 lockdown, and there are plenty of multimedia widgets embedded within stories that allow me to put in my postcode and answer the question "How many cases are there in my area?"

When it comes time for the budget, the BBC will offer a similar function that asks for my salary, number of children, how much I drive, smoke and drink. It will use this information to answer the question "Will I be better or worse off after this budget?"

We know that proximity and impact are key to identifying news values and both of these examples highlight these elements of a story for their readers.

Help me to take action

The mark of a really great feature is one that encourages readers to take action. For some features, practical advice is an important component of the feature. So back to our feature on running your first marathon, we could answer the question "How do I train for my first race?" with an online training plan.

If we are running a feature about the impact of plastic in the ocean, then a boxout telling the reader how to reduce their plastic consumption would be of value. If you are reading about the guitarist Brian May, you may want the answer to the question "How do I set up my guitar to sound like him?" Deciding whether to do this in video or words is less important than clearly identifying the function and value of that content.

Key message

Always start by articulating the function and value of your multimedia content clearly: this is often best done in the form of a question. When you have your questions identified, then you can decide what type of boxout or multimedia content will deliver the strongest final package.

Remember that this content could be the first thing that many readers see, so it needs to work for people who haven't read your article. Don't assume knowledge tucked away in your feature. Multimedia content has the potential to pull in much bigger audiences, so it needs to work in isolation from your main feature but still offer that important link back.

Exercise 2: Planning your feature package

You have been asked to write a feature on initiatives to get young women playing more football. Your main feature involves interviews with three women at different stages of involvement in the game, as well as coaches and campaigners trying to get more women into football.

Sketch out how that feature would look across six pages.

What boxout content would you add with it?

What images would you want in the feature and to illustrate the boxouts?

What additional multimedia content would you require to deliver that feature online?

14
The professional writer

What kind of journalist do you want to be?

Most people associate the word "brand" with million dollar marketing campaigns for global corporations like Coca-Cola, Nike and Audi. It's a neat trick, performed with slogans, logos and advertising, to get millions of customers reaching for Coke rather than Pepsi (or vice versa). It is what allows these two companies to dominate the global soft drinks market.

Clearly writers aren't the same as sports cars, expensive trainers or fizzy drinks, but you still have a brand. It is what comes to mind when an editor hears your name. It is what encourages them to hand you a potential commission or to pass it over to someone else. You can either let your brand develop accidentally or make a conscious decision to shape the way that people see you as a journalist and a writer.

So what do you want editors (and eventually readers) to think when they hear your name? Perhaps it's "Trustworthy, Creative and Authoritative" or "Analytical, Resourceful and Proactive." It's definitely not "Sloppy, Thoughtless and Unreliable."

I'm not saying you have to only be three things. While that kind of brevity can be really useful in a large organisation, you can treat yourself to a full sentence. This is your mission statement that sets out the kind of stories you want to work on, and the professionalism and creativity that you aim to bring to your work.

You build your brand with everything you do: every time you post on Twitter, approach an editorial team, offer a proposal, sit in on an editorial meeting or deliver on a commission.

According to the NCTJ (National Council for the Training of Journalists), between 2000 and 2015, there was a 67% increase in the number of freelance journalists in the UK (Spilsbury 2016). That's 25,000 people all looking to pitch ideas. With a growing number of young writers starting out as freelancers, competition is increasingly tough and it is more important than ever for you to actively shape the way others see you.

In very simple terms, it's about being professional: turning in sharply edited copy on time, and as per your commission. It's about how you add value to your own and others' feature ideas, your attention to detail and your ability to overcome problems.

Building your brand online

No matter where you are in your career, every writer should have a presence online, says digital lecturer Simon Williams. "If you're applying for a new job, seeking clients or chasing a commission, having a professional online presence is essential," he explains. "Make sure that it includes a portfolio of your strongest work. People giving away dream jobs are likely to be busy, so send them one link, so that in just a few clicks they're convinced it's you they're looking for."

Bethan Rose Jenkins has worked as a staff writer for magazines like *Red*, *Good Housekeeping* and *Prima* and now works on *BBC Gardener's World* and *Radio Times*. Her website has played a key role in getting work as a journalist. "I set up my portfolio website while on my journalism course and, a couple of years into my career, I still use it as my main platform for showcasing my work," she says.

"When I was applying for my first roles in journalism I included the link on my CV. Employers could easily scroll through examples of my work and see that I had the skills to create and manage a website. I also had it ready on an iPad during interviews so I could quickly bring up relevant work to different questions they had.

"I always include the link in my email signature and direct commissioning editors towards it when I'm pitching freelance articles. From my online portfolio they can see what sort of work I've had published before."

There are a range of free online tools available to set up your website. "You don't need to spend much time or money to get the job done," says Simon. "With the free versions of **www.journoportfolio.com** or **www.clippings.me** you can be up and running with a simple home page and links to online articles in an hour or so. The site **www.wordpress.com** has the most functionality, especially if you intend to use your portfolio site for blogging – but it does have a steeper learning curve to get started and doesn't have the best portfolio features."

Whatever platform you use, there are three key sections that need to appear on your site.

Welcome to my portfolio

See Bethan's professional website at bethanrosejournalist.wordpress.com

About me

This tells a potential editor who you are, the kind of journalism you do and what motivates you. Show some individuality and remember that your ability to write needs to leap off the page. So while you do need to talk about your professional experience, don't just treat it as a CV. "Editors know the best work comes from writers who are interested and passionate, so make sure that comes across in your writing," says Simon.

Portfolio

Use this to highlight your best pieces, show your range and offer links to the original stories. "It's best not to fully reproduce articles that are online elsewhere," explains Simon. "So have a headline and a picture that links to the original. Someone's unlikely to click through to more than one or two stories, but have enough to show the range and extent of your published work. If you've created videos, podcasts or infographics, show some of these too. These skills are in demand and you may find that they are lacking in some established editorial teams."

Contact

"This page should allow an editor to get in touch via email and mobile phone and it needs to include links to your professional social media accounts," says Simon. "You need to be found easily with your name, 'journalist' and location. So find out about search engine optimisation (SEO), and make sure your site is properly optimised."

Your contacts page should link to social media, so consider setting up professional accounts on platforms. An Instagram full of pictures of you partying in various locations won't win you a lot of work, and nor will a Twitter account that is engaged in furious political rants and name calling with people you have never met.

Exercise 1: About you

Find five professional websites from other journalists and identify what they do well. Then write your own 150-word "About Me" section that sums up your mission statement as a writer and journalist.

Turn rejection to your advantage

You can't just sit back and wait for a website to do its job. You need to proactively approach potential commissioning editors, either through a feature proposal or a more speculative conversation.

Your proposal may not turn into an immediate offer of work, but if you show potential it can start a useful conversation. So if you get a "no," ask what it is they do need. Quite often it's the smaller, regular sections that cause editorial teams difficulty and this can be a way in for some writers. The publication may have a complete editorial plan for the next 12 months but be struggling to fill online news content: you'll only know if you ask.

When I edited *Trail*, our routes section at the back was a way in for many new writers. On *BBC Wildlife*, most feature proposals were from people heading to Africa or South America asking if we needed anything from these areas. The answer was almost always "No." Very few potential writers bothered to ask what we were actually looking for, which were news and science stories. Some of those who did developed a long-term relationship with the publication.

Work hard, be nice

If you are lucky enough to get a commission or secure a staff position, you still need to shape the way people see you. Mike Hill, former editor of the *South Wales Echo,* asked his editorial team to follow a simple mantra of "work hard and be nice to people" that builds your brand both within an editorial team and with potential sources for stories.

"I wanted to get the message across to trainees that there are no shortcuts in journalism and that working hard – knocking on doors, scouring through messages on social media and reading lengthy documents – will provide your breakthrough, or at the very least, a decent tip for where to go next," says Mike. "Being pleasant, polite and decent to people also goes a long way in persuading them to talk to you, and helping them to remember you when they have got a story."

Ethics and media law

As a journalist you should have a working knowledge of the legal and ethical requirements of the job. Media law means, most importantly, an understanding of libel and defamation; privacy, copyright and freedom of speech. The book *McNae's Essential Law for Journalists* is a good place to start (page 233).

You should be familiar with the relevant ethical guidelines. For print and online journalists in the UK that means the IPSO Editors Code of Practice, or for anyone working on a BBC brand, the BBC Editorial Guidelines, which was the case when I worked at both BBC *Wildlife* and Lonely Planet. If you are a member of the NUJ you also need to sign up to their code of conduct.

There are hundreds of guidelines on good media practice around the world, but they focus on five key areas, according to the Ethical Journalism network.

Truth and accuracy – information you provide should be honestly delivered, accurate and fair.

Accountability – you should be accountable for mistakes you make: correct inaccuracies quickly and offer a right of reply when appropriate.

Independence – You should report on behalf of your readership and not special interest groups, whether they be political, cultural or business interests. This includes your own interests, especially if you find yourself writing about issues such as finance, shares and securities.

Fairness and impartiality – you should differentiate between facts and opinion and offer all sides of a story. You should be fair to sources specifically with respect to their privacy, says IPSO: "Everyone is entitled to respect for his or her private and family life, home, health and correspondence, including digital communications."

Humanity – no matter how much you need a story you should not resort to "intimidation, harassment or persistent pursuit," say the IPSO guidelines. In addition, journalists "should take care when reporting on grief and loss and take particular care with how they report on suicide." You need to be aware of guidelines when reporting on issues that involve children and vulnerable people, particularly those who have been witnesses or victims of sexual offences. And your reporting should not expose anyone to "hatred or discrimination on the grounds of a person's age, gender, race, colour, creed, legal status, disability, marital status, or sexual orientation," say the NUJ guidelines.

Hitting deadlines

Time management is a vital skill for any journalist. I have worked with some brilliant writers in my career but a number of them were surprisingly reluctant to hit deadlines. Freelancers who did this were unlikely to be used again.

The key to hitting deadlines is planning. To do this, you need to identify all the stages to completing this task. Let's assume it's Monday morning 9am, and you have just been given a commission for a feature about the impact of air pollution on young people in some of the UK's most deprived urban areas. You need to deliver this for the following Monday by 12pm.

To write this feature we will need to…

- Do background research
- Find and contact potential interviewees
- Set up and conduct interviews
- Transcribe interviews
- Write first draft
- Edit work
- Submit

Some of these tasks are within your control. I decide when I do my background research and how long I'm going to spend on it.

Other tasks are less controllable. I cannot force an interviewee to speak to me, and even if they do agree to the interview, they may not be available this week. Equally, we might book an interview for the Wednesday morning and something may happen to force them to cancel or delay.

So not only do we need to identify the stages to completing the piece, but we also need to identify any potential risks. Doing this allows us to identify a plan B (i.e. another interviewee or a phone, rather than face-to-face, interview). You can also identify strategies to minimise risk (i.e. emailing the interviewee the day before to check everything is still looking OK).

The key is to set yourself a series of mini-deadlines.

The first thing I am going to do is to bring my main deadline back to Sunday evening 6pm. This means that the story will be waiting in my commissioning editor's inbox when they get to work on Monday morning rather than having to chase it up at 12pm.

Monday 5pm: Start background research, identify and contact all primary interviewees
Wednesday 5pm: all interviews completed and transcribed, background research complete
Thursday 5pm: plan and write first feature draft
Friday 5pm: edit and rewrite
Sunday 6pm: final read and submit
Monday 11am: call office to check everything OK

This plan prioritises the most problematic elements of the feature first: finding and interviewing your sources. It sets a number of smaller internal deadlines to keep me on target. If one interview slips to the Thursday, that's not a massive problem, but if they all slip to Friday, then I am going to have a stressful weekend.

To avoid that I need a plan for getting in touch with interviewees. If you just send an email, then you are likely to still be waiting for a reply on Friday morning. A telephone call is likely to get you an answer more quickly. So send an email first then follow up with a telephone call later that day.

And get into the habit of using a phone to talk to real people. Too many aspiring journalists seem to be phone-phobic: they send an email and then just wait. Set yourself apart by getting on the phone to get interviews and the answers you need.

If you have exhausted ways to approach interviewees and still haven't had a response, make sure you have other potential people ready to go.

Weather can ruin an outdoor photo shoot and travel congestion can mean that interviewees run late. If you are reviewing a car, it needs to be delivered on time. Anticipate potential problems and you are more likely to find solutions.

Commissioning editors like working with people they can trust to solve problems and deliver.

This plan leaves plenty of time for editing your work. You should aim to get a first draft together quickly, and then take your time to edit thoroughly. Ideally, you want to be able to leave your copy for 24 hours before you submit, but that depends on your deadline.

Your final read on the Sunday evening should be simply to spot any typos and make sure that everything is in order. Depending on the length of your piece it shouldn't take too long. Having left your copy for over 24 hours will help you to spot any glaring errors (see below). Send an email with your word document properly laid out as an attachment.

Your commissioning editor will find it in their inbox when they arrive at work the following morning and know that they don't have to chase up copy.

How to edit your own work

You should aim to write your first draft quickly. The real work of writing will come in your rewrite.

"It can be pretty daunting when you're faced with a blank word document and a flashing cursor," says travel writer Phoebe Smith. "I always do a brain dump first and get ideas on the page, without worrying too much about grammatical issues or writing. The intro is so important and quite often you'll find a gem of an idea, or a sentence in this first draft. I aim for a strong intro and a sense of where I want to finish my piece. Then it's simply a case of how I'm going to get there."

Your first draft is all about getting the structure and shape that your feature needs: identifying the key ideas and making sure that they link and flow carefully from one to the next. It will not be perfect, but it should be engaging, be rich in information, and have a logical structure.

"When I've finished my first draft, I'll go and do something completely different," explains Phoebe. "It might just be for an hour but when I come back, I can almost look at it as thought it's not my own work. I've spent plenty of time editing other writer's work, which helps me to view my first draft relatively dispassionately."

Rewriting is when you aim to strengthen this structure and deliver a feature with pace and style.

Everyone will approach editing their own work slightly differently and you need to find the approach that is right for you. Here's how I would spend my Friday afternoon…

1. **First edit with the reader in mind:** We start out assuming that our reader doesn't know and doesn't care. Each part of your feature has to move them along the spectrum towards "I care, I'm interested, and I feel more informed." Make sure that each paragraph has a clear purpose and that the feature flows logically from one idea to the next. Are quotes strong and well used? Are you delivering on the commission you were given?
2. **Hand it to a critical friend:** I hand anything I have written to my wife, who as an ex-journalist can be fairly blunt with her feedback. When you are starting out a good critical friend can be invaluable. Deal with any issues, specifically elements they find confusing.
3. **Read it out loud:** This will help you to spot repetition, awkward phrases that you trip over or pompous words that you would never dream of using in conversation. Highlight anything that you are not happy with and any sections that need significant revision.
4. **Read it to check facts**: Go back through your copy and check the spelling of every name, every location, every number or piece of data. Factual errors can seriously undermine your readers' confidence in you as a journalist and the publication you are writing for.
5. **Check spelling and punctuation**: The majority of grammatical errors are depressingly common and very easy to miss when you are reading for the 20th time. So always check "its" and "it's." Make sure their, there and they're are used correctly. Double-check advice and advise, effect and affect. Using a ruler to keep your focus on just one line at a time can really help.
6. **Final read:** Leave the feature for as long as you can and then read it out loud once again. This is also a good opportunity to spot any final glaring errors you may have missed.

Keep it conversational

Kent Brockman is the TV news anchor in *The Simpsons*, apparently based on Los Angeles TV anchors Hal Fishman and Jerry Dunphy. While he's clearly a parody of local TV journalists, it surprises me how often new writers seem to fall into a similarly pantomime tone, as if they are trying to mimic what they think a journalist should sound like.

Equally, there are those writers who adopt an overly formal writing style or who try to impress with lots of long words and complicated ideas. This approach is likely to confuse and put your reader off, no matter how good your story.

Instead, imagine yourself telling the story over a pub table, or via a phone conversation. Aim for writing that is conversational, clear and easy to understand.

There's nothing new here. William Strunk, whose book *The Elements of Style* was later revised by E B White, wrote in 1918: "Young writers often suppose that style is a garnish for the meat of prose, a sauce by which a dull dish is made palatable. Style has no such separate entity; it is non-detachable, unfilterable. … The approach to style is by way of plainness, simplicity, orderliness, sincerity."

So don't try to sound like someone else. If your work sounds right as you read it out loud, you are probably in the right area. Trust your ability to tell stories, and be honest with yourself if it's not working. If that's the case, you need to rework it, but if you come across something that you are particularly proud of, then you should potentially do the same.

Quoting a college tutor, the writer Samuel Johnson (1709–1784) pronounced, "Read over your compositions, and where ever you meet with a passage which you think is particularly fine, strike it out."

And echoing Dr Johnson, Sir Arthur Quiller-Couch told Cambridge undergraduates in 1913, "Whenever you feel an impulse to perpetrate a piece of exceptionally fine writing, obey it – whole-heartedly – and delete it before sending your manuscript to press. *Murder your darlings.*"

Style is not something to be strained for or added on. Your aim should be plainness, economy, precision – above all, clarity. What is not needed is rhetoric or embellishment.

Avoid cliché

We looked at travel writing clichés in Chapter 9, but journalism has its own batch of clichés that need to be on your watchlist. Here are a few that you may recognise…

On the brink
Breathe a sigh of relief
Humiliating U turn
Brutal dictator
Ill fated policy
Only time will tell
Double down
Game changer
The new normal
Withering criticism

Unsung hero

When you spot phrases like these, recognise that they are actually rather vague approximations of what you want to say. Replace them with words that offer precision and information, delivering facts that are specific to the story you need to tell.

Word counts and writing tightly

If you have been asked for 1,200 words of bodycopy but deliver 1,600 words, do not think that equates to 30% of extra value for free. What it means is an additional hour's work for an already busy sub-editor who now needs to tighten your copy.

Hitting your word count is vital, but it's not just about the number of words you deliver. Writing tightly and with purpose should be your goal. Cutting empty words and phrases allows you to include more content of value and delivers sharper and more stylistically pleasing copy.

If you can cut a word, then do so. If you aren't sure whether a sentence is required in your piece, then it probably isn't. Cut this too. Cut out every word and every phrase that isn't required, that doesn't serve a very clear purpose. If a paragraph doesn't talk directly to the angle of your feature, then question whether you need it in your story.

Active voice

In the active voice, the subject of the sentence performs the action (see page 15). It encourages tighter writing, is easier to understand and is less likely to deliver grammatical errors. Most of all, journalism is about people doing things. Active voice encourages a more dynamic narrative that tells your story through people.

Avoid jargon

We have seen approaches to dealing with jargon in scientific and business reports (see Chapter 12). You'll find technical language in all walks of life. Your aim should be to make your writing as accessible as possible for the widest possible audience. Aim to avoid jargon all together.

George Orwell

All of these points were identified in George Orwell's "six elementary rules" from his famous essay, "Politics and the English Language," published in 1946:

1. Never use a metaphor, simile or other figure of speech which you are used to seeing in print.
2. Never use a long word where a short word will do.
3. If it is possible to cut out a word, always cut it out.
4. Never use the passive where you can use the active.
5. Never use a foreign phrase, a scientific word or a jargon word if you can think of an everyday English equivalent.
6. Break any of these rules sooner than say anything outright barbarous.

Developing a personal style

Good writing should be clear, but it should also have a flair and style that makes it worth reading. A news story in your local newspaper needs to inform, but a review of a new album or film needs to entertain as well.

An opinion piece needs to get people thinking, a satirical political sketch has to make them laugh and both probably aim to flatter the reader's intelligence. A travel story should transport people to another place, an interview should make them feel they've spent time in that person's company.

You have the option to SHOW, TELL and QUOTE, so mix up these different building blocks in your story. Use each of these to build an authoritative piece that draws on different sources of information, and that changes the flow and pace of your writing.

And good writing should have a rhythm to it. It should not only sound conversational but feel like it is meant to be read with elements of a sentence hitting a certain beat. You may want to place emphasis on things that matter, build ideas and create a certain atmosphere to take the reader deeper into a piece of writing. Literary devices like alliteration, assonance, consonance and sibilance can all be used to build a scene and create atmosphere in your copy.

When you read your piece of writing out loud on your final edit, there should be a cadence and a rhythm that sounds right. So while you want to write as you speak, you should really aim a little higher. You need to strike that perfect balance of things sounding conversational but also being perfectly weighted and sharply delivered.

If the tone you are looking to strike is a conversation across a pub table, then really good writing should make the reader feel like they are sat with the smartest, most insightful and engaging group in the pub that evening.

There are two things you need to do to develop your own writing style: read a lot and write as much as you can. You'll find a list of great reading at the back of the book (page 232).

Here's a former colleague of mine on how he looks for inventive writing approaches as he reads.

Why you should keep a word book

Simon Ingram

UK editor of *National Geographic* and author of *Between the Sunset and the Sea*

Writing has no secrets. It's not like physics, or architecture where everything is underpinned by storeys of invisible workings. You can understand everything about the mechanics of a particular piece of writing on a purely visual level. It's right in front of you on the page. The skill comes in clarity of purpose and a lucid assembly. The only equipment is words.

I started keeping a book of words as a companion to a notebook. When reading, or listening to audiobooks, if a certain word caught my eye or ear, I'd make a note of it. If I immediately thought of an application, I'd make a note of that, too. A tool to describe a person, or place. Good or unexpected use of colour, or sound, or smell. A metaphor, or comparison. A deft sidestep of a cliché.

The best writers use descriptive words that are non-standard descriptors, but completely normal words. Nothing archaic, or unfamiliar. Just well-chosen ingredients of normal language. This is especially important in non-literary journalism, where engagement is paramount but a pretentious phrase can de-rail an entire piece. These can be as basic as single words, or phrases that offer a way of capturing an image. Or demonstrations of the way a writer uses a particular dialogue tool, or structures a sentence.

By connecting with a particular description, you have captured the heart of what that writer has been learning to do throughout their career. Now it's for you to absorb, and develop. Good words are still just words: ingredients, like atoms, like notes in a song. If they work in a description they will work in most, if used right. You're being taught, in the most direct way possible.

What the word book really becomes is a crutch to guide you towards your own stride. Yes, it's a good hack if inspiration is lacking. But mainly it's a way to force a habit, which over the years becomes a methodology, and eventually an absorbed reflex. You end up unconsciously changing the way you write from the outset. And eventually you end up using the word book less and less. But it's always good to know it's there.

And that's why you should keep it somewhere where you read, not where you write. That way it's there when you need to record something, but you have to think for yourself just a little bit before you reach for it.

Exercise 2: Finding your own voice

Identify five journalists whose work you admire. What is it that they do well? What value do their articles offer readers? What is it about their writing that you find appealing and engaging? What could you learn from them? If you need some inspiration see page 232.

This book in five steps

In this book, we set out to give you an approach to news and feature writing. It draws on experience of professional journalists and the lessons I've learned from almost 20 years of helping to develop editorial talent. It aims to build from the basics but it can be boiled down into five simple rules…

Understand your readers: Know who they are, what they need from you and why they'll be interested in your news story (see page 8) or feature (page 73).

Be clear on your story: You have to be able to explain what your article is about in a single sentence. A feature standfirst (page 80) and the opening par of a news story (page 11) should show that clarity of thought.

Keep it simple: If your story is important, then you need to get that across with clarity. Keep jargon out of your copy (page 169), keep a news intro simple (page 24) and use the paragraph to develop your piece one idea at a time (page 99).

Tell your story through people: Good storytelling needs characters (page 115), so bring people to the top of your story and aim to get a quote high in your news (page 26) or feature (page 95).

Mix showing, telling and quoting: to make your story authoritative and engaging, and to give it pace (page 88) and understand the role that different interviewees play (page 106).

Because it's all about people

Writing is about words, sentences, paragraphs and ideas, but most of all it is about people.

Stories are commissioned by editors, generated by interviews and read by readers. Publications are bought, and stories are liked, shared and retweeted by people. So you need to be able to persuade an editor to commission you, coax people into talking to you and then into revealing something of importance in an interview. And most of all you have to encourage readers to take time out of their busy lives to engage with what you have written.

So do obsess about sentence structure, storytelling and word use, but most of all you should focus on what it is your readers need from you.

This is the key to being a really effective writer.

Bibliography

BBC (2020) *Editorial guidelines* <www.bbc.co.uk/editorialguidelines>

Ethical Journalism Network (2020) *Five principles of journalism*. <ethicaljournalismnetwork.org/who-we-are/5-principles-of-journalism>

Ipso (2020) Editors' Code of Practice <www.ipso.co.uk/editors-code-of-practice>

National Union of Journalists (2020) *Code of conduct* <www.nuj.org.uk/about/nuj-code>

Orwell, G. (2013 [1946]) *Politics and the English language*, London: Penguin Classics

Spilsbury, M. (2016) *Exploring freelance journalism 2020, National Council for the Training of Journalists* (Accessed 8 September 2020) <www.nctj.com/downloadlibrary/EXPLORING%20FREELANCE%20JOURNALISM%20FINAL.pdf>

Strunk, W. and White, E.B. (1959 [1918]) *The Elements of Style*, New York: Allyn & Bacon.

Glossary of terms used in journalism

Journalism is rich in jargon. Some of it comes from printing (book for magazine), or survives from the pre-computer age (spike for rejected copy), or is imported from the United States (clippings for cuttings). It is often punchy and graphic (ambush, bust, fireman). But if it crops up in copy (e.g. in stories about the media), the sub will usually have to change it (replace "story" by "report") or explain it (after "chapel" insert "office branch" in brackets). The obvious exception is in publications for journalists such as *Press Gazette* and the *Journalist*.

ABC Audit Bureau of Circulations – source of independently verified circulation figures

A-B testing Comparing two versions of something (e.g. a headline) to see which one delivers the best result.

ad advertisement

add extra copy to add to existing story

advance (1) text of speech or statement issued to journalists beforehand; (2) expenses paid before a trip

advertorial advertisement presented as editorial

agencies news agencies, e.g. PA and Reuters

aggregation process of combining data from various sources into a single new one

aggregator organisation that collects and combines data from various sources

agony column regular advice given on personal problems sent in by readers; hence agony aunt

algorithm procedure or formula for solving a problem

ambush journalists lying in wait for unsuspecting, unwilling interviewee

ampersand & – symbol for "and"

analytics systematic analysis of data, particularly statistics about digital engagement

angle particular approach to story, journalist's point of view in writing it

art editor editorial lead responsible for design and layout of publication

artwork illustrations (e.g. drawings, photographs) prepared for reproduction

ascender the part of a lower-case letter (e.g. b and d) that sticks out above the x-height in a typeface

attribution identifying the journalist's source of information or quote

back of the book second part of magazine (after the centre spread)

backbench, the senior newspaper journalists who make key production decisions

backgrounder explanatory feature to accompany news story

bad break clumsy hyphenation at the end of a line

banner (headline) one in large type across front page

basket where copy goes – once a physical basket, now a digital folder

bastard measure type set to a width that is not standard for the page

beard the space between a letter and the edge of the base on which it is designed

beat American term for specialist area covered by reporter

black duplicate of written story (from colour of carbon paper once used with typewriter)

bleed (of an image) go beyond the type area to the edge of a page

blob solid black circle used for display effect or to tabulate lists

blog regularly updated website or webpage consisting of separate entries (posts)

blow up enlarge (part of) photograph

blown quote another term for pull quote

blurb displayed material promoting contents of another page or future issue

body copy the main text of a story, as opposed to page furniture

body type the main typeface in which a story is set (as opposed to display)

bold thick black type, used for emphasis

book printer's (and so production journalist's) term for magazine

bounce rate indicates how many people visited a web page and then read nothing else. This may indicate that the reader has found exactly what they were looking for.

box copy enclosed by rules to give it emphasis and/or separate it from the main text

breaker typographical device, e.g. crosshead, used to break up text on the page

brief (1) short news item; (2) instruction to journalist on how to approach story

bring up bring forward part of story to earlier position

broadsheet large-format newspaper

bullet (point) another term for blob

bureau office of news agency or newspaper office in foreign country

business-to-business (b2b) current term for what were once called "trade" magazines, i.e. those covering a business area, profession, craft or trade

bust (of a headline) be too long for the space available

buy-up interview exclusive bought by publication

byline writer's name as it appears in print at the beginning of a story

call out another term for pull quote

calls (also check calls) routine phone calls made by reporters to organisations such as police and fire brigade to see if a story is breaking

camera-ready (e.g. artwork) prepared for reproduction

caps capital letters

caption words used with a picture (usually underneath), identifying where necessary and relating it to the accompanying story

caption story extension of picture caption into a self-contained story

cast off estimate amount of printed matter copy would make

casual journalist employed by the shift

catch(line) short word (not printed) identifying different elements of a story in the editorial process

centre set type with equal space on either side

centre spread middle opening of tabloid or magazine

chapel office branch of media union (the shop steward is the father, FoC, or mother, MoC, of the chapel)

character unit of measurement for type including letters, figures, punctuation marks and spaces

chequebook journalism paying large sums for stories

chief sub senior sub-editor in charge of the others

churnalism recycling of, e.g. press releases and pre-packaged material, without further research

city desk financial section of British national newspaper (in the US the city desk covers home news)

classified advertising small ads "classified" by subject matter, grouped in a separate section

clippings/clips American term for cuttings

close quotes end of section in direct quotes

close up reduce space between lines, words or characters

CMS (Content Management System) It is the software application running your blog or website. It is what allows you to publish your stories to the web.

CMYK cyan, magenta, yellow and black, the process (basic printing) colours

colour piece news story written as feature with emphasis on journalist's reactions

colour sep(aration)s method by which the four process colours (CMYK) are separated from a colour original

column (1) standard vertical division of page; (2) regular feature by journalist often encouraged to be opinionated and/or entertaining

column rule light rule between columns of type

concurrents How many people are reading your article or site at any one time

conference meeting of editorial staff to plan current/next issue

consumer magazines the category includes specialist titles (e.g. *Angling Times*), women's magazines and those of general interest

contact sheet photographer's sheet of small prints

contacts book a journalist's list of contacts with details of phone, fax, email, etc

contents bill *see* bill

content can include words, video, photography or other multimedia.

controlled circulation free distribution of specialist title to target readership by geography (free newspapers) or interest group (business-to-business magazines)

convergence merging of media forms and platforms

copy text of story

copy taster *see* taster

copyright right to reproduce original material

copytaker telephone typist who takes down copy from reporter

correction published statement correcting errors in story

correspondent journalist covering specialist area, e.g. education

coverlines selling copy on front cover

credit (line) name of photographer or illustrator as it appears in print next to their work

crop cut (image) to size or for better effect

crosshead line or lines, taken from the text, set bigger and bolder than the body type and inserted between paragraphs to liven up page

cut shorten or delete copy

cut-out illustration with background masked, painted or cut to make it stand out on the page

cuts cuttings

cuttings stories taken (originally cut) from newspapers and filed electronically under subject

cuttings job story that is over-dependent on cuttings

dateline place from which copy is filed

deadline time story (or any part of it) is due

deck originally one of a series of headlines stacked on top of each other; now usually used to mean one line of a headline

delayed drop device in news story of delaying important facts for effect

delete remove

descender the part of a lower-case letter (e.g. g and j) that sticks out below the x-height in a typeface

desk newspaper department, e.g. picture desk

deskman American term for male sub-editor

device The tool to access digital content, can include desktop, mobile or tablet

diary, the list of news events to be covered; hence an off-diary story is one originated by the reporter

diary column gossip column

disclaimer statement explaining that a particular person or organisation was not the subject of a previously published story

display ads ordinary (not "classified") ads which appear throughout a publication

display type type for headlines, etc

district reporter one covering a particular area away from the main office

doorstepping reporters lying in wait for (usually) celebrities outside their homes

double a story published twice in the same issue of a publication

double-column (of text, headline, illustration) across two columns

double page spread (or DPS) two facing pages in a magazine, whether advertising or editorial

downtable subs those other than the chief sub and deputies

drop cap, letter outsize initial capital letter used to start story or section; it drops down alongside the text which is indented to accommodate it

drop quotes outsize quotes used to mark quoted matter

dummy (1) pre-publication edition of new publication used to sell advertising and experiment editorially; (2) blank version of publication, e.g. to show quality and weight of paper; (3) complete set of page proofs

dwell time How long a reader spent on your site overall once they had found their way in.

edition version of newspaper printed for particular circulation area or time

editor senior journalist responsible for publication or section

editorial (1) leading article expressing editorial opinion; (2) content that is not advertising

editor's conference main planning meeting for next issue

em, en units of measurement for type – the width of the two letters m and n

embargo time before which an organisation supplying material, e.g. by press release, does not want it published

ends the story ends here

engaged time/rate This measures how people interact with your article: how long they spend on the page, whether they comment, share or like it, or click on hyperlinks

EPD electronic picture desk

EPS file Encapsulated PostScript file

exclusive claim by publication that it has a big story nobody else has

face type design

facing matter (of advertising) opposite editorial

facsimile exact reproduction, as with electronic transmission of pages

favourite (to) to mark a tweet as a favourite

feature article that goes beyond reporting of facts to explain and/or entertain; also used of any editorial matter that is not news or listings; hence feature writer, features editor

file transmit copy

filler short news item to fill space

fireman traditional term for reporter sent to trouble spot when story breaks

fit (of copy, etc) to occupy exactly the space available

flannel panel magazine's address, contact information and list of staff

flash brief urgent message from news agency

flatplan page-by-page plan of issue

flip (of picture) transpose left to right

flush left or right (of type) having one consistent margin with the other ragged

fold, the centre fold in a newspaper so that only the upper half of the paper ("above the fold") is visible at the point of sale

folio page (number)

follow up take published story as the starting point for an update

format (1) size, shape or style of publication or section; (2) computer instruction; hence to format

fount (pronounced font and now often spelt that way) typeface

free(sheet) free newspaper

freebie something useful or pleasant, often a trip, supplied free to journalists

freelance self-employed journalist who sells material to various outlets

freelancer American term for freelance

galley proof typeset proof not yet made up into a page

gatefold an extra page which folds out from a magazine

ghost writer journalist writing on behalf of someone else, often by interviewing them; hence to ghost (e.g. a column)

gone to bed passed for press so too late for corrections

grams per square metre (gsm; g/m2) the measure used to define the weight of paper

graphics visual material, usually drawn

grid design skeleton specifying (e.g.) number and width of columns

gutter space between two facing pages; can also be used of space between columns

H & J (of copy on screen) hyphenated and justified, so in the form in which it will be typeset

hack, hackette jocular terms for journalist

half-tone illustration broken into dots of varying sizes

handout printed material, e.g. press release, distributed to journalists

hanging indent copy set with first line of each paragraph full out and subsequent ones indented

hard copy copy on paper, e.g. printout, rather than screen

hashtag the # symbol used to mark key words or topics in social media

head, heading headline

heavy broadsheet newspaper

heavy type thicker than standard

hold (over) keep material for future use

hot metal old typesetting system in which type was cast from molten metal

house ad publisher's advertisement in its own publication

house journal publication for employees of a particular organisation

house style the way a publication chooses to publish in matters of detail

hyperlinks clickable links within your article which link through to other articles

imposition arrangement of pages for printing

imprint name and address of publisher and printer

in-house inside a media organisation

in pro in proportion (used of visual material to be reduced)

indent set copy several characters in from left-hand margin

infographic graphic visual representation of data

input type copy into computer

insert (1) extra copy to be included in existing story; (2) printed matter inserted in publication after printing and binding

intro first paragraph of story; also used (confusingly) in some magazine offices to mean standfirst

italics italic (sloping) type

jackline another word for widow

journo jocular term for journalist

justified type set with consistent margins

kern reduce the space between characters in typeset copy

kicker introductory part of caption or headline. Can be used to boost SEO at the front of a web headline

kill drop a story; hence kill fee for freelance whose commissioned story is not used

knocking copy story written with negative angle

label (of headline) without a verb

landscape horizontal picture

layout arrangement of body type, headlines, etc and illustrations on the page

lead (1) main story on a page; (2) tip-off or idea for story (in the US the intro of a story is called the lead)

leader leading article expressing editorial opinion

leader dots three dots used to punctuate

leading (pronounced "ledding") space between lines (originally made by inserting blank slugs of lead between lines of type)

leg column of typeset copy

legal send material to be checked for legal problems, e.g. libel

legal kill lawyer's instruction not to use

letter spacing space between letters

libel defamatory statement in permanent or broadcast form

lift (1) use all or most of a story taken from one newspaper edition in the next; (2) steal a story from another media outlet and reproduce it with few changes

ligature two or more joined letters

light face type lighter than standard

likes a social media metric: weak indicator as people often like articles without reading them

linage (this spelling preferred to lineage) payment to freelances by the line; also refers to classified advertising without illustration

line drawing drawing made up of black strokes

listicle list-based article, e.g. "10 things you need to know about computers"

listings lists of entertainment and other events with basic details

literal typographical error

lobby, the specialist group of political reporters covering parliament

local corr local correspondent

logo name, title or recognition word in particular design used on regular section or column; also used on magazine's front-page title

long-tail effect publishing content online and keeping it available in an archive

lower case ordinary letters (not caps)

make-up assembly of type and illustrations on the page ready for reproduction

mark up specify the typeface, size and width in which copy is to be set

masking covering part of photograph for reproduction

masthead publication's front-page title

measure width of typesetting

medium type between light and heavy

merchandising details of stockists and prices in consumer features

metric a system or standard of measurement

mf more copy follows

model release contract signed by photographic model authorising use of pictures

mono(chrome) printed in one colour, usually black

more more copy follows

mug shot photograph showing head (and sometimes shoulders)

must copy that must appear, e.g. apology or correction

mutton old name for an em

neg photographic negative

news agency supplier of news and features to media outlets

news desk organising centre of newsroom

newsman American term for male reporter

newsprint standard paper on which newspapers are printed

newsroom news reporters' room

nib news in brief – short news item

night lawyer barrister who reads newspaper proofs for legal problems

nose intro of story; hence to renose – rewrite intro

NUJ National Union of Journalists

nut old name for an en; hence nutted, type indented one en

obit obituary

off-diary *see* diary, the

off-the-record statements made to a journalist on the understanding that they will not be reported directly or attributed

on spec uncommissioned (material submitted by freelance)

on-the-record statements made to a journalist that can be reported and attributed

op-ed feature page–facing page with leading articles

open quotes start of section in direct quotes

originals photographs or other visual material for reproduction

orphan first line of a paragraph at the foot of a page or column

out take another term for pull quote

overlay sheet of transparent paper laid over artwork with instructions on how to process it

overline another word for strapline

overmatter typeset material that does not fit the layout and must be cut

overprint print over a previously printed background

PA Press Association, Britain's national news agency

package main feature plus sidebars

page furniture displayed type, e.g. headlines, standfirsts and captions, used to project copy

page plan editorial instructions for layout

page proof proof of a made-up page

page views how many times a page has been viewed: but remember one person can view the same page multiple times so these are distinct from unique views (see unique users)

pagination the number of pages in a publication; also a newspaper system's ability to make up pages

panel another word for box

parallax scrolling fluid scrolling that creates an illusion of depth with text overlaid on pictures or multimedia

par, para paragraph

paparazzo/i photographer(s) specialising in pursuing celebrities

paste-up page layout pasted into position

patch specialist area covered by reporter

pay-off final twist or flourish in the last paragraph of a story

peg reason for publishing feature at a particular time

photomontage illustration created by combining several photographs

pic, pix press photograph(s)

pica unit of type measurement

pick-up (of photographs) those that already exist and can therefore be picked up by journalists covering a story

picture desk organising centre of collection and editing of pictures

piece article

plate printing image carrier from which pages are printed

platform computer's operating system

point (1) full stop; (2) standard unit of type size

pool group of reporters sharing information and releasing it to other media organisations

post blog entry

PostScript Adobe's page description language

PR(O) public relations (officer); hence someone performing a public relations role

press cuttings *see* cuttings

press release written announcement or promotional material by organisation sent to media outlets and individual journalists

profile portrait in words of individual or organisation

proof printout of part or whole of page so it can be checked and corrected

proofread check proofs; hence proofreader

publisher (1) publishing company; (2) individual in magazine publishing company with overall responsibility for title or group of titles

puff story promoting person or organisation

pull proof; to pull is to take a proof

pull (out) quote (blown quote, call out, out take) short extract from text set in larger type as part of page layout

pullout separate section of publication that can be pulled out

pyramid (usually inverted) conventional structure for news story with most important facts in intro

query question mark

queue collection of stories held in a computer

quote verbatim quotation **quotes:** quotation marks

ragged (of type) with uneven margin

raised cap outsize initial capital letter used to start story or section; it is raised above the text

range left or right (of type) have one consistent margin with the other ragged

recirculation Did readers of your article then go on to read other articles on your website, or did they simply read the one article and then leave the site?

referrers other publishers that have linked to your article on their own website or in one of their articles, which is delivering bonus traffic to you

register alignment of coloured inks on the printed page

rejig rewrite copy, particularly in the light of later information

renose rewrite intro of a story

repin copy onto somebody else's board

reporter gatherer and writer of news

repro house company that processes colour pictures ready for printing

retainer regular payment to local correspondent or freelance

retouch alter photograph to emphasise particular feature

Reuters international news agency

reverse indent another term for hanging indent

reversed out (type) printed in white on black or tinted background

revise extra proof to check that corrections have been made

rewrite write new version of story or section as opposed to subbing on copy

ring-round story based on series of phone calls

river white space running down a column of type, caused by space between words

roman plain upright type

rough sketch for layout

round-up gathering of disparate elements for single story

RSI repetitive strain injury, attributed to overuse and misuse of computer keyboard, mouse, etc

rule line between columns or round illustrations

run period of printing an edition or number of copies printed

run on (of type) continue from one line, column or page to the next

running foot title and issue date at the foot of the page

running head title and issue date at the top of the page

running story one that is constantly developing, over a newspaper's different editions or a number of days

running turns pages with no paragraph breaks on first and last lines; also used of columns

rush second most urgent message from news agency (after flash)

sans (serif) plain type (*see* serif) – this is an example

scaling (of pictures) calculating depth

schedule (1) list of jobs for (eg) reporters; (2) publication's printing programme

scheme make a plan of page layout

scoop jocular word for exclusive

screamer exclamation mark

screen the number of dots per square inch of a half-tone

section (1) separately folded part of newspaper; (2) complete printed sheet making up part of magazine

sell another word for standfirst, often used in women's magazines

SEO (Search Engine Optimisation) optimise an article so that it can be found easily on a search engine

serif decorative addition to type – this is an example of serif type

set and hold typeset and keep for use later

setting copy set in type

shareability extent to which digital content is easily discovered and shared by others

shares a social media metric that is a stronger indicator of quality as people share thinking – "This is the sort of thing I'd like people to think that I read."

shift daily stint worked by staff journalists and casuals

shoot a photographic session

shovelware derogatory term for software notable for quantity rather than quality

shy (of headline) too short for the space available

sidebar subsidiary story or other material placed next to main story, usually in box

sidehead subsidiary heading, set flush left

sign-off writer's name as it appears in print at the end of a story

sketch light-hearted account of events, especially parliamentary

slip newspaper edition for particular area or event

small caps capital letters in smaller size of the same typeface

snap early summary by news agency of important story to come

snapper jocular term for press photographer

snaps press photographs

social media websites and applications (apps) that enable users to create and share content or take part in networking

solid (of type) set without extra leading

sources of traffic Where is your traffic coming from? Is it coming from Google or Bing? From Facebook, Twitter or TikTok? Are people coming directly to your website to read it?

spike where rejected copy goes (originally a metal spike)

splash newspaper's main front-page story

splash sub sub-editor responsible for tabloid's front page

spoiler attempt by newspaper to reduce impact of rival's exclusive by publishing similar story

spot colour second colour (after black) used in printing publication

spread two facing pages

s/s same size

standfirst introductory matter accompanying headline, particularly used in features

stet ignore deletion or correction (Latin for "let it stand")

stone bench where pages were made up; hence stone sub – sub-editor who makes final corrections and cuts on page proofs

stop press small area on back page of newspaper left blank for late news in days of hot metal

story article, especially news report

strap(line) subsidiary headline above main headline

Street, the Fleet Street, where many newspapers once had their offices

stringer local correspondent; freelance on contract to a news organisation

style house style

style book/style sheet where house style is recorded

sub sub-editor

subhead subsidiary headline

subtitle another word for standfirst

tab(loid) popular small-format newspaper such as the *Sun*

tagline explanatory note under headline

take section of copy for setting

take back (on proof) take words back to previous line

take over (on proof) take words forward to next line

taster production journalist who checks and selects copy; also coverline

template a document or file with a preset format

think piece feature written to show and provoke thought

tie-in story connected with the one next to it

tint shaded area on which type can be printed

tip(-off) information supplied (and usually paid for) whether by freelance or member of the public

titlepiece traditional term for name of magazine as it appears on the cover – now replaced by masthead and logo

TOT triumph over tragedy, feature formula particularly popular in women's magazines

tracking space between characters

trade names product names (e.g. Hoover, Kleenex, Velcro)

traffic the amount of people crossing through your website or story

trans(pose) reverse order

turn part of story continued on a later page

tweet 140-character message sent via Twitter

Twitter online social networking service

typeface a complete range of type in a particular style, e.g. Times New Roman

typescale measuring rule for type

typo American term for typographical error

typography craft of using type

u/lc upper and lower case

underscore underline

unj(ustified) text set flush left, ragged right

unique users (UU)s This records how may individual browsers visited a site or page. One user can visit a page multiple times, but that reader will only be counted once.

upper and lower case mixture of capitals and ordinary letters

upper case capital letters

url uniform resource locator – the address for a file that is accessible on the internet

vignette illustration whose edges gradually fade to nothing

visitors the number of people reading your site or article

visits Amazon's Alexa support page notes that if a person clicks another web page on your site within 30 minutes of the last click, that is counted as one visit. If the second click comes after 30 minutes, it is a separate visit.

vox pop series of street interviews (Latin: *vox populi* – voice of the people)

weight thickness or boldness of letters in a typeface

white space area on page with no type or illustration

widow single word or part of word at the end of a paragraph on a line by itself; originally the last line of a paragraph at the top of a page or column

wire a means of transmitting copy by electronic signal; hence wire room

wob white on black – type reversed out

wot white on tone

x-height height of the lower-case letters of a typeface (excluding ascenders and descenders)

Recommended reading

In Chapter 1, we emphasised the importance of reading to develop your journalistic skills. This section gives you some of the best books on journalism, as well as reading suggestions for specialist areas such as sports, business, politics and science.

We've also flagged up journalists, publications and podcasts that we think you should follow. You'll find many of these as Twitter lists on my account, so if I'm missing someone important, drop me a line to let me know.

@MattSwaine

English usage and writing style

Burchfield, Robert, *Fowler's Modern English Usage* (third edition), OUP, 2004

Evans, Harold, *Essential English for Journalists, Editors and Writers*, revised by Crawford Gillan, Pimlico, 2000

Gowers, Sir Ernest, *The Complete Plain Words* (third edition), Penguin, 1987

Hicks, Wynford, *English for Journalists* (fourth edition), Routledge, 2013

Hicks, Wynford, *Quite Literally: Problem Words and How to Use Them*, Routledge, 2004

Strunk, William, *The Elements of Style* (third edition), revised by E B White, Macmillan (New York), 1979, also available free at www.bartleby.com/141/

Print journalism

Adams, Sally, *Interviewing for Journalists* (third edition), Routledge, 2017

Frost, Chris, *Reporting for Journalists* (second edition), Routledge, 2010

Holmes, Tim, *Subediting and Production for Journalists*, Routledge, 2016

Keeble, Richard, *Ethics for Journalists* (second edition), Routledge, 2009

Hanna, Mark and Dodd, Mark, *McNae's Essential Law for Journalists* (25th edition), OUP, 2020

Mason, Peter and Smith, Derrick, *Magazine Law a Practical Guide*, Routledge, 1998

Journalists on journalism

Books suggested by Cardiff University Journalism lecturers

Ayres, Chris, *War Reporting for Cowards*, Grove Press, 2006

Barber, Lynn, *Demon Barber*, Viking, 1998

Bernstein, Carl and Woodward, Bob, *All the President's Men*, Pocket Books, 1994

Boynton, Robert, *The New, New Journalism: Conversations with America's Best Nonfiction Writers on Their Craft*, Vintage, 2005

Davies, Nick, *Hack Attack: How the Truth Caught up with Rupert Murdoch*, Chatto & Windus, 2014

Evans, Harold, *Do I Make Myself Clear?* Little Brown, 2017

Evans, Harold, *Good Times, Bad Times*, Weidenfeld & Nicolson, 1983

Evans, Harold, *My Paper Chase*, Abacus, 2010

Marr, Andrew, *My Trade: A Short History of British Journalism*, Macmillan, 2004

Rusbridger, Alan, *Breaking News*, Canongate Books Ltd, 2019

Wolfe, Tom and Johnson, EW, *The New Journalism*, Harper & Row, 1973

Numbers in journalism

Suggested by Dr Aidan O'Donnell (ch 12) given in order of increasing complexity…

Blastland, Michael and Dilnot, Andrew, *The Tiger that isn't: Seeing through a World of Numbers*, Profile, 2008

Cohen, Sarah, *Numbers in the Newsroom. Using Math and Statistics in News* (second edition), IRE, 2014.

Cohn, Victor, *News and Numbers* (third edition), Wiley-Blackwell, 2012

Spiegelhalter, David, *The Art of Statistics: Learning from Data*, Pelican, 2019

Reinhart, Alex, *Statistics Done Wrong: The Woefully Complete Guide*, No Starch Press, 2015

Rowntree, Derek, *Statistics without Tears: An Introduction for Non-Mathematicians*, Penguin, 1981

Meyer, Philip, *Precision Journalism. A Reporter's Guide to Social Science Methods* (fourth edition), Rowman & Littlefield, 2002

Science and the environment

An entirely subjective list that sets the standard for engagement and clarity of writing but that in no way captures the breadth of writing on science and the environment.

Bryson, Bill, *Short History of Time*, Black Swan, 2004

Carson, Rachel, *Silent Spring* (new edition), Penguin Classics, 2000, originally published 1962

Dawkins, Richard, *The Selfish Gene*, Oxford University Press, 2016

Diamond, Jared *Guns, Germs and Steel*, Vintage, 1998

Kahneman, Daniel, *Thinking Fast and Slow*, Penguin, 2012

Monbiot, George, *Feral*, Penguin 2013

Mukherjee, Siddhartha, *The Emperor of All Maladies: A Biography of Cancer*, Fourth Estate, 2011

Roberts, Alice, *The Incredible Unlikeliness of Being*, Heron Books, 2014

Sagan, Carl, *Cosmos: The Story of Cosmic Evolution, Science and Civilisation*, Abacus 1983

Young, Ed, *I Contain Multitudes*, Vintage, 2017

Science journalism Twitter list

@NatureNews – Tweets from the news team at Nature, the international journal of #science

@newscientist – The place to find out what's new in science and why it matters

@theAliceRoberts – Professor of Public Engagement in Science at University of Birmingham

@carlzimmer – @nytimes columnist and specialist on science communication

@edyong209 – Science writer at The Atlantic and author of *I Contain Multitudes*

@hannahdev – Science Correspondent for *The Guardian*

@SoMe_Lilian – Award-winning health & science journalist, assistant news editor @ newscientist

Environment journalism Twitter list

@GeorgeMonbiot – journalist, campaigner, advocate for rewilding and author of *Feral*

@AkshatRathi – Climate and energy specialist at Bloomberg News.

@AlexCKaufman – Senior reporter @HuffPost on the climate, energy, and environment

@catBrahic – Environment editor @TheEconomist

@HirokoTabuchi – Reporter at the @NYTimes covering climate

@NadaFarhoud – Environment Editor and columnist @dailymirror

@patrick_barkham – Natural history writer for *The Guardian*: books on badgers and butterflies

Books on UK and general politics

Suggested by colleagues at both Cardiff University's Journalism and Politics departments

Crick, Bernard, *In Defence of Politics*, Continuum, 2005

Freeden, Michael, *Ideology: A Very Short Introduction*, Oxford University Press, 2003

Gunn, Sheila, *So You Want to be a Political Journalist*, Biteback Publishing, 2012

King, Anthony, *Who Governs Britain?* Pelican, 2015

Mudde, Cas and Kaltwasser, Cristóbal Rovira, *Populism - A Very Short Introduction*, Oxford University Press, 2017

Mulgan, Geoff, *Good and Bad Power*, Penguin: First Thus Edition, 2007

Rawnsley, Andrew, *The End of the Party*, Penguin, 2010

Sobolewska, Maria and Ford, Robert, *Brexitland: Identity, Diversity and the Reshaping of British Politics*, Cambridge University Press, 2020

Toynbee, Polly and Walker, David, *Unjust Rewards: Exposing Greed and Inequality in Britain Today*, Granta Books, 2008

Wright, Tony, *British Politics: Very Short Introduction*, Oxford University Press, 2020

Books on America and its politics

Cramer, Katherine J, *The Politics of Resentment: Rural Consciousness in Wisconsin and the Rise of Scott Walker*, University of Chicago Press, 2016

Dionne, EJ, Ornstein, Norman J and Mann, Thomas E, *One Nation after Trump: A Guide for the Perplexed, the Disillusioned, the Desperate, and the not-yet Deported*, St. Martin's Press, 2017

Grossman, Dave, *On Killing: The Psychological Cost of Learning to Kill in War and Society*, Back Bay Books, 2009

Hochschild, Arlie Russell, *Strangers in Their Own Land: Anger and Mourning on the American Right*, New York: New Press, 2016

Mayer, Jane, *Dark Money: The Hidden History of the Billionaires behind the Rise of the Radical Right*, Penguin Random House, 2016

Marietta, Morgan and Barker, David C, *One Nation, Two Realities: Dueling Facts in American Democracy*, New York: OUP, 2019

O'Rouke, PJ, *A Cry from the Far Middle: Dispatches from a Divided Land*, Grove Press, 2020

Reid-Henry, Simon, *Empire of Democracy: The Remaking of the West since the Cold War, 1971–2017*, John Murray, 2019

Younge, Gary, *Another Day in the Death of America*, Guardian Faber Publishing, 2017

Books on world affairs

de Burgh, Hugo, *China's Media in the Emerging World Order*, University of Buckingham Press, 2017

Edkins, Jenny and Zehfuss, Maja, *Global Politics: A New Introduction*, Routledge, 2019

Galeano, Eduardo and Allende, Isabel, *Open Veins of Latin America: Five Centuries of the Pillage of a Continent*, Serpent's Tail, 2009

Halliday, Fred, *Islam and the Myth of Confrontation: Religion and Politics in the Middle East*, I.B. Tauris & Co, 2003

Jones, Branwen Gruffydd, *Decolonizing International Relations*, Rowman & Littlefield Publishers, 2006

Roberts, JAG, *A History of China*, Palgrave Macmillan, 2011

Robinson, Neil, *Contemporary Russian Politics: An Introduction*, Polity, 2019

Rodney, Walter, *How Europe Underdeveloped Africa*, Verso, 2018

Thomson, Alex, *An Introduction to African Politics*, Routledge, 2016

Verini, James, *They Will Have to Die Now: Mosul and the Fall of the Caliphate*, Oneworld Publications, 2019

Politics Twitter list

@MarinaHyde – Guardian columnist and sharpest satirical writer around

@johnestevens – Daily Mail's deputy political editor "Always looking for stories"

@MrHarryCole – political editor @TheSun

@peterwalker99 Guardian political correspondent, books on cycling (page 101)

@afuahirsch Columnist @guardian: made documentary Enslaved with Samuel L Jackson

@katyballs deputy political editor @spectator and @ipaper columnist

@thejonnyreilly – Political columnist @TheSun

Books on business and economics

Appelbaum, Binyamin, *The Economists' Hour: False Prophets, Free Markets, and the Fracture of Society*, Hachette, 2019

Bootle, Roger, *The AI Economy: Work, Wealth and Welfare in the Robot Age*, Nicholas Brealey Publishing, 2019

Chang, Ha-Joon, *Kicking Away the Ladder*, Anthem Press, 2002

Kessler, Sarah, *Gigged: The Gig Economy, the End of the Job and the Future of Work*, Random House Business, 2019

Klein, Naomi, *The Shock Doctrine: The Rise of Disaster Capitalism*, Penguin, 2008

Landsburg, Steven E, *The Armchair Economist: Economics and Everyday Life*, Simon & Schuster, 2012

Lubin, David, *Dance of the Trillions: Developing Countries and Global Finance*, Brookings Institution, 2018

Raworth, Kate, *Doughnut Economics: Seven Ways to Think Like a 21st-Century Economist*, Random House Business, 2018

Sanderson, Henry and Forsythe, Michael, *China's Superbank: Debt, Oil and Influence - How China Development Bank is Rewriting the Rules of Finance*, Bloomberg, 2013

Tooze, Adam, *Crashed: How a Decade of Financial Crises Changed the World*, Allen Lane, 2018

Business and economics Twitter list

Twitter list with thanks to Nigel Stephenson (Chapter 12)

@fletcherr – Richard Fletcher Business editor of @thetimes

@ChrisGiles_ – Economics Editor, FT

@PhilAldrick – Economics Editor. The Times

@faisalislam – Economics Editor, BBC

@BBCSimonJack – Business Editor, BBC

@ReutersMikeD – Editor at Large, Finance and Markets, Reuters

@tim – Tim Bradshaw, Global tech correspondent, FT

Travel Twitter list

@PhoebeRSmith – Editor at large for Wanderlust, podcast host and writer (page 205)

@olivertomberry – Writer and photographer. Lonely Planet, BBC, Guardian, Independent (chapter 12)

@Nature_Traveler – Lavanya Sunkara writes for @nytimes, @travelleisure_ and USA Today

@MrSimonIngram – Online editor @NatGeoUk @Guardian Country Diary writer (page 210)

@RobGMacfarlane – Books include Underland, The Lost Words, The Old Ways, Landmarks

@OliSmithTravel – Four-time Travel Writer of the Year: Outside, Nat Geo, BBC, etc

@BudgetTraveller – Kash Bhattacharya was the NatGeo blogger of the year

Sport books

Suggested by Cardiff University senior lecture Mike Hill who teaches sports journalism (see Chapter 14)

Hamilton, Duncan, *Provided You Don't Kiss Me: 20 Years with Brian Clough*, Harper Perennial, 2008

Imlach, Gary, *My Father and Other Working Class Football Heroes*, Yellow Jersey, 2005

Krakauer, John, *Into Thin Air*, Pan, 2011

Lewis, Michael, *Moneyball: The Art of Winning and Unfair Game*, W. W. Norton & Company, 2004

McGinniss, Joe, *The Miracle of Castel di Sangro*, Sphere, 2000

McRae, Donald, *Dark Trade: Lost in Boxing*, Hamilcar Publications, 2019

Moore, Richard, *Slaying the Badger*, Yellow Jersey, 2011

Remnick, David, *King of the World: Muhammad Ali*, Picador, 1999

Krien, Anna, *Night Games: Sex, Power and a Journey into the Dark Heart of Sport*, Yellow Jersey, 2014

Walsh, David, *Seven Deadly Sins: My Pursuit of Lance Armstrong*, Simon & Schuster, 2013

Sports Twitter list

@natcoombs – Hosts @thencshow covering all the latest from the #NFL

@OllieHolt22 – Chief Sports Writer, The Mail on Sunday

@SiClancy – Ex BBC Sport writer @Gridiron Magazine, Sports Illustrated, NY Times, Independent.

@amy_cricket I write stories and sometimes talk @bbcsport

@guardian_sport – Sport news from @Guardian with accounts for US and Aus sports

@thesetpieces – Quality football storytelling | Part of the @Guardian Sports Network

@blzzrd Sharing football stories you won't find anywhere else

Great podcasts

A selection of podcasts that are worth subscribing to alongside this book

The Tip Off Podcast

Award-winning podcast that gives you "the stories behind some of the most compelling investigative journalism"

@TipOffPodcast

Foreign Correspondence Podcast

Hour-long interviews with journalists around the world

@foreignpod

The Media Insider

Each episode interviews a commissioning editor, writer or producer to find out how and why they commission a story

www.themediainsider.fm

The Long Read Podcast

Guardian long reads in audio format: listen to 'The man who sleeps in Hitlers Bed' if nothing else

@gdnlongread

BBC In Our Time

A brilliant Radio 4 discussion programme presented by Melvyn Bragg that covers everything from classics and philosophy to science and evolution and beyond

@BBCInOurTime

Long Form Podcast

A weekly conversation with a non-fiction writer: or "an hour-long meditation on the craft of writing, as well as the people behind the stories that are dominating the news cycle," according to *the Guardian*

@longformpodcast

More or Less – BBC

Tim Harford explains – and sometimes debunks – the numbers and statistics used in political debate, the news and everyday life.

@BBCMoreOrLess

Documentaries and films on journalism

Suggested by Dr Janet Harris who runs MA in Digital Documentaries at Cardiff University

A Thousand Cuts – Ramona S. Diaz
The Dissident – Bryan Fogel
All the President's Men (1976)
Killing Fields (1984)
The Post (2017)
Frost/Nixon (2008)
Citizenfour (2014)
We steal Secrets: The story of WikiLeaks (2013)
Spotlight (2015)
*Don't F**k with cats: Hunting an internet killer* (2019)

Literary journalism

Suggestions by Cardiff University's Dr Janet Harris…

Alexievich, Svetlana, *Voices from Chernobyl: The Oral History of a Nuclear Disaster*, Picador, 2006

Behr, Edward, *Anyone here Been Raped and Speaks English?* Penguin, 1992

Capote, Truman, *In Cold Blood*, *Penguin Classics*, 2000, originally published in 1965

Colvin, Marie, *On the Front Line: The Collected Journalism of Marie Colvin*, HarperPress, 2012

Crawford, Alex, *Colonel Gaddafi's Hat*, Collins, 2012

Gardner, Frank, *Blood and Sand*, *Bantam*, 2014

Hemmingway, Ernest, *By-line*, *Arrow*, 2013, originally published in 1967

Kapuscinski, Ryszard, *The Shadow of the Sun: My African Life*, Penguin, 2002

Thompson, Hunter S, *Hell's Angels*, Penguin Classics, 2003, originally published in 1967

Waugh, Evelyn, *Scoop*, Penguin Classics, 2000, originally published in 1938

Storytelling

Books that will sharpen your sense of storytelling and what it means for your writing

Campbell, Joseph, *The Hero with a Thousand Faces*, Princeton: Princeton University Press, 2004

Gottschall, Jonathan, *The Storytelling Animal: How Stories Make Us Human*, Boston: Houghton Mifflin Harcourt, 2012

Hart, Jack, *Story Craft: The Complete Guide to Writing Narrative Nonfiction*, University of Chicago Press, 2012

King, Stephen, *On Writing: A Memoir of the Craft*, New York: Scribner, 2000

Kramer, Mark and Call, Wendy, *Telling True Stories: A Nonfiction Writers' Guide*, Nieman Foundation at Harvard University, 2007

Yorke, John, *Into the Woods: How Stories Work and Why We Tell Them*, Penguin, 2013

Suggested answers

Chapter 2

Exercise 3

1. A Leeds primary teacher has won first prize in a leading literary award for nature writers with her first novel.
2. Russian interference in our elections poses the biggest threat to UK democracy, according to government minister Keith Hounslow.
3. People with strong northern or rural accents are less likely to get a job offer, according to latest research.
4. A woman is recovering in hospital and another ten were seriously injured after a coach crashed through the barriers on the M4 near Swindon today
5. British drinkers will pay more for a pint after a poor harvest of hops, say farming unions.
6. Over 450 people in Indonesia were evacuated from their homes after a month's worth of rain hit their island in just three days.
7. Over 40,000 people die each year due to air pollution, according to latest research.

Chapter 3

Exercise 2

Why is this news: 650 people to lose work due to Covid lockdown
Who: at least 650 workers
What: to lose jobs
When: next month
Where: in the UK
How: 47 store closures
Why: downturn sparked by lockdown

Over 650 workers face redundancy as the bakery chain Crumbles announced the closure of 47 stores hit by falling sales during the coronavirus lockdown.

The first wave of redundancies is expected at the end of next month as the business that has 2,670 stores nationally revealed a 78% drop in sales in some of its city outlets.

CEO Thomas Bloxworth said: "This is devastating news for our workers. We have made every possible effort to keep stores open by but sales figures make it impossible to avoid redundancies. We have to take this step today to ensure the long-term health of the business."

Chapter 5

Exercise 1

1. "Jackie Traction strike donation: Generous Holt Harriers star donates £5,000 to Bangyong Electronic staff"
2. "Harriers' Traction in 5k strike donation"

Index

Printed in Great Britain
by Amazon

67648275R00149